The Teachers

The Teachers

A Year Inside America's
Most Vulnerable,
Important Profession

Alexandra Robbins

DUTTON

DUTTON

An imprint of Penguin Random House LLC
penguinrandomhouse.com

LIBRARY OF CONGRESS CATALOGING-IN-PUBLICATION DATA

Names: Robbins, Alexandra, 1976– author.
Title: The teachers: a year inside America's most vulnerable,
important profession / Alexandra Robbins.
Description: First Edition. | New York: Dutton, [2023] | Includes bibliographical references.
Identifiers: LCCN 2022042500 | ISBN 9781101986752 (Hardcover) | ISBN 9781101986769 (eBook)
Subjects: LCSH: Teachers—United States—Case studies. |
Teachers—United States—Interviews. | Teaching—United States—Case studies. |
Teaching—Vocational guidance—United States.
Classification: LCC LB1775.2 .R63 2023 | DDC 371.100973—dc23/eng/20221125
LC record available at https://lccn.loc.gov/2022042500

Printed in the United States of America

1st Printing

To my family, past and present, with unconditional love
and
to the educators who taught me,
the coworkers who supported me,
and the teachers who inspired me

CONTENTS

Contents

The Teachers

Prologue

You may think you know what's inside, but you don't.

You see the boxy buildings, brick or concrete—flanked by lush green athletic fields, a primary-colored playground, or a crumbling blacktop spiked with rusted basketball hoops—in front of which yellow buses groan exhaustive sighs before depositing or collecting lines of chattering bag-backed students.

Look deeper.

Long locker-lined corridors or tiled halls studded with bulletin boards, smelling of poster paint, cleaning products, or perhaps faintly of feet funnel children into classrooms at the trill of the bell.

Teenagers watch raptly as their science teacher demonstrates her favorite experiment.

An unflappable paraeducator expertly soothes an elementary school student behind the cubbies so the rest of the class can continue learning undisrupted.

Look deeper.

A school librarian is teaching technology, teaching an information literacy class, teaching animation, teaching other teachers.

The gymnasium echoes the class's boisterous cheers as the PE teacher's fists rise in triumph when the child on the spectrum sinks his first basket.

A student is struck by the magical pierce of recognition and relief the moment they are introduced to a book featuring a character who is a lot like them.

A teacher giddily hightails it back to her classroom after orchestrating a prank on a coworker to brighten his day.

Look deeper still.

Marginalized students gather, finding acceptance, solace, and camaraderie during lunchtime in the library.

A teacher spends her planning period, then her lunchtime, subbing unpaid for a coworker's class—for the third time in a week.

A parent spews obscenities at staff members in a windowless conference room.

Teachers congregate in the lounge to console a colleague who has just found out that her father passed away.

A music teacher gives his student the gloves off his hands for the wintry walk home.

A math teacher stays after school to provide extra support to a student before rushing home to her own ailing immunocompromised child.

A kindergarten teacher meticulously creates sight word cards, laminating them with a machine she personally purchased to teach a certain child to read when others could not.

English teachers grade essays, painstakingly refining adolescents' writing, long after the sun has dipped below the treetops, in classrooms where the only sounds are the thwonks from the clunky, broken HVAC and the hum of outdated fluorescent lights.

A veteran history teacher with a master's degree calls a blood donation center, desperate to pay the bills because her teaching salary and part-time second job aren't enough to live on.

You may think you know what lies beneath a school's façade, how to interpret the bustle, where the system's gone wrong. But unless you're an educator, you don't.

Look deeper, here, and learn.

Prologue

The truth is that you don't know what it's really like to be a teacher—the inspiration and frustration, the humor, the tears, the joys—unless you've stepped into their shoes. In this book, teachers invite you to do just that. As a journalist who has written several books about students and education, even I was surprised by what teachers shared.

To get an uncensored, no-holds-barred look at their lives, I followed three teachers' stories over the course of a school year. You'll meet Penny, a southern middle school math teacher, who grappled with a toxic culture at the big school in a small town; Miguel, a special ed teacher in the western United States, who fought for his students as both educator and activist; and Rebecca, an East Coast 4th grade teacher, who struggled to schedule and define a life outside of school. I also interviewed hundreds of other teachers, many of whose voices appear in the essays that anchor each chapter.*

Let these teachers take you behind the scenes to join their classrooms; watch parent-teacher conferences, staff meetings, and student behavioral meetings; eavesdrop in the staff lounge and teacher happy hour; take a field trip; witness teacher pranks. Learn teachers' secret codes and strategies and what they think about parents, ride along with the highs, feel the weight of the pressures, lose your heart to the kids.

While this book does address COVID-19's effects on teachers, particularly in chapter 4, I have chosen not to focus extensively on COVID because the pandemic did not cause the underlying problems in U.S. school systems—it simply exacerbated them, laying

---

* Some identifying details, including Rebecca's, Penny's, Miguel's, and their colleagues' and students' names, have been changed or omitted to protect individuals' privacy. Some events are not in chronological order.

them bare for all to see—and to suggest otherwise would be a disservice to the teaching profession. Teachers' working conditions had deteriorated before the pandemic and won't resolve unless decision-makers commit to making sweeping long-term changes. "Other countries treat teachers like doctors and lawyers: true experts of their subject and craft," a Pennsylvania AP English teacher said. "In the U.S., they say things like 'Those who can't, teach.'" After the teachers in this book escort you through their year-in-the-life stories, our hope is that you'll never tolerate that message, or anything like it, again.

CHAPTER 1

August

A Maryland administrator to a group of female math teachers: "Long-term subs are really hard to find, so I need you to not get really sick or pregnant this year."

A district arts coordinator to a Texas high school art teacher: "We don't need to give you money for art supplies because you can repurpose found objects, like toilet paper cores and cereal boxes!"

A parent at a parent-teacher conference, banging his fists on the table and screaming at a Michigan high school English teacher: "I'm coming to get you, little girl. Just wait. I am coming to get you."

Rebecca Abrams   Elementary School Teacher

Ah, summer, that long relaxing stretch during which the nation's teachers, freed from all classroom and contractual obligations, spend the entirety of their "summers off"*—"they're off four months a year"—on a "paid vacation" (after working their "part-time job" for "only 180 days" during which all they have "to do is show up the next

---

* All actual quotes from public sources. See notes for citations.

year, teach the same class, and do the same job, and they automatically get a cost of living increase") either partying with abandon, three sheets to the wind, or generally loafing about, comatose on the beach.

Haha, not.

Following a month of lesson prep and continuing ed coursework, Rebecca Abrams met with Yvonne, Eastern Elementary School's instructional coordinator, to go over the gifted English language arts curriculum requirements. After two years of teaching 4th grade (following stints in 3rd and 1st), Rebecca felt confident that her gifted math lesson plans were effective and fun, and she was well prepared for her on-grade-level social studies and science classes. But she hadn't taught gifted ELA before and the curriculum, set by a combination of district and state entities, was a beast.

During their nearly four-hour session, Yvonne handed Rebecca endless packets, too thick to staple, of the units and strategies the class was expected to cover, each accompanied by a teacher's guide and student workbook or dozens of pages listing URL links for teachers. The district provided no direction explaining the order in which to teach the units or how to incorporate the strategies. The preassessment for one unit analyzed a poem that Rebecca, a lifelong literature buff, didn't fully understand, but somehow the county expected nine-year-olds to comprehend it before the class covered its first poetry unit.

"You'll be so good at this!" Yvonne said.

"I'm going to die!" Rebecca announced. She shook her mop of untamable copper curls, which along with her general zaniness had led many students over the years to refer to her as Ms. Frizzle, of Magic School Bus fame.

For three summer weeks after that meeting, Rebecca struggled to figure out how to integrate the mountain of advanced requirements into the general ed curriculum she was supposed to teach the gifted ELA class. The units and strategies did not overlap. She had never even heard of some of the strategies.

In August, when Rebecca learned there would be a professional development session on 4th grade gifted ELA, she was delighted—and not because she enthusiastically considered herself a big dork (though she did). PDs, which had varying levels of usefulness, could span anywhere from a one-hour workshop to a yearlong class. To keep their licenses, teachers had to accumulate continuing education credits, which they often earned over the summer.

In a classroom at a nearby elementary school, the curriculum guides were spread out on a table. *Awesome, they're explaining the guides!* Rebecca thought. *I'm so glad they're having this PD.*

The facilitator introduced herself to the three dozen seated teachers. "Here are a bunch of links," she said, gesturing to a Smart Board. "You should bookmark them. They're important. And here's an online community. You should join it. Okay, go ahead!"

The teachers continued to look expectantly at the facilitator. While some had taught gifted ELA before, many of the attendees were either new to the program or, like Rebecca, had taught only gifted math.

"This is your time to look through it all. You can talk to each other about it!" the facilitator prodded.

I thought you were going to train us to make sense of this, Rebecca thought. She had already reviewed every page of the resource materials several times.

As the facilitator strolled around the room talking to participants, Rebecca raised her hand to request help designing lessons. The facilitator started toward her, then turned to talk to another table. While she waited, Rebecca reviewed the Google Docs links, which emphasized, yet again, just how much material there was. She raised her hand once more when the facilitator turned in her direction, but the presenter suddenly veered off as if pulled by a magnet. The third time this happened, Rebecca's tablemates giggled. Now hands were going up across the room.

"I give up, I give up," Rebecca muttered, thinking, *I don't know where to start. This is the worst PD of my teaching career.* Rebecca was generally confident, bubbly, upbeat, and loud, but now she stared forlornly at her laptop. The veteran teachers at the table talked about happenings at their school. Looking beaten, the other new gifted ELA teacher at the table took out her phone to text.

Rebecca lowered her hand. Her tablemates noticed her dejection and stopped chatting. "Hey, we can get her attention for you, don't worry," one offered.

"Nah, forget about it," Rebecca said in her strong New York accent, worried she'd choke up if she said anything further because she was so passionate about giving her students the best possible educational experience. ("I'm a crier. All my emotions come out my eyeballs," she told me later, laughing at herself.)

Her tablemates peered at her more closely. Their hands shot up at the same time. "She has a question!" they shouted, pointing to Rebecca. "She's been trying to get your attention!"

"Oh, I'm so sorry!" the facilitator said, hurrying to their table. She looked at Rebecca, waiting.

"I'm so overwhelmed, I don't know what to do," blurted Rebecca, mortified when a few tears rolled down her cheeks.

The veterans jumped in. "Oh hey! It's not that bad!" "It's like a big mishmash of things!" "She's right, this PD would be more helpful if it included lessons or a calendar or something more concrete."

"Why don't you just pick one or two things to focus on this quarter," the facilitator said.

"But which ones?" Rebecca asked.

"That's up to you!"

Rebecca didn't challenge her. She left the meeting feeling no more informed. In her car, she blared her version of "angry music"—

some Linkin Park, "Smash the Mirror" from the musical *Tommy*, "Good for You" from *Dear Evan Hansen*—and sang along at the top of her lungs. To boost her mood, she drove to Eastern, where she could "do something productive that I'm good at: setting up my classroom." She arranged her classroom library, hung bulletin board borders, and organized desk supplies and cabinets, physical tasks that calmed her because she could methodically cross them off her to-do list.

This was "summer vacation" for a teacher, the time when the general public seemed to believe teachers did not work. Certainly, teachers who weren't in classrooms over the summer could have less day-to-day stress, and some teachers made the most of the season by recharging, as they deserved to, because they were paid only 10 months of the year. But most teachers' work continued with second jobs or required certification courses, compliance trainings, PDs, planning meetings, creating new classroom resources, learning new curricula, and developing and revising lesson plans and strategies. Because of nonsensical district training schedules, Rebecca had even been required to sit through the same online training on a new textbook twice this summer.

In Rebecca's district, teachers' yearly contracts stipulated that they could be asked to work beyond stated working hours for school-related activities; those who refused were breaking contract. Rebecca had been half amused when she saw a mandatory district training presentation slide stating unironically that the teachers' workweek ended at midnight on Fridays and began at 12:01 a.m. on Saturdays.

It was no wonder Rebecca didn't have time for the life she thought she wanted. At the start of her teaching career, she'd tried to date, do community theater, and sing in her synagogue's chorus. But when her principal switched her to different grades in consecutive years, finding work/life balance became impossible. Last year, Rebecca had been frustrated that she couldn't often help her siblings with their children, attend dance classes, or spontaneously see friends on weekends. She'd given up Nacho, a dog she'd loved and fostered for a few months. She had to back out of auditioning for a musical. All because teaching dominated her life.

Rebecca missed the camaraderie, culture, and inside jokes of what she called her "strange and glorious" musical theater community. And at 29, she thought that perhaps five years without a date was her limit. Her last relationship ended when her boyfriend moved out because Rebecca, at 24, was always working. After they broke up, he told her he'd almost ended the relationship several times before that because she wasn't home or paying attention to him.

This summer, Rebecca's best friend, Aiko, had cajoled her into making a pact that they would both try online dating. Rebecca loved her work, but she wanted her life back. *I can't believe I haven't dated in five years. This is the year,* she vowed as she got her classroom in order. *I'm going to have a social life again.* Was that really too much to ask?

Rebecca was shaking her booty and singing inappropriate lyrics about half an hour before the start of the first day of school when the assistant principal stuck her head in Rebecca's classroom. "Hi, I'm glad you're here. I want to introduce you to some people," the AP said. She led a mom and two kids into the room. "This is Holly. She's new to Eastern and she'll be in your class." Holly peered shyly from behind her mother.

"Holly, hi! It's so great to meet you!" Rebecca enthused, overexuberantly shaking hands with Holly and her little brother. "So listen— SNEAK PEEK: I sing and dance in class all the time because I'm a Disney princess."

Holly, still hiding, laughed. The AP agreed: "That's true. Sometimes I'll be walking down the hallway and I'll hear singing coming from here. Really, really loud singing."

"It's a good thing you didn't come into my room five minutes earlier," Rebecca said to the adults, who snickered because they'd heard her.

The AP looked at Holly. "You know what else Miss Abrams does? She walks down the hall reading her Kindle. I'm amazed she doesn't walk into things."

"Oh, I totally walk into things!" Rebecca told Holly. "That's another sneak peek. But it's worth it because I lo-ove reading!"

"Me too!" Holly exclaimed.

Rebecca chatted in her usual boisterous way with Holly and her brother. When they left, she resumed singing. As she usually did in the minutes before the first day of school, Rebecca double-checked her giant first-day to-do list to determine whether she needed to make copies, bring home papers to cut for projects or books to judge for potential read alouds, and so forth. She admired how neat her room looked because it definitely would never look that nice again for the rest of the year. Today she also worried about doing the gifted ELA program justice and whether parents might complain to administrators that she wasn't offering students enough of a challenge.

At least her colleagues had her back. Rebecca loved most of her coworkers. Her closest friend at school, Trixie, was a fellow 4th grade teacher. They helped each other at every turn, moving furniture together during classroom setup, dropping off surprise funny pick-me-ups, pooling classroom supplies, and vetting each other's emails to parents and administrators. Rebecca was also tight with Evangeline, Eastern's music teacher, with whom she had a history of Prank Wars.

Later that morning, when her students had settled and put away their supplies, Rebecca gave her annual spiel, which she'd previewed for Holly. "I have four very important things to tell you," she announced. "First, I spontaneously burst into song and dance. If anyone says anything that makes me think of a song, I'll sing. Sometimes I'll even have a dance routine that goes with it." She couldn't help it; whenever she heard something that reminded her of a song—and with her extensive musical background, she knew a *lot* of songs— Rebecca sang. She'd never gone longer than a week without singing in class. Sometimes she burst into song during Eastern's weekly team meetings. Her colleagues were used to it.

"Number two: I'm very clumsy. I'll trip over the computer cord, fall onto your desks, trip over air." The kids laughed. "When I'm trying to toss you things, I will accidentally hit you. You will all get hit by a flying whiteboard marker sometime this year. You're allowed to laugh as long as you're laughing *with* me, not at me."

"Three: I'm really forgetful. I have some strategies that help me work around it, like writing notes on my hand and Post-it notes. So you might need to help me remember things."

"Four: I have very high expectations." As happened every year, the students' faces fell. "What I mean is, I expect you to try your best and take learning seriously. That doesn't mean we won't have fun. I just expect you to do your best and not give up. *Can you all do that?*"

The kids looked relieved. "Oh! Yeah!" "We can do that!"

"I'm going to challenge you. I'm not going to let you sit on your bippies!" Rebecca said. "But you will all learn in my class."

At a staff meeting after school that day, administrators discussed building relationships with students and their families. "Just to show how this is already happening at Eastern, I'm going to out Rebecca," the AP said from the front of the cafeteria. Everyone turned and looked at Rebecca.

"Ohh, Rebehhccaa, what'd you doo," Trixie singsonged.

Rebecca, who had no clue, offered a hammed-up shrug.

"Rebecca doesn't know I'm about to say this," the AP continued, "but she's already started building a relationship with a student new to the school. Let me tell you about this visit." She told the group that Holly had come from a small private school where she didn't have positive relationships with her classmates or teachers. She was anxious about attending a new school—and then she met Rebecca. The AP explained how Rebecca quickly and warmly established a rapport with the student. Rebecca was surprised; she hadn't thought about the interaction all day.

"As I walked the family back down the hallway," the AP said, "the student stopped dead in the middle of the hall while I was talking to her mother and announced, 'I think this is going to be my best school year ever!'"

"Aww," chorused the teachers.

A few days later, as Rebecca walked her students to their weekly library class, two girls admitted they had been afraid of 4th grade. "But now we've met you and we're so happy!" said Mia.

"Why were you scared of fourth grade?" Rebecca asked.

"Because the tests are harder!" said Luci, Mia's best friend. "Also! I talked to Anamaria! She was in fourth grade last year! She said you and Ms. B."—that was Trixie—"were real witches! But now that I'm actually in your class? You're not bad at all!"

Rebecca snort-laughed, her unintentional signature. "Oh, I can be a witch when I have to be." She belted out lines from *Into the Woods*: "I'm not good / I'm not nice / I'm just right / I'm the witch!" Later, she'd share the exchange with Trixie.

That day, Rebecca had planned a purposely challenging math task so the class would struggle enough to launch an interesting conversation about math strategies. Mia tried to avoid tackling the problem by repeatedly getting up to sharpen her pencil and retrieve her water bottle.

"Mia, sit back down. Let's talk about the math," Rebecca said.

She couldn't hear what Mia said. Mia was a mumbler. "Say that again?"

"This is really hard," Mia mumbled.

"Yes, I know. I told you it would be hard, remember? I want you to practice talking about math with your teammates. If the problem were too easy, you wouldn't have anything to talk about. And remember the first day of school? I warned you I have high expectations and would challenge you!"

Mia gave Rebecca a big smile. "Anamaria was right, Miss Abrams. You really *are* a witch!"

Rebecca tapped her fingers together, cackled, "Muahahahaha! Now do your math!" and shimmied away.

Penny Davis   6th Grade Math Teacher

As soon as Penny entered the auditorium, Southern Middle School felt different than it had in years past. Usually, she began Work Week excited to start the school year. Every year on the first August workday before school, the principal had greeted teachers with games and gift cards, music, a school spirit staff T-shirt, and a sprawling breakfast buffet over which colleagues chatted about their summer. Penny, a 6th grade math teacher, hoped the new principal would carry on the positive legacy of the previous administration, particularly now, when teachers' morale was sagging beneath the weight of continued pandemic fallout. But the faculty meeting atmosphere felt cold and sterile. There was no food, music, or swag. The staff's conversations were hushed. The new principal, who, at 40, was the same age as Penny, stood aloof in front of the room, her nose high, her back straight.

Penny missed her favorite coworker at Southern, who'd left over the summer for a position at the district's central office. She spotted Birdie, a new inclusion* teacher, and chitchatted to make her feel welcome. When a few teachers joined them, the women murmured about the changes they feared the principal would implement. The faculty was already unhappy about the new principal, who they believed was unqualified. Disruptions to routines made Penny nervous.

There were a few new teachers this year. Savannah and Vivian, who were on Penny's 6th grade team, were young twentysomethings who must have met over the summer because they were already joined at the hip.

"Who is *that?*" Savannah said, chin-pointing to a man in the doorway.

The man, who had floppy black hair and deep chestnut eyes, looked out of place. There were only a few male teachers at Southern, all currently clad in their regular hometown gentleman uniform of khakis, a neutral polo shirt, and loafers. The new guy sported a pink button-down shirt and a whimsical tie. He looked around the room with a lost smile, saw James, a custodian, cleaning up in a corner, and ambled over to strike up a conversation with him.

"Never mind, not my type," Savannah said, eyeing his dad bod.

"That must be the new Spanish teacher, Ed," said Jan, a friendly 8th grade math teacher. "I heard he just moved from New York City."

Penny didn't know many northerners. She was intrigued by the prospect of meeting someone with a worldview different from her own. She looked back at the guy, who caught her glance. When she smiled in greeting, regretting as she did so that her wide, toothy smile got wider and toothier when she felt awkward, he flashed her a relieved grin that carved unexpected dimples.

---

* Birdie worked with special education students in general ed classes. For more details about inclusion and current special ed practices, please see page 41.

Soon after the principal began her presentation, she talked about tightening the budget. Penny grew more uneasy. Southern teachers were already short on funds. Many of Penny's colleagues were on the borderline of the cutoff for qualifying for government assistance. Single-parent teachers spent almost their entire paycheck on health insurance premiums. Paraeducators often worked only for the insurance and took home no pay; some still had to pay the school system an additional monthly fee to cover their insurance contributions. Penny had teacher friends who worked two or three extra jobs to support their families and pay for their children's sports teams and extracurricular activities. Penny, a veteran teacher with 18 years' experience, had a salary of $47,000.

Penny wondered what more the principal could possibly cut from the budget. Last year, the school had given teachers only $100 for classroom supplies and books for the entire year. One year, Penny had spent $2,000 of her own money on those items. Southern also already set its heat and air conditioning to objectionable levels to save money; Penny had to keep a fan, heater, and jacket in her room. The Southern building had leaks and there was mold in Penny's classroom—really, there was mold all over the school—even though every year she asked the school to eliminate it.

Yet Southern and the high school it fed into were the crown jewels of their conservative rural county. Among other accolades, the high school football team was a perennial playoff contender and the middle school usually won local band competitions. They were known by other district communities as "the rich schools." Many Southern families were comfortably middle or upper middle class, but the district also included a few blue-collar neighborhoods where families couldn't afford school supplies.

After the meeting, as Penny stood up to leave, she saw Nel, the administrative secretary, and Blair, a 6th grade science teacher, side-eyeing her and whispering. This treatment wasn't new. Plenty of times last year when Penny was checking her mail in the office, Nel or Blair would say to a handful of teachers, "Hey, we're going to lunch, want to come?" or "We're ordering takeout—anyone want anything?" blatantly ignoring Penny. When Penny picked up lunch or ran to the convenience store, she made sure to ask everyone within sight if they needed something.

Penny was used to "not fitting into their little bubble," as she put it, but it still hurt. People told Penny, who was petite and chesty with long, shiny dark hair, that she was pretty, but when she looked in the mirror, she still saw the awkward teen whom middle school classmates made fun of. To this day, Penny didn't feel like she'd ever had a true best friend. The women in her small town were interested in such stereotypically southern-belle fripperies that Penny had difficulty finding common ground. They sure didn't like Star Wars like Penny did.

Penny saw herself as a "math nerd," though she was intellectually curious and well-read in so many subjects that she could clear a *Jeopardy!* board any night of the week. Penny had never really met anyone else like her and wouldn't have had an active social life if not for her husband, Kent.

Kent and Penny had met in high school—the same high school their kids now attended—a golden couple from the start. At least, that's what other people believed. Even now, Penny's colleagues seemed to think she led a charmed life, with two strapping football player sons and a husband who could win over anyone. Maybe that was why some coworkers kept their distance from her. Blair called Penny "Princess Perfect." Penny once overheard Nel tell a teacher, "Penny's just too perfect: perfect wife, perfect kids, perfect husband. I can't deal with that." Penny's colleagues had no idea what was actually going on behind closed doors.

The abuse had started early on, before Penny knew enough to realize that the way Kent treated her was wrong. She longed for the kind of passion she saw in *Dirty Dancing*, her favorite movie outside the Star Wars canon. She'd grown up believing the movie showcased what love (and sex) should be. Life with Kent wasn't like that at all. She'd read enough articles about how love didn't mirror movie portrayals to convince herself that Kent was good enough. In Penny's town, women were expected to marry young and get crankin' on the babies right away. Penny always had tried to do what was expected of her.

When Penny was seven months pregnant with the twins, she and Kent got into an argument about Kent's pickup truck. Kent refused to get a new car and hadn't allowed Penny to get a master's degree so that she could eventually earn more money as a teacher to pay for a used, safer car herself. Penny showed Kent a spreadsheet she'd made to illustrate that they could afford a safe car to protect their boys. Suddenly it was as if a switch had flipped. Kent screamed at Penny, accusing her of being raised poorly, of being spoiled—this from the man who bought himself a $400 coat. Penny had never seen Kent rage this way before. Afraid he would hit her, she fled the house in the dark, wearing only her nightgown on the coldest night of the year.

He didn't go after her. Eventually, when she worried the twins could freeze, she walked the dozen blocks back home. He was still angry when she returned. That night, she asked herself, "Should I leave him?" *No,* she decided, *his temper is just flaring. He'll be better once we have the boys.* She made excuses like that for years.

Now, Kent yelled at her every week. He saved his physical aggression for video games. One time he got so angry during a game that he kicked a hole in the wall and needed surgery on his foot. After that incident, Penny fixed up a man cave in the basement to give him his own space—and so the kids would be less likely to hear their dad bellowing at a screen.

Kent still found ways to control her. Sometimes he gave her

an afternoon curfew. When they were out in public, whether in town or their front yard, if she stopped to greet a friend or neighbor, he'd hiss that she wasn't "being courteous" to him. Penny told herself daily she could stick out the marriage until the boys turned 18, which was now two years away. Kent was a decent father, mostly. But she lamented that her boys knew her as someone who was always on edge.

⤫

The first family to enter Penny's classroom for Open House was the family who'd known Penny the longest. Penny had grown up with Skylar's mother, Kitty. While they'd been friendly as children, it would be a stretch to say they were friends now. Kitty was, in Penny's opinion, "a cross between a Stepford wife and a helicopter mom."

Kitty owned an enormous house in the city, where the schools were not top-notch. Until now, she'd sent her four children to private school. Although she technically lived out of district, she'd asked school officials for years to waive her family in. She wanted her kids to attend the most prestigious public schools in the county, where her sons could play on the football team and her daughter eventually could join the high school's award-winning cheer squad. Southern's new principal had agreed to put a word in with the school board for a transfer.

The moment the transfer was approved, Kitty lobbied the principals at the middle and high schools to put her kids in the "best" teachers' classes. At Southern, that included Penny for math. Over the summer, Kitty barraged Penny with texts, though they hadn't hung out in years. "Skylar's coming to Southern next year and I've already requested that she'll be in your class!" the first one said.

Ohh boy, this might not be a good idea, Penny thought. Teaching the children of people she'd grown up with added extra pressure. Their parents usually assumed they'd have an in with Penny. If she could do it all over again, Penny wouldn't have stayed in her hometown. Teaching where she grew up blurred too many lines.

"Can you email me a list of the students in each of Skylar's classes?" Kitty texted in July. "I want to look up where they all live and make sure Skylar's only going to be with the good kids."

"No, I can't do that," Penny replied, and promptly forwarded the text to her mom so they could have a good laugh.

At Open House, Kitty was flanked by her daughter and her mother, all three wearing head-to-toe Lilly Pulitzer, sauntering down the hallway, blessing all the hearts, looking like they sashayed "straight out of Bravo's *Southern Charm*," Penny told me later. Skylar's outfit cost exponentially more than Penny's black slacks, low heels, and green top, which she'd found on sale at Target.

Skylar's grandmother gave Penny a southern hug—a side hug with her hand on Penny's shoulder—and an air-kiss, touchy-feely without smudging her lipstick. "We are so excited y'all are going to be Skylar's teacher," she announced.

"Anyhoo, we know you're the best teacher here, and my Skylar just had to be on your team because if there are any problems, I know who to call immediately," Kitty gushed.

Greeaat, Penny thought. She turned to Skylar. "Hi, Skylar, I'm looking forward to having you in my class."

"Yes, ma'am. Thank you, ma'am," Skylar said. Penny smiled at her and moved on to Asher's dad, another parent she'd grown up with.

Later, a mother approached Penny, leaving at the door a pale boy whose auburn hair fell messily in his face. "Hello, my son Zach is a selective mute. He won't talk to you no matter what you do. He will talk to other kids and he will talk to me. That's it," she said matter-of-factly.

Penny was a deer in headlights. Neither the school nor the district had provided her with any information about this student. Penny was confident she could teach any child, but she liked to be thoroughly prepared. She'd been at school since 7 a.m. to finish decorating her meticulously organized classroom, which was so colorful that students had remarked, "It looks like a pack of highlighters threw up."

"Also, Zach is shaky in math," his mother said. She explained that she wanted Zach to have accommodations, but the district refused to give him an Individualized Education Program (IEP) because selective mutism wasn't officially recognized as a disability. It would have been helpful if the Southern administration had assigned Zach to an inclusion class. Penny had Birdie, the inclusion teacher, only two periods a day.

The rest of Open House plodded along, with a few memorable doozies. One parent told Penny, "I'm not buying school supplies. You should be buying the school supplies because I pay your salary because I pay taxes." Penny didn't mention that she'd spent hundreds of dollars on supplies already this year, and that for the first time any Southern teachers could remember, the administration gave them no money for their classrooms.

A nurse, smiling radiantly with a large gift bag and three well-behaved kids, introduced her son, Darren, and said, "I thought you might need extra glue sticks, paper, and pencils, so this is for you. If there's anything I can do to help you, let me know. Anything you need, please call." It occurred to Penny that unlike this single parent, Kitty, whose family was the wealthiest at Southern, hadn't brought or offered a thing. Darren's mom was the antidote to other parents at Open House; Penny carried her kindness with her for the rest of the interminable day.

Before Open House ended, Kitty texted Penny: "We're very concerned because Asher and Skylar are in the same class. They're such good little friends, we're worried they're going to misbehave."

Penny rolled her eyes. "Class schedules are set. I'll put them on opposite sides of the room. They'll be fine."

That afternoon, Penny had to attend an IEP meeting for one of her students. During IEP meetings, staff reviewed and updated customized educational plans for students with special needs. In this case, the student struggled with ADHD.

The school counselor introduced the teachers to the parents and passed out copies of an evaluation report. As the meeting began, the central issue crystallized: The parents wanted their son diagnosed with a learning disability that he didn't have and placed in special ed classes with more accommodations than he needed. The parents didn't listen to the counselor's gentle hints that the child belonged in general ed, where he already received accommodations for mild ADHD.

After about 10 minutes of observing the group talking in circles, Ed, the new Spanish teacher, spoke for the first time. "The counselor's report says right here that your child does not have a learning disability," he said, pointing at the page.

The student's mom bristled. "He *does* have a learning disability."

"The tests indicated otherwise," Ed said. "But he might benefit from medication for his ADHD."

"We don't have to give him medicine if we don't want to," the mom said, crossing her arms and shooting an accusatory look at the school counselor, who nodded.

"That's true, you don't," the counselor agreed.

"There's nothing any of us can do to make your child have a learning disability. Your child actually tests above average," Ed said.

The other participants looked warily at one another or down at their laps. *Wow, Ed is kind of a jerk*, Penny thought. *People here are raised to not be that blunt.*

After the meeting, Penny finished diligently writing her meeting notes. She looked up to see Ed waiting for her. "Golly, you were aggressive with those parents," she said.

"The report and the student's prior teachers said he could do the work."

"I agree, but we sugarcoat it with parents. You were very blunt. Maybe that's a New York City thing."

"Have you ever been to Manhattan?" Ed asked.

"Oh, my husband, Kent, took us there for his job once," she said, defensive. "He has a big fancy office overlooking the park and they put us up at a ritzy hotel."

Ed cocked his head. "You're big on bragging about your life, aren't you."

Penny scowled. "Uhh, okay. You asked." She gathered her things and strode out of the room, shaking her head at the audacity of the city guy who thought he was all that.

The 6th grade teachers and students were divided into three teams. At Penny's team's meeting the Friday before school, the other teachers carped about Zach.

"If he's not going to talk to us, how do we communicate with him?" asked Wilma, a history teacher. Wilma and Blair were considered the "mean teachers" at Southern, stern to students and tough with grades.

"He needs to be removed from the classroom immediately if he won't talk," Blair said. "He's deliberately disobeying teachers. He's being obstinate. That's oppositional defiance."

Oppositional defiance is a behavioral disorder, Penny thought. *That's totally different from selective mutism.* "It's going to be tricky, but if he'll write us notes or talk to other students, it could work out," Penny said. "He's been doing this for years, so I think he'll know how to communicate with us. We could even email his teacher from last year for advice." Although Blair, Wilma, and Celia, an English teacher, were older than Penny, teaching was their second career. Penny, who started teaching right out of college, was the veteran on the team.

"But why isn't he in special ed? Why doesn't he have an IEP?" Savannah asked.

"Because it's not considered a disability," Penny said.

"Then if he chooses not to speak, his parents need to force him to speak or punish him until he does," Blair said.

"I agree. How am I supposed to reach this child?" Wilma groused.

"You ask him yes-or-no questions. Or have him write on a whiteboard," Penny said.

Penny went to the office after the meeting to ask if the school had Zach's file yet. Nel grudgingly dug a folder out of a cabinet.

"You had this the whole time? Why didn't we get his file before Open House?" Penny asked.

Nel shrugged.

Penny flipped through the pages. There it was: selective mutism. She could have been prepping for this for weeks. The file also showed that Zach was a B student who passed the state tests. "He's smart! Blair, Wilma, and the others feel like Zach doesn't belong here. I was appalled," Penny told me later. "Teachers make accommodations for kids a whole lot. I may not have an IEP saying this child needs accommodations, but if I see a child struggling, I'm going to accommodate that child."

Miguel Garcia   Middle School Special Ed Teacher

Miguel Garcia laid his head on his desk. Even though he was a veteran National Board–certified special education teacher and former union representative, even though he'd grown up in poverty in a rough neighborhood, even though he was grateful to be in a position in which he could help students who lived in unfathomably difficult circumstances, this week had been too much. *If I were a first-year teacher*, he thought, *I would have quit today.*

Half a dozen opened textbooks blanketed Miguel's desk. It was 8 p.m. on a Thursday, the latest Miguel had ever stayed in his classroom, so late that the rest of the Western Middle School building was empty. He had lost sleep over his job all week, and he still didn't know where to begin. *I'm drowning in paper*, he thought. *How the hell do I do this?*

This was an entirely new set of problems from the ones Miguel had encountered the previous year, when the moderately to severely disabled students in his special ed classes constantly bit, hit, or spit on him. This year, Miguel was teaching one general ed elective video production class and four periods of special ed classes for mildly to moderately disabled students. He had switched to the less severely disabled population only because his doctor told him he must.

Miguel had enjoyed working with the moderate to severe population. He always rooted for the underdog; As the son of impoverished Salvadoran immigrants, he'd been an underdog himself. When he was a first generation college student, he'd devoted his free time to volunteering with kids from the projects. "I'm drawn to public service with populations that are overlooked, maybe because I was overlooked sometimes and was always super grateful when someone noticed me," he said. "My job would be so much easier if I dealt with all really well-behaved kids from upper-class neighborhoods, but that's not what I got into this for." He also chose to work in special ed for the same reason he left the entertainment industry more than two decades ago. When his mother had a brain hemorrhage, her resulting disabilities included severe communication and mobility issues. Her treatment and rehabilitation inspired Miguel to leave a much more lucrative career for teaching: He wanted to help the people who most needed help.

Miguel loved teaching students with mild to moderate disabilities, too. The kids tugged at his heartstrings, like Eli, a 6th grader who bolted from the classroom practically every day last year but had a dry sense of humor that Miguel found irresistible. And Dewayne, a good-hearted 7th grader whose distracting behavior, fueled by severe ADHD, led some of his gen ed teachers to kick him out of class.

Western was an urban Title I school* with a diverse population of mostly Black and Latino children. Many students had permits to attend Western rather than their local schools because their parents worked nearby as nannies, housekeepers, home health aides, or nursing home assistants. Local families who had the money usually sent their kids to private schools. While Western had struggled in the past, recently it had turned around under Frank, a congenial new principal and former teacher whom Miguel had befriended. Western had a large number of homeless students, kids expelled from other schools, students in single-parent families, and children who came from neighborhoods so unsafe that their parents bused them in. "Our school," Miguel said fondly, "is the Island of Misfit Toys," where students were accepted, nurtured, and given second chances.

Which made it all the more galling that school district officials were trying to destroy it.

In late spring, the Western community had been stunned to learn that district officials held secret meetings with parents at wealthier elementary schools about taking over Western and turning it into a charter-school-like academy. Schools invited to the meetings were as far as four miles away from Western. Closer-in schools, where parents were more likely to know Western families, were not invited. No Western families attended the schools that would feed into the

---

* Title I schools have a high percentage of students from low-income families.

academy. No Western families were informed by the board about its plans to snatch away a crucial anchor in their lives.

Western and Central, the other public middle school in the area, had plenty of space for more kids. Rather than prioritizing its current students and welcoming new ones, the school board was capitulating to private-school parents who wanted a free middle school in the neighborhood "for *our* kids." The academy would be 75% white, Miguel estimated, based on the elementary school populations invited to apply. Western and Central averaged more than 80% minority students. The new academy would eliminate Western, divert resources away from Central, and end a special education program that families relied on.

Locals didn't trust Chad Tucker, the school board member with gelled inky hair who was leading the charge. He was a young white elite and former investment banker whose exorbitant campaign funding came from out of state. His education inexperience, out-of-touch proposals, and seeming affinity for charter schools led some educators to refer to him as "Betsy DeVos, Jr."

Over the summer, Miguel had devoted himself to opposing the takeover, though he didn't have the time. His mother was dying in hospice and in addition to his usual summer prep work and side jobs to supplement his teaching salary, he took a training course on teaching mildly to moderately disabled students. Miguel traveled back and forth across the country to be with his mom, while also fighting the school board: writing letters, rallying community members, researching policies.

Miguel's mother had died earlier in the month. Frank had called to check on him every day.

Miguel didn't want to be involved in politics. He went into teaching solely to help disadvantaged kids. "But when the board encroached on my corner of the world, it made my blood boil. I think they've been trying to starve out our school for the last two years so they could take over. One way is trying to get rid of our teachers," he told me. The district had transferred several excellent teachers away from Western when it technically didn't have to. This year, just before school started, officials transferred a terrific longtime Western math teacher elsewhere because of "lower enrollment projections." The district easily could have floated Western the teacher's salary for the first few weeks of school until student numbers rose, as they did every year. Western needed only a few more students to reach the threshold. Instead, a PE teacher and a science teacher were assigned the math classes, a long-term sub took two science classes, and other teachers' class schedules were changed at the last minute to accommodate the switch. While the district officials were at it, they also axed Western's school band.

Miguel was one of the few teachers who wasn't afraid to speak out against the district to defend his school. He was willing to risk being fired if he could save Western in the process. Teaching was not his first career, and it likely would not be his last.

Miguel had attended a notoriously bad inner-city public elementary school. His parents worked extra jobs to scrape together enough money to send Miguel and his sister to a poorly run Catholic school where, Miguel remembered, "some of the nuns were downright abusive, mentally and physically. I hated school. I was bored. Rote learning and nineteen-forties teaching methods were the norm. Curiosity and freethinking weren't allowed. I'd get so depressed on Sunday nights. But my parents were doing their best and at least I wasn't getting jumped every day anymore."

Even now, in his fifties, Miguel cringed when he recalled his student days. He aimed to give his students the opposite experience. "The most wonderful thing about being a teacher is that I get to go back to school and try to be the teacher I wish I had. I try to make things fun," he said. Miguel was known as a charismatic, innovative teacher. He had gotten a master's in education specifically to learn new strategies to engage students.

Once, a student informed a new classmate, "Don't worry, we don't do a lot of work. We play a lot of games." Miguel loved to hear that the kids thought his lessons were games. Even when he let his students play actual games, like Uno and Connect 4, after lunch to transition them back into the classroom, they didn't realize he was assessing their academic and social-emotional skills. He moved kids from table to table to determine who needed to be closer to him and whether certain students would learn better if they were separated. This week, Miguel quickly realized that Eli couldn't stand Laurent, a 6th grader who was habitually contrarian. Miguel separated them because Eli responded with cutting insults that Laurent didn't understand.

As a teaching mentor in a district teacher training program, Miguel mentored 15 teachers, mostly at night. Every year, he taught the new teachers that the first two weeks of school were "an investment. Don't feel like you have to start teaching academics right away. First you have to get to know your students. Talk about their favorite TV shows, things like that. As I start them doing team games, apps, and Smart Board stuff, I do formal assessments for groupings. I just assume the first two weeks are going to be mostly observing and developing a consistent routine." He strove to "trick my students into learning by playing. I love to see them excited about learning, especially because my students have learning disabilities and for many of them, school has always been a dismal chore, like it was for me as a kid."

Now Miguel was the one faced with a dismal chore. He looked helplessly at the books that had been scattered across his desk since the end of the school day. His teaching schedule had already changed three times in only the first week of school. Miguel was expected to teach history, science, English language arts, and math to special ed students, plus his video elective. His special ed classes combined 6th to 8th grades. Today, the district had placed two new students with complicated IEPs, a 6th grader and an 8th grader, in his classes without any notice or support staff.

The district demanded the impossible: Miguel had to prep curricula for essentially 13 different classes in three different grade levels—and he had to do it without proper resources or a teaching assistant because officials claimed to have no funding for the kids who needed it most. The district didn't give Western money for new textbooks, and the special ed language arts books were unusable. Western didn't even have a nurse more than once a week, though some Western students had seizure disorders so severe that they required an ambulance. Funny how the board could find the money to create a new academy for wealthy white families. The district's inequitable policies were preventing Miguel from meeting his students' needs. *If I feel this way after twenty-plus years of experience, a new teacher would be crushed*, he thought. Lesson planning was going nowhere tonight. Miguel forced himself to pack up and go home.

On Friday, Miguel was in the middle of teaching second period math when Eli reluctantly trudged in, late for the third time that week (the other two days he was absent). Eli's behavior needed adjusting and he knew it; he said during a class discussion, almost as a warning, "I have this anger issue. And people in my family have it." Eli's last teacher, who had left special ed because she was fed up with the paperwork, had informed Miguel that Eli was difficult. "I can see why teachers are like, 'I can't deal with him,'" Miguel told me. "Teachers talk, and then kids travel from one class to another with a reputation. But I'm going to act like I don't know anything. I'm going to validate him and be really positive. He's smart and no one's seen his potential. He can be defiant, but it's self-protection. He's resilient. He's a good kid. I just think he's had a tough go for a while." Academically, Eli was a strong reader, but he refused to write or do homework.

Eli had mentioned in passing on separate occasions that he had to sleep on the floor or a couch. Miguel guessed he was homeless, perhaps staying with relatives or friends, constantly on the move. Western teachers weren't allowed to ask students about their home lives or medications.

"Hey, Eli, hi, I'm glad you're here," Miguel said warmly. He thought Eli likely got grief last year for being late, but the obstacles homeless students faced getting to school each morning would be daunting for an adult, let alone an 11-year-old. "We just did a worksheet on graphs; here, I'll get one for you."

The other students talked loudly. Miguel pointedly stared at the class. He tried never to raise his voice to students unless he had to short-circuit a behavior loop. With older kids, like his video students, he simply clapped sharply once and said, "Eyes." Tall and clean-cut, with close-cropped hair and a baby face, Miguel looked much younger than his age, but his theater training had taught him how to command a room.

A few students noticed Miguel's stare. "Come on, shut up," someone said.

"I'm going to have to yell at you guys if you don't listen. Do you want me to yell?" Miguel asked.

"Yeah!" several kids replied. They'd never heard him yell before.

"Okay," Miguel said. "I WANT YOU ALL TO BE QUIET!"

Startled, the kids busted out laughing.

"Do you want me to do that again?" Miguel asked.

"No!"

"Okay." Miguel shrugged so they'd know he wasn't angry. "When I'm talking, don't talk," he said. "This is a skill you're going to have to learn for high school. You appear rude when you talk while someone else is talking. I'm sure you're not trying to be rude. So you need to whisper so you don't interrupt me. Do you know how to whisper?"

The kids played it off as if the question were silly, but Miguel caught enough uncertain looks that it hit him: Maybe no one had taught them how to whisper. Miguel had learned from teaching autistic kids that what neurotypical children learned practically through osmosis, some children needed to be taught specifically, step by step. Miguel thought this strategy could benefit all kinds of special ed students.

"When you whisper, you can't talk from your stomach. You have to talk from your throat. So let's practice whispering." Now the students looked at him as if he were crazy. "Talk about whatever you want, but whisper," he said. "Here, if you don't know what to talk about, tell the person next to you what your favorite cereal is." Miguel circled the room, alerting kids when they were too loud. Eventually, their chatter reached an appropriate volume level.

Experts call it "the hidden curriculum," the things students learn that they aren't specifically taught. This is a particular concern for students with special needs. One of the most important examples Miguel ever heard was at a special ed conference. The presenter said that as a woman, for years she didn't think twice about telling her students that when they speak to someone, they should make eye contact and say hello. She told the audience she hadn't considered that she was putting her male autistic students at risk because in public bathrooms, men usually don't talk to or look at one another. Since that conference, Miguel had instructed his male special ed students that in public bathrooms, they should "do your business and leave. Don't look at anybody. And if anyone talks to you in the bathroom, ignore them until you get outside. Then, if there are other people around, you can talk."

They need to be explicitly taught these things, Miguel thought as he crossed the classroom. Maybe, he realized, he should adopt the same back-to-basics outlook for his curriculum planning. What if he tossed out the district's grade-level academic requirements and focused more on catching students up on the basic executive functions necessary for school? He could teach them how to interact and how to be successful students.

Because prepping 13 classes wouldn't help his students, Miguel would consolidate subjects. He'd prioritize the language arts basics—reading comprehension, fluency, and grammar—in history and science. Instead of teaching three grade levels of science at once, he'd rotate every two weeks: earth science, life science, physical science. He'd teach the other periods at a 6th grade level, simultaneously emphasize more advanced techniques for the 7th and 8th graders, and improve all the students' life skills to prepare them for next year. His decision made, Miguel relaxed. He would cover as much as he could. He would not be beholden to district requirements. If district officials came after him, so be it. He'd go down knowing he did right by the kids.

Miguel resumed his math lesson. He drew a graph on the whiteboard. "All right, let's vote on . . . doughnuts! Yeah, that's a good one. What's your favorite doughnut?"

Instantly the class perked up. "I love Krispy Kreme glazed doughnuts!" someone proclaimed.

"I really like Dunkin' chocolate-covered," another student said.

"Nah, man, glazed!"

"Chocolate!"

Before the debate intensified, Miguel interrupted. "Okay, okay, let's do a vote. Who here likes glazed? Raise your hand." He graphed the result. "Chocolate-covered? And who likes cream-filled?"

"Eww, that's nasty! I hate cream-filled," someone piped up.

"Yeah, when you squeeze it, it's like pus coming out a pimple."

A chorus: "Eww!"

As the conversation devolved, Miguel wrote the data on the board. *They are super into doughnuts*, he thought. *Aha*. Miguel had devised a reward system this year: Students could earn points by turning in homework, giving thoughtful answers in class, and so forth. At the end of the day, he gave the student with the most points a treat: a Pop-Tart, granola bar, or whatever Miguel picked up at the grocery store. For every five points, Miguel gave out paper tickets, but he hadn't yet figured out what the kids would be able to buy with the tickets, until now.

Miguel often felt like a club DJ in the classroom, continuously changing tracks, managing the vibe, keeping the room moving and motivated. "It's like you do a set, and if a song doesn't work out or kills the mood for some reason, you have to be prepared with options B, C, and D," he told me. "I'm lucky I have a great principal who understands this. Especially in special ed, you have to make decisions on the spot. And what works one year might not work the following year."

"By the way," Miguel informed his class, "Monday I'll give double points if you get your assignment planner signed and triple points if you do your homework. And"—the plan formed quickly—"we're going to have a Doughnut Day based on this graph right here. I'll use the data to pick the flavors. If you want a doughnut, it'll cost you twenty tickets. Yeah, we're going to have a doughnut store every Friday." Boom. The kids' eyes lit up. They had never been so attentive and engaged during a lesson.

Every Friday before school, Miguel bought freshly baked doughnuts. He picked up extras for his 10-year-old daughter to eat in the car on the way to her elementary school on the days she wasn't at her mom's. (Miguel and her mom were both now married to other people.) Miguel stored the box atop his bookcase so his students could smell the doughnuts all morning.

Miguel used the store as a learning activity: One week he'd increase the price to 25 tickets as an opportunity to explain inflation; another week he'd announce a 10% discount and the students had to calculate the new price. Eventually he added Yu-Gi-Oh! cards and mechanical pencils to the store. At the end of the month, he bought pizza, a bigger-ticket item. All of this was out of Miguel's pocket; he had paid for almost everything in his classroom.

The system worked. When kids asked to use the bathroom at inopportune moments, Miguel would say, "That's fine, but you have to pay me five tickets." Ninety percent of the time, they opted to save their tickets. They learned to wait until breaks or lunch.

As the school year got going, Miguel quickly grew attached to his kids. Each child's unique blend of strengths and challenges was like a puzzle, and he was confident that by the end of the year he'd get his students to the point where they'd be ready to learn in their special ed classes the following year.

And then the district dropped another bombshell.

To save money, district administrators told some staff members they would eradicate special ed classes for mildly to moderately disabled students beginning the following school year. The students would be mainstreamed, while special ed teachers would rove among classes as helpers. Miguel was devastated. Not only were his students getting squeezed out of their school, but now they'd get lost in larger classes of strangers with gen ed teachers overloaded with too many students to give special ed students the extra time they needed. "It's going be a nightmare. Disastrous. I shudder to think what's going to happen to my kids next year," Miguel told me. "In a small, structured class, I can get their behaviors under control. But the gen ed environment is wide open and they're going to get in trouble again all the time. I can't properly do behavior modifications and social supports if I'm not consistently their teacher."

As much as Miguel treasured his students, he was disenchanted by a system that wasn't working and a district leadership that didn't seem to care. The system asked too much of teachers, gave back too little, and frequently threw roadblocks in their way. While he knew he was making a difference in his students' lives, the district's obstacles prevented him from making the kind of impact his students deserved. He expected this year of teaching would be his last.

Introduction
"It Makes My Soul Happy": What Teachers Endure and Why They Stay

LeVar's workday didn't end when the Texas school bell rang at 3:20. On days when the full-time PE and health teacher wasn't coaching middle school football, soccer, or basketball, he drove straight to his next job as a carpet cleaner from 4 p.m. to 7 p.m., a job he also worked all day Saturdays. For a long time, every weekday he came home to grade papers, prepare lessons, and sleep for a couple of hours before working the 10:45 p.m. to 6:45 a.m. shift as a hospital tech. He was back at school at 7:15. He barely saw his wife and two young daughters.

Eventually, LeVar's high blood pressure led his doctor to tell him to quit the night shift or he'd have a stroke. After LeVar left that job, his physical and emotional strains continued as he struggled to figure out how else to supplement his teacher salary of about $30,000 after taxes and insurance payments. At various times both his water and cell phone were cut off. He thought he tore knee ligaments, "but I can't get it looked at because who is going to work if I can't? I've had to act like I ate somewhere else just so my girls can eat more," LeVar told me. "I've shed a tear or two. I'm always thinking, *How am I going to feed my family?*"

In the years before the COVID-19 pandemic, the education landscape had already darkened considerably for the nation's approximately four million K–12 teachers. "Teachers feel more voiceless than ever. There's a lack of community support and understanding of how difficult it can be to serve children's educational, emotional, and psychological needs," a South Carolina elementary school librarian told me in March 2020.

The pandemic further exposed the nation's shameful mistreatment of teachers, which remains underaddressed. As school staff fled the profession, districts ordered teachers to take on additional roles, such as substituting for other educators during their lunch and planning periods or supervising students from other classes alongside their own. By 2022, when there were 567,000 fewer public school educators than before the pandemic, a National Education Association (NEA) survey found that three-quarters of its members were handling extra responsibilities and/or covering for coworkers.

During the 2021–22 academic year, a Maryland school pulled its interventionist almost every day for four months to cover other teachers' classes. Rather than teach her special ed and struggling students, she had to sub for most classroom grades, as well as art and PE and as a counselor. Administrators continued to yank her even after she told them their actions demonstrated that they thought "my job is not important and neither are my students." She was frustrated that her intervention students were "missing out. I feel like I've failed my students by not seeing them. They're not getting the support they desperately need. I leave at the end of the day completely drained and usually end up crying on my way home. The feeling of inadequacy is overwhelming."

In interviews, teachers nationwide repeatedly echoed the sentiments of a New York middle school art teacher, who said that teaching is "a very different profession than I signed on for twenty years ago."

Despite ever-expanding responsibilities, teachers remain underpaid. U.S. teachers' salaries compared to those of workers in other professions with similar education levels are worse than in every other industrialized nation surveyed by the Organisation for Economic Cooperation and Development—and U.S. teachers work more hours than most. In the 2010s, the national average teacher salary dropped 4.5% at the same time as college costs and student loans ballooned. The "teacher pay gap" hit a record high in 2021, when the Economic Policy Institute reported that teachers were paid 23.5% less than U.S. professionals with similar education and experience—and that the pay gap was a major reason why the "teacher shortage" is "real, large and growing, and worse than we thought." For comparison, the teacher pay gap was 6% in 1996. In Alabama, Arizona, Colorado, Oklahoma, and Virginia, the pay gap exceeds 30%.

The average teacher's starting salary is less than $40,000 in more than half of public school districts. Like Penny, even the highest-paid, most experienced teachers with advanced degrees make less than $50,000 per year in more than 1,000 school districts. "I'm a single mom. I work other jobs to make ends meet. I work summer school," said a 20-plus-year veteran Missouri middle school teacher with a master's degree in special education. "I will be lucky to make what a friend's son started out making as an accountant fresh out of a five-year bachelor's program. I feel like a fool. I am bright. I am educated. I work hard. I can't get ahead."

To make things worse, the average health insurance family plan premium for teachers is more than $7,000 per year—about $1,300 higher than premiums for other state and local employees—and teachers contribute both a higher amount and a higher percentage of premiums than they did 10 years ago. As if that weren't enough, in California, Oklahoma, and some districts in other states, teachers must pay for their own substitutes when on extended medical leave, which in some areas can cost up to $240 to $260 a day. "There's a lot of pressure to go to work sick so I can stay home with my kids when they are sick," said a Pacific Northwest high school science teacher with three children. During the pandemic, teachers in some districts had to use their sick leave days to quarantine or test when they caught or were exposed to COVID at school. When Penny got COVID and was still sick after her isolation period ended, her district stipulated that she had to return to school the next day or they would dock her pay.

These were only a few of the factors that led to what the Associated Press in 2021 called "a shortage of teachers and staff the likes of which some districts say they have never seen." "Teacher shortage" may be the popular term, but it's a misleading one. There is not a shortage of potential qualified and aspiring educators. There is a shortage of teaching jobs that adequately treat and compensate bachelor's- to master's-level professionals such that they would want to be teachers. Miguel, a trained, willing, superb educator, planned to leave teaching only because his district made the job so unpalatable that the stress of the role outweighed his passion for the work.

Demand for U.S. teachers outgrew supply by more than 100,000 for the first time in 2019, while enrollment in and completion of teacher preparation programs each dropped by approximately a third between 2010 and 2018. In 2021, 13% of educator preparation programs surveyed by the American Association of Colleges for Teacher Education had "significant declines in the number of new graduate students due to the pandemic."

The pandemic also hastened the exodus from the field. A 2022 NEA survey found that 55% of educators said they would leave the profession earlier than planned—nearly a 20% rise over the rate reported in August 2021. "Teachers, as well as building and district leaders, are retiring at unprecedented levels, and there simply aren't enough new educators to replace them," Tina Kerr, executive director of the Michigan Association of Superintendents and Administrators, told *PBS NewsHour* in late 2021. "We're seeing schools close, the state is begging retirees to return, and too many students—especially students of color and those living in poverty—are being taught by long-term subs, and we're seeing a shortage of them too."

The substitute pool shrank so precipitously that states took drastic measures to recruit bodies. In October 2021, Oregon issued a statewide emergency order reducing the qualifications for subs: Candidates needed only to be "at least 18 years old, sponsored by a participating district or charter school, and have 'good moral character' with the 'mental and physical health necessary' to teach," *The New York Times* reported. "Teachers are drowning," Charlie, an Oregon high school teacher, told me. "Students in high school see their teachers struggle, especially in our small town, and they don't want that life. How are we supposed to attract talented and professional employees? The people we need are passing this profession up for others that allow them to have the personal lives they want."

Teachers are approximately five times more likely than average full-time workers to take on an additional part-time job; nearly 70% of teachers have needed a second job to make ends meet. Most teachers I contacted said they and/or colleagues had to work a side hustle. Several teachers agreed with a Kansas special education teacher who said, "The only teachers I know who don't work second jobs married someone wealthier." Teachers told me about working retail, cleaning houses, farming hay, walking dogs, selling beauty products, DJing weddings, tutoring, working in fast food, waitressing, bartending, painting houses, and staffing amusement parks, among other jobs.

A Texas history teacher whose only meal of the day sometimes consists of food left over in the teachers' lounge said, "My greatest fear is my next ride request will be from a group of my students coming back from a social engagement. That would be mortifying." The 20-year teaching veteran drives for Uber because it's one of the few gigs that jibe with his teaching schedule, thanks to "the extreme burden of take-home work in planning, grading, and professional development. This situation gets complicated with even a single problem student who negatively impacts the classroom environment. It can consume a teacher's take-home work, having to figure out ways not just to ensure students learn important objectives, but also how to strategize so that disrupters don't disrupt the learning."

Many teachers are also concerned about the scarcity of special education and English language learner support staff and resources,* which a Florida elementary school teacher said is a "major cause of stress and anxiety among teachers I know." When Charlie taught sophomore history, she could have a student reading at 3rd grade level, a first-year English language learner, an advanced student at a

---

* A brief introduction for readers who aren't up-to-date on special education practices: Approximately 14% of students ages 3 to 21 are in special education programs. The Individuals with Disabilities Education Act (IDEA) ensures that students with disabilities receive a "free appropriate public education" that, when possible, must be provided in the "least restrictive environment" alongside children who are not disabled. The federal law also requires that eligible students have an Individualized Education Program (IEP); among educators, "IEP" can refer to the plan, the document, or shorthand for the required meetings with staff and parents that occur at least once a year.

About 65% of six- to 21-year-old students served under IDEA spend at least 80% of their school hours in a "general class," according to the National Center for Education Statistics. "Inclusion" is the practice that educates special ed students in classrooms with their general ed peers. Some gen ed classes have aides, paraprofessionals, or teachers, like Birdie, who support special ed students, as at Penny's school, but other gen ed classes, such as some at Miguel's school, do not.

junior reading level, "a student with an unstable home so they're on the verge of meltdown, another student who needs emotional support for autism, add in twenty-four other kids with their individual strengths and weaknesses. Now I need to be able to teach all of them, repeat six times with one fifty-five-minute period to prepare, grade, contact parents, and attend meetings."

As the stories in this book illustrate, teachers are among the most vital, hardest working, passionate, and selfless members of the workforce—yet they are also among the most disrespected and undervalued. "I'm really over being treated as if I'm disposable," a North Carolina middle school English teacher told me. A Maryland middle school science teacher said many people have patronizingly edu-splained to her that "'teaching is so easy: You play all day with kids and you have your summer off.' Or they say, 'Teaching is so easy, anyone could do it.' I always invite them to come spend a day in my shoes, in my classroom, and then come talk to me. My kids can make me smile and laugh, and they can make me want to cry. But I will teach the children, I will build relationships with them, and god forbid, I would protect them with my life."

Schools don't provide teachers similar protections. Many teachers confronted the chilling dilemma of whether to leave classroom doors and windows open to help protect against COVID spread or keep them closed to help protect against school shooters. *New York* magazine national correspondent Gabriel Debenedetti tweeted that some teachers weren't given the choice: They were "told they can't leave classroom doors open to promote better air circulation, because that would circumvent the school's automatic locking system that's in place for active shooter situations."

Other teachers lack even basic proper working conditions. Teachers in some schools must bring their own toilet paper, paper towels, and hand soap to work. Maryland's largest school district grants teachers a ridiculously paltry two days of paid maternity leave—zero employer-paid days for adoptive leave, paternity leave, or other family leave issues—and actively opposed a state bill to improve paid family leave. An Iowa high school teacher said her district's superintendent "spent thirty-two thousand dollars cosmetically renovating the cafeteria, a room that students spend twenty-two minutes a day in, when several classrooms' doors don't lock and the ceiling collapsed in our student center." A Texas art teacher's high school had so many rats that one jumped on her desk and she frequently had to clean droppings out of her desk drawers, though she was severely allergic to rodents. An Idaho English teacher's school doesn't have air conditioning and the heating system is faulty, "so my room is either freezing or so warm it puts my students to sleep. The building is incredibly old, so the floors are chipping, desks are broken, and I'm using a square of shower board as a whiteboard," she said.

Without enough support staff, resources, and time, teachers are hamstrung, desperate to reach all their students but unable to stretch any further. "I see the difference I make in just one year for my students. Imagine classrooms around the country filled with teachers who have support. With the right support, I could help every student I see, and I know most teachers feel the same," Charlie said. "My hands are tied. I watch kids I know could be saved drop out, commit petty crimes, use drugs, and make bad choices. We could fundamentally change the lives of millions of children, but we're simply too overwhelmed to meet their needs in the way we know we should."

LeVar is trying. Like many teachers, his heart is with his students, and he deprioritizes his own financial needs to focus on their well-being. He often spends the little spare time he has hunting for donations for classroom supplies and clothes for students; he provided shoes and football cleats to a student whose only footwear was a pair of flip-flops. Despite his struggles, LeVar has no plans to leave teaching, a profession he loves. "I didn't have when I was growing up. So

I like being there for these kids because they don't have," he said. "Kids will have plenty of opportunities to do the wrong thing, but I want them to hear my voice saying, 'Hey, you will be great someday,' and make the right choice. I love being a teacher because I get the chance to make a difference in someone's life. Seeing kids' futures get brighter makes it all worthwhile. Teaching can be hard, but it makes my soul happy."

⤙⤚

Four years ago, I was surprised to read an article about a local public school district's glaring lack of substitute teachers, which wasn't a well-known issue to noneducators before the pandemic. After asking administrators, an assignment secretary, and teachers if the situation was dire (it was), I applied to be a sub. This decision was coincidental and separate from this book; I want to be clear that the teachers and students in the schools where I worked, and still work, are not a part of the narratives and essays that follow.

I'd intended to substitute perhaps once every couple of weeks, but the experiences with students and educators were so rewarding and the school system's need so great that I accepted assignments much more frequently. In my first few months, I subbed for PE, music, and classroom grades from kindergarten through 8th. During one stretch back then, I subbed for seven different classes on six consecutive school days—and that was at only one school. I've since subbed in person, virtually, and hybrid; as a teacher and paraeducator; for lunch duty, bus duty, and hall duty; for four children in a special ed ESOL class and for more than 40 4th graders in an overcrowded portable during indoor recess.

While I became a sub just to help out, my personal experiences informed the depth and understanding of this book, and the "characters"—real teachers—were instrumental in making me a better sub. For example, after observing students' good-natured banter when I substitute-taught 7th and 8th grade special ed classes, I knew to ask Miguel specific questions about his students' rapport. When Miguel shared strategies he used with Dewayne, I adapted them to keep a student with similar difficulties on task; I also found Penny's methods with her inclusion students helpful. Inspired by Rebecca's constant singing to engage kids, I taught students raps to remember math and reading techniques. And I learned quickly that lunch and planning periods are so packed with prepping, grading, meetings, or administrative work that teachers almost never get a break.

Just before the start of the 2021–22 academic year, an East Coast elementary school where I short-term subbed was allotted a new class at a time when its district had almost 1,000 unfilled staff positions, partly because of the latest COVID variant wreaking havoc before five- to 11-year-olds could get vaccinated. Unable to find a teacher, the school asked me to fill in as a long-term sub. This was how I unexpectedly ended up full-time teaching a 3rd grade class for nearly an entire semester, starting the day before the August Open House, at a time when I couldn't fall behind on my work deadlines. I woke up at 4:30 in the morning to write, got to school between 7:00 and 7:30 to prep, and came home after school to work and prep additional hours into the night. Stressed about not having enough hours in the day for two jobs, I was short with family members, left laundry piles unsorted until weekends (and sometimes—okay, often—beyond), frequently served the same dinner leftovers two or three nights in a row, and pretty much neglected my marriage. When I sustained what I later learned was a ligament tear in my foot, I didn't seek medical attention until Winter Break (a decision I regretted later). There wasn't any time.

I'm glad that situation arose because I got the barest inkling of what daily life can be like for the many teachers who work extra jobs specifically so they can afford to continue teaching. Still, I would never presume to think that because I sub, I personally know what it's like to be a teacher. As Miguel once remarked, "I didn't feel like a real teacher until I was ten years in."

But despite inadequate pay and resources, unrealistic workloads, and pervasive disrespect for the profession, I understand firsthand why teachers stay. There are moments from even my first year of subbing that I still remember vividly: the time I made an eight-year-old laugh so hard he fell off his chair (and kept laughing); the lunch period I graded math tests after I'd spent a week teaching a unit—and realized the kids had mastered it; the 5th graders who hung out with me in "my" kindergarten classroom during recess just because; the countless times teachers kindly went out of their way to help me; the day a 2nd grade boy interrupted a reading lesson to say, "You're the best sub we've ever had because you're funny *and* you make us learn."

These moments of connection, to use a teacher phrase, "fill my buckets." Those are the memories that linger, that propel me to accept 6 a.m. sub calls, forget my epic embarrassing sub fails (I keep a list for comedic value), or return to difficult classes. That feeling of reaching people, the junctures of kinship, mutual learning, growing, and understanding—those moments are powerful enough to redirect a life. At least that's what happened to me.

And while I am not a "real" teacher, my experiences have shown me that LeVar's description of teaching concisely and eloquently explains the allure: It makes my soul happy.

CHAPTER 2

September

Why teachers shouldn't give their cell number to parents (actual texts from a mother to a Virginia middle school teacher):

Hey! Did Kayci do ok on the math test last week? I'm keeping my eye on those grades 😉

Have dates been set for [state] testing?

Hi there! Has Kayci taken the practice [state standardized] math test yet?

Just curious—how could Kayci get tested for the gifted program?

When's the [state] math [test]?

Hope the [state test] went well! When will we know?

Will you send the percentages and breakdown of the [state test]? Thanks!

Hi! Will kids get math [state test] scores today?

Rebecca Abrams   Elementary School Teacher

The air conditioning didn't work in Rebecca's hallway, as usual, and the heat index topped 100 degrees. Students draped over their desks, heat fatigued.

Why wasn't a basic problem fixed in a school building that served more than 700 people daily? Rebecca knew her school wasn't an exception. Her previous school's heating system was broken. For a week there, Rebecca had to relocate her classroom, which was so cold that students could see their breath, to the school's multipurpose room and abandon lesson plans that required an overhead projector the multipurpose room didn't have. She'd heard of schools that had no air conditioning, schools with moldy water fountains, and worse. While the COVID pandemic exposed many schools' HVAC systems' inability to ventilate properly, Eastern's couldn't cool a room at all.

"How do you even learn in these situations?" Rebecca asked me. "How do legislators and school board members get away with it? Why aren't the parents protesting? I guess parents like ours don't have the time or language to protest, maybe that's how." Eastern was a diverse suburban school that encompassed both tree-lined neighborhoods of single-family homes and a sizable low-income apartment complex. The majority of students were Hispanic, nearly two-thirds received free/reduced-price meals, and a high percentage were ESOL students.

At an after-school happy hour, several teachers commiserated about their sweltering classrooms. Rebecca and Trixie laughed about how they had coincidentally worn the same outfit to beat the heat: white camis beneath white sleeveless tops, shorts, and goofy knee socks to justify wearing shorts to school. "We're twinsies!" Trixie told their colleagues. Teachers often accidentally dressed similarly—that was a thing. At least once a month, a couple of Eastern educators would come to school in nearly the same outfit, unplanned.

September

The teachers swapped classroom stories, which was usually how their gatherings began. A 3rd grade teacher said she'd reminded a student daily not to walk backward in the halls, but the student didn't respond to the teacher's increasingly urgent warnings until she whipped around and slammed her face directly into a maintenance cart. She had a black eye for a week. Trixie shared that she'd privately named one of her students "Satan," leading her husband and kids to ask at dinner, "What did Satan do today?"

Then a teacher brought up Oliver, a 4th grader. His 1st grade and 2nd grade teachers grimaced. "Who has him this year?" warily asked a 3rd grade teacher who hadn't had him last year, but knew him nonetheless. Most teachers did. He was one of the most difficult students in the grade.

"Partly me," Rebecca said.

The teachers visibly relaxed. "Oh, you'll be so good for him!" "You'll be the perfect match!" "I hoped he'd be with you!"

Oliver was one of the few students who had Rebecca for both gifted math and ELA and wasn't in her homeroom; he was in Grace's room the rest of the day. When his parents discovered this during Open House, they angrily demanded a meeting with administrators. The admins explained that Oliver often cried or stared robotically in the classroom. In 3rd grade, he was bullied occasionally by a student who was now in Rebecca's homeroom, which was why Oliver was placed elsewhere. His parents had not heard this information before. Despite Oliver's many social and executive functioning issues, Fiona, his 3rd grade teacher, apparently had given them only rosy reports. They didn't appreciate being blindsided now. They didn't know that Oliver had one friend, who was not as academically advanced. Oliver had been assigned to a homeroom with that friend.

Rebecca had made an effort to connect with Oliver starting on day one, when she complimented him on his Roblox shirt so he'd know he had an ally. Since then, she'd spent extra time each class to

49

get him back on track after daydreaming or experiencing one of his funks. Her goal was to keep him engaged without stressing him out or making him feel "different." But he was easily agitated in a way that led classmates to keep their distance.

Rebecca foresaw another major challenge in her class: The gap between the gifted and other students was pronounced. During social studies and science, some of Rebecca's non-advanced students floundered while others needed only moderate support. The advanced students finished assignments early and, without more tasks, monkeyed around while their classmates weren't halfway through the original assignment. JJ, a student whose academics surpassed even his brightest classmates', finished assignments well before the advanced students. After Rebecca administered math unit pretests, she'd outline for Camille, the math specialist, "Most of the group needs to work on this, this small group needs to work on that, a lot of kids need help with that. And then there's JJ, who already knows everything." How could she find time for his enrichment?

"The much larger, angrier issue," according to Rebecca, was the way the district tracked these students. The kids who were identified as "advanced" in 3rd grade tended to stay in advanced classes through middle school. Other students could apply if they had an advocate, but the core group, mostly white English speakers, who were designated by peers "the smart kids," typically remained the same.

During a rare weekend lunch out, Rebecca's friend Aiko, who was not a teacher, tried to steer the conversation toward their pact to start online dating, but Rebecca kept talking about her students. "For years, these kids learn only with each other, hearing the same ideas, living out the same power dynamics, and drinking the Kool-Aid of being 'better' than others, while the other kids believe they're *not* smart. These are eight- to twelve-year-olds! No, no, no. Just no."

The man at the next table kept glancing at them. When Aiko

went to the bathroom, he leaned over. "I have to tell you, I was listening to your conversation because I'm a teacher, and boy, what you're saying sounds familiar," he said.

They ended up talking for 10 minutes about how their county's school board and parents didn't listen to the teachers. The man, a high school art teacher, told Rebecca that even prior to the COVID pandemic, he'd been required to teach English, math, biology, and other subjects outside his expertise because the district didn't hire enough teachers. "Teachers are the ones on the front lines," the man said.

"Yep, we're the ones who actually know what the kids need as learners," Rebecca agreed.

"It's ridiculous how often the people who make decisions about schools and the education system either don't bother asking teachers for their input or ask and then totally ignore it," he said.

Aiko asked Rebecca later if the guy was a romantic prospect. "No way," Rebecca said. "While it would be nice to date another teacher who knows what it's like to be a teacher, then there'd *really* be no getting away from work."

When the PTA president came in during recess to pick up folders to fill with school papers, she said to Rebecca, who was grading at her desk, "While I'm in the building, I thought I'd stop by to ask you how Daisy's doing . . ." After school, when she dropped the folders off, she initiated another impromptu conference about her daughter. Several Eastern PTA officers had children in Rebecca's classroom. *This is going to happen all the freaking time this year while I'm trying to get stuff done*, Rebecca realized.

Many parents would "just stop by" if they were in the building, with "a quick question," forgetting that teachers had limited time to eat, work, or go to the bathroom. "If it's truly just a quick question, fine, but sometimes they actually want a full conversation about how their kid's doing, which is a conference. We're not always prepared for that, and we have other things to do," Rebecca told me. "So we need to pick between answering as best we can, then rushing, or saying we can't talk but we can set up a conference, and then feeling rude."

With two gifted classes this year, Rebecca had received more parent emails in one month than she usually received in five. Parents emailed her at all hours of the night. Rebecca carefully crafted each response, which she proofread several times before sending. She desperately needed that time to work on things for school—such as planning gifted ELA lessons. Since the PD session, Rebecca hadn't received further guidance on the curriculum. A few weeks into the year, she realized the district was putting the onus on teachers to structure the class. She would continually have to sift through the curriculum materials to figure out which units and strategies to teach, when, and for how long, as well as how to fit in separate class-wide, small group, and individual reading and writing lessons for every two- to five-week unit. "I really don't want to give up on my goal of actually having a social life for the first time in five years, but I'm already worried," Rebecca told me.

One morning, when Rebecca walked her kids to the music room as she did every Wednesday, they found a sign on the door: "Music class closed."

The kids reacted immediately: "Wait, what?" "AWW!" "Why isn't there music?" "I don't understand!"

Rebecca was suspicious. "No, no, I don't know what's going on, but I know she's here. We'll get to the bottom of this," she reassured them. She raised her voice in case Evangeline was behind the door: "I'M SURE THERE'S SOME GOOD EXPLANATION."

Rebecca opened the door to see Evangeline standing there laughing. "I was just messing with you!" Evangeline told Rebecca. "I'm very happy to have music class with you today!" she told the students.

"Kids, this year's Prank War is on!" Rebecca announced. "To taste revenge will be so sweet," she sang as she left the room.

When she got to her desk, she paused. Something was awry. After a few moments, she realized the manatee sticker that hugged the left corner of her desk was missing. Rebecca collected manatee merch because her favorite animal was fun and weird. She checked the floor, under her desk, in her bag, and on her chair, but the sticker wasn't there.

When Rebecca picked up her kids from music, she asked Evangeline if she'd also pranked Rebecca by hiding her sticker. Evangeline hadn't seen it.

"Miss Abrams," a student interjected. "What's an STD?"

Rebecca imagined herself yanking her eyeballs back into their sockets. "Something you'll learn about in fifth grade. Why are you asking about that?"

"Because Joaquin thinks it's Stinky Toilet Diapers. But *I* know that STD means—"

"OKAY LET'S LINE UP FOR LUNCH!" Rebecca shouted.

Miguel Garcia   Middle School Special Ed Teacher

Miguel was running a third period Kahoot, a create-your-own on-line quiz game, when Eli came in late again. He'd been late or absent about four times each week, usually arriving during second or third period. "Hey, Eli, I'm so glad you're back," Miguel said. "Have a seat, grab an iPad. You can jump in next round."

The kids didn't realize Kahoots were lessons in disguise. Because the players' real-time rankings were visible to all, the students desperately wanted to do well. Miguel took advantage of this. He'd say, "Take notes: I'm going to give you some clues to help you do well on the Kahoot."

Eli's last teacher had warned Miguel that Eli's mother was difficult to communicate with. When the teacher had suggested, "You should read with your son every night," Eli's mother had retorted, "You're the teacher. That's your job."

Sure enough, in their only phone conversation thus far, she'd said to Miguel, "I haven't had a good experience with teachers," and expounded at length. "I'm sorry to hear that," he'd replied before breezily changing the subject. He would be as accommodating and respectful as possible. He hoped she'd come around.

So far, a month into the school year, she had not. For example, Miguel gave his students a planner in which they recorded their homework assignments. Miguel didn't believe in homework, but because some parents did, he gave students easy assignments to get them in the habit of writing down their tasks. He instructed them to ask their parents to sign the planner daily—he periodically wrote notes to parents there—and bring it back to school for reward points so they would learn to advocate for themselves and be accountable for their schoolwork. Eli's mom rarely signed. She didn't seem the least bit interested in her son's education, and Eli's grades suffered because he missed so many lessons.

But Miguel didn't treat Eli like the student he was. He treated Eli like the student he wanted the boy to become. He saw in Eli the kind of sparks that made more privileged students stand out in gen ed. Bright, funny, and motivated by Miguel's point system, Eli was starting to participate more in class.

During the next Kahoot, the kids ribbed one another as they usually did. A few questions in, Gabe saw the results and called out, "Hey! Hey, look!" Gabe, a 7th grader, had regular sessions with the counselor at Western. At his former school, his gen ed classmates had bullied him mercilessly. "Haha, look, Eli got it wrong!" Gabe observed. Students looked at Eli in surprise. "Haha, see, you couldn't get this one," another student chimed in. "Eli got it wrong, Eli got it wrong!" Gabe repeated.

Miguel heard kids teasing because they were surprised Eli got an easy question wrong. But Eli heard something else. He slammed his fists onto his desk. "I guess I'm wrong. I guess I'm always gonna be wrong," he said, his voice rising. The class quieted. Eli had dished it out plenty of times.

"No, what we were saying was just . . ." Gabe began.

"What you were *saying* was I just can't do this," Eli retorted.

Miguel tried to head off Eli's catastrophizing: "All right, moving on, now we're going to—"

"Mr. Garcia," Eli interrupted. "I'm getting really mad. I'm getting ANGRY."

Here we go, Miguel thought. *He's going to either explode or bolt like he did last year.* "Do you need to take a walk?" Miguel asked.

"Okay."

"Great, I'll see you when you're ready," Miguel replied, pleased, and redirected the class back to the Kahoot.

Within five minutes, Eli returned to his seat and calmly resumed the game.

A few days later, Miguel wrangled his students onto a school bus and directed them to seats. "You go here, you go there. Gabe, get your hands off Kavon." Miguel had seated Gabe in front on purpose to keep an eye on him. Gabe kept initiating a hand-slapping game with Kavon, a 7th grader who was easily distracted.

"Oh god, what a nightmare," Harriet, a history teacher, said miserably from the front seat.

Great attitude, Miguel thought, annoyed that she wasn't helping manage the students. This outing wasn't for her. He'd personally set up this field trip to a large museum, applying for a grant for enough buses that a third of the school could attend. *Field trips like this are what these kids are going to remember when they're forty. These disadvantaged kids hardly ever get to go anywhere.*

"I can't deal," Harriet said to the teacher next to her, although she was doing nothing but sitting and complaining. "I hate this."

"Gabe, I need you to stop. Please keep your hands to yourself," Miguel repeated, catching him hand slapping again. "You can sit there, you go down there . . ." A teacher had inexplicably changed the bus seating chart and wasn't helping to execute it. Miguel coldly took the clipboard from his coworker to check off students' names, wordlessly conveying that her refusal to assist was duly noted. Miguel was already exhausted and battling a fierce headache.

Gabe, squirming, double-slapped Kavon. This was how fights started.

"GABE, I *SAID* KEEP YOUR HANDS TO YOURSELF!" Miguel yelled.

His students froze. They had never seen Miguel diverge from his nice-guy teacher persona. While Kavon shrugged off the scolding, Gabe stiffened, lowered his head, and stared intently at the seat in front of him. Miguel knew immediately that yelling at him was the wrong tactic. *I can't lose him this early in school year*, he thought.

When the bus started, Miguel leaned over from his second-row seat. "Hey, I want to apologize," he told Gabe. "I was really stressed out. I broke one of the rules: I was not respectful to you and that's not okay. I wanted you to stop because it's a safety issue on the bus, but I shouldn't have yelled."

"Okay." Gabe looked like he didn't want to discuss the matter. Miguel dropped it.

At the museum, despite Harriet's dread, the students did fine. A

PE teacher and LaShonda, an art teacher who was one of Miguel's close friends, stepped up to help manage the group. It was magical to observe the kids staring at a 400-year-old painting while a docent shared stories that made it come to life.

When the classes piled back onto the buses to return to school, Miguel did a head count. All his students were present; he'd counted them constantly since the trip began. He checked on another bus, where students were noisily cavorting in the aisle. "All right, are we all set to go? Did we do a head count?" Miguel asked the teachers in front.

"I think so?" a teacher said.

"You don't know?" Miguel said. He rubbed his forehead.

She explained that the numbers were unclear because a girl had informed them that she saw two kids ditching school back at Western. (Within days, classmates would target the girl so viciously—"Snitches are bitches"—that she left the school permanently.)

Miguel took the clipboard from the teacher across the aisle. "ALL RIGHT, EVERYONE QUIET," he bellowed. Immediate silence.

Miguel counted three students short, not including the kids who'd ditched. His heart raced—a museum staffer just today had told him about a school that left a kid at the museum. Miguel recounted but got the same number. "You have no idea where these students could be?" he asked the teachers in front. *This is my nightmare*, he thought. *We're going to leave someone behind.*

Penny Davis   6th Grade Math Teacher

"Zach's poking me!" Brentley called out in the middle of a lesson. Only a couple of weeks into the school year, Penny already could tell that Brentley, who sat in front of Zach, would be a problem. Penny shot both students a look. At the next break, Zach handed Penny a Post-it note. Penny had told him on the first day of school, "I know you don't want to talk to me. Write me notes, communicate through another student, whatever you need to do to feel comfortable in this room is what you should do." Zach wrote notes infrequently; when he wasn't whispering to classmates, he was usually quiet and expressionless.

The note read, "He's lying." Penny kept a closer eye on the two of them.

Eventually, Brentley again yelled, "Zach poked me!"

"No, he didn't," Penny said. "Why don't you and Zach switch seats."

Brentley and his twin sister, Addison, who were both in Penny's class, could not have been more dissimilar. Their mother had friend-requested Penny on social media promptly after Open House. Her posts heralded her son's athletic accomplishments. Her daughter, also an athlete, was strangely absent from her mother's feed. Addison was a good-natured, humble girl who always completed her assignments. Brentley was an egotistical piece of work.

Apparently, his attitude came from home. In early September, the twins' mom had emailed all their teachers a list of their various fall sports schedules. "My children like it when their teachers attend their sports events," she wrote. "Your attendance at all of the attached games would be appreciated."

Penny's jaw had dropped. *Seriously?* she thought. *Even if I weren't attending my own children's games, you think I'd have time to attend all your children's?*

That was only the start of the emails from the woman Penny referred to as Helicopter Mom. She often emailed Penny during school: "My Addison had a headache today so I'm just checking on her." "How is my Brentley doing today? He had a sore throat this morning."

September

Toward the end of September, Helicopter requested referrals from Addison's teachers for special ed services. Because Addison wasn't making straight As, Helicopter was convinced her daughter had a learning disability. But Addison was pulling Bs and occasional As on tests and assignments in every class. Penny wasn't surprised when a committee reported that Addison had no disability.

Penny was surprised, however, to hear what Helicopter did next: She found an IEP form online, changed some of the wording, created a document supposedly signed by a psychologist, and forged an IEP for Addison, complete with "necessary" accommodations. The document was obviously fake; IEPs came from the district, not a doctor. Administrators called Helicopter to a meeting and told her politely, "Ma'am, we can't find any records from this particular doctor"—he didn't exist, for one—"so this IEP is not going to work."

At first, Penny was mystified. Addison was a good student and would get better; Brentley was the twin who didn't do his homework. When Penny collected assignments, sometimes she'd say, "Your sister's right next to you. Why don't you do your homework together and check each other's answers?"

"I had football," he'd say   or baseball, or whatever was the sport of the day. It turned out that the twins' parents were convinced Brentley would be a professional athlete.

Penny had heard from a lot of parents lately. Her high school acquaintance, Kitty, texted her constantly, even though her daughter had no issues at school. "Skylar's just getting over a cold. Can you keep an eye on her today?" she'd text. "How'd Skylar do on the quiz today?" And "Can you get us Skylar's missed work from all her classes and something she left in her locker?"

One warm evening while watching her sons play football, Penny spotted Ed, the Spanish teacher, sitting alone in the stands. She wondered why he was there until after the game, when a cheerleader skipped into the bleachers to hug him.

At school the next day, Ed found Penny in her classroom during lunch. "Your sons had a great game," he said.

"Was that your daughter cheering?" Penny asked.

"Yes. I never miss a game," Ed replied.

"Why were you sitting by yourself?"

"Well, we moved here this year for my wife's job and she works all the time," Ed said.

"She doesn't go to the games?"

"I don't think Ellen's ever been to any of Claudia's performances."

At Penny's raised brow, he added, "It's all right. I love being there for Claudia. The hard part is getting to know the other parents. Or my coworkers. Everyone here all went to high school together or they're still wrapped up in their glory days. It's very difficult as an outsider to make friends here. Dads aren't usually the primary parents. And, well, Ellen and I are separated but she doesn't want people to know, so we don't tell anyone. So we're not going out with friends together."

Penny hadn't considered how challenging it was for Ed to try to fit into her small town when, as an insider, she had a hard time herself. "It's not you," she said. "Well, maybe it is. You're very blunt"—Ed laughed—"but it's not easy to make friends even if you grew up here. I don't have a lot of friends, either. A lot of my friends are through Kent."

As they chatted, they found they had some things in common: They liked the same bands, tried to get outdoors as often as possible, and couldn't imagine making a living doing anything other than teaching because they were so devoted to their students.

Penny did not have those kinds of conversations at home.

The next evening, Penny stood stock-still, weeping as her husband screamed at her again. As usual, he yelled at her for not being sexually adventurous enough for him, that she wasn't spending enough time cleaning the kitchen until it gleamed, and that she wasn't always home the minute she said she would be. He usually demanded that Penny return home by a certain time when she was out for work or with friends. When Kent was angry at her, the only guaranteed way to soften him up was to have sex with him. She was caught in what her therapist told her was a cycle of abuse: He'd rage, she'd sleep with him to get a few days' break from his anger, and then he'd rage again. She knew their relationship wasn't healthy, but she was afraid to leave him.

Kent's behavior had been escalating recently. For the last six months, Penny had returned to therapy, which Kent had allowed because he said Penny needed to learn "why you act this way." After every appointment, Kent sat Penny down and insisted she tell him every word the counselor said. Then he'd claim the therapist was wrong and call her a "liberal radical" or tell Penny, "You make me do that."

This time, after Kent ended his tirade and stomped downstairs, the twins found Penny in the bathroom, where she usually retreated to compose herself.

"Mom, we heard Dad yelling."

"Yes, he yelled at me, but he's still your dad and he's a good dad. You don't need to worry about it, it's okay. Moms and dads sometimes disagree." It was difficult to strike a balance between reassuring her children and teaching them that yelling was unacceptable.

"We have three options for you," Justin said.

"One, Dad gets counseling and we stay in the house," Jack said.

"Two, we stay in the house and try to make it through," Justin said.

"Or we move out."

Penny wiped her eyes. "How would you feel about going to live at Nana and Grandaddy's house for a while?"

The twins nodded eagerly. "Yes," Justin said.

"Let's go," said Jack.

A week later, Penny slowly stepped into the kitchen, feeling nauseous after planning for this conversation every spare minute of the last seven days. She didn't know how Kent would respond. She did know he would somehow punish her.

"I'm unhappy," she said. "I'm tired of being humiliated. I can't take the yelling. It's not all my fault."

Kent barely reacted. "You need to tell me what you want to do."

"I'm going to move into my parents' house. I'm leaving and the boys are coming with me."

"If you're leaving, we need to divide up the bills," he said, icy. He opened his laptop and created a spreadsheet. "This is what you're going to be responsible for." He listed bills including house payments for the house she would no longer be living in.

Although she had almost nothing in her savings account and her salary was a fraction of Kent's, Penny agreed, relieved the conversation was over. *After all, I am the one leaving*, she thought.

⁓

This year, Penny was teaching all the inclusion math students (special ed students taking gen ed math) in the grade. Other teachers had made excuses: "This is only my second year at this school, so I don't think I should teach them," "I don't have the training," and so forth. Penny loved teaching kids with special needs because she valued their perspectives. "Give *me* the kids who can't do. I will work with them," she had told the assistant principal.

One of her inclusion students this year was Robert, a student on the autism spectrum. His father was in prison. His mother hadn't graduated from high school. During Open House, despite his mom hollering at him to stop, he zoomed around Penny's classroom, sticking his hands into whatever he could find.

With Penny's patient behavioral reminders and Birdie's help, he'd improved slightly. He could sit in his chair for the full period now, but sometimes he blurted things out in class, and when his work was challenging, he threw up his hands and groaned, "I can't do this!"

Penny could see in his files that Robert had never passed a state-mandated standardized test, which kids began taking in 3rd grade, in any subject. Penny desperately wanted him to pass one for his self-esteem.

The district was no help. When the school system had instituted a new, more intense set of curriculum standards for classes and tests, it didn't provide schools with any new resources to cover those lessons, though the current textbook didn't address all the new standards. Penny had written her own multimonth spiral-bound textbook aligned with the new standards.

One day, Penny noticed that her only copy of her book was missing from her desk. Fortunately, she'd taught long enough that she could run the day's lessons without her notes. "I can fly by the seat of my pants," she told me. "You have to be able to do that if you want to be a teacher."

None of the teachers were prepared, however, when Southern's new principal visited each grade level's biweekly meeting with a surprise change in school grading policy. She didn't put the policy in writing and told teachers not to record her instructions in the meeting minutes. From now on, she said, teachers were required to give students a score of 60 or higher. If a student earned a 10 out of 100, teachers had to bump it up to a 60. If students didn't turn in their work, teachers could not give them a zero, the principal said, "so these kids have a chance to pass and get some credit." Furthermore, she "strongly" encouraged teachers to find ways to "make students who are discipline issues pass to the next grade or move to the next school."

Behind closed doors, the teachers vented about their opposition to the policy. "If we didn't do our job, we wouldn't get a paycheck," Blair said. "If students don't do what's expected of them, why should we hand out a grade?"

"We're going to reward these kids for doing nothing? You can't expect kids to perform if there aren't some kind of consequences," said Wilma.

"At what point in this world are students going to be held accountable for their actions?" Celia asked.

At first, Penny didn't comply with the policy. How would it help students to move to 7th grade without learning the 6th grade math they needed as a foundation? When Brentley didn't bring in homework ("I had football"), Penny gave him a zero. When Diamond, who was a year older than the average 6th grader, got every answer wrong on tests, Penny gave her zeros, too.

The principal called Penny into her office. She pointed to Brentley's grades on her computer. "You need to bump these grades up to sixties," she said.

Brentley's mom had apparently seen the grades and complained to the principal. Parents had 24/7 online access to their children's grades. "It's terrible. I'll be in the middle of teaching and a parent will send an email the second I post a grade, wanting to know what's going on or accusing me of something," Penny told me. "Like, 'Why did my child get this grade?' 'How can we get this grade back up?'"

Helicopter was the worst offender. As soon as she saw a new grade, she'd either make excuses for her son or blame Penny. Once, she emailed Penny, "Did you get the homework out of Brentley's locker?"

"Ma'am, it's not my responsibility to go into the child's locker and get their work," Penny replied.

Another time, Helicopter said, "I check his homework every night, and I know he did it."

"If he did it, that's great, but I have to be able to see it," Penny answered.

Helicopter started taking pictures of the homework so that if Brentley forgot to turn it in, she had proof that he had done it. "I need him to turn in the paper because I have to grade it," Penny told her. "I can't grade it over a picture."

The principal also ordered Penny to bump zeros to sixties for Diamond, one of the few Black students at Southern. The principal, who was white, said, "Shanaynay was up in here having drama with the other girls."

"That's kind of racist," Penny protested.

"Oh, I'm just kidding."

Penny did as she was told because she couldn't risk losing her job, especially now that she had to support herself and her boys alone. Too often it felt like teaching involved a precarious balance between keeping administrators happy and parents content. If a principal didn't like a teacher, she could make the teacher's job unbearably difficult. At the same time, Penny had observed several situations where parents bypassed the principal and complained to the superintendent. "If the superintendent is contacted, the parent's almost always 'right' and the teacher's 'wrong' and must cave to the parental demands," Penny said. "I've seen parents go to school board members about something that didn't occur, and the teacher was forced to participate in extra professional development."

The next time a student scored a 10 on a test, Penny recorded the grade as a 60. "It's demeaning," she told me. "If we're just going to let kids get grades without effort, why should I stand up here and waste my breath? But at the same time, I stand up here and waste my breath because I love what I do and I love my kids."

"STOP TOUCHING MY CAR": Parent Aggression and the Culture of Teacher Blaming

One day after school, a Pennsylvania high school English teacher was walking to her car in the parking lot when a Mercedes rolled into her. Luckily uninjured, the teacher jumped back in surprise. The parent driver, still on her cell phone, lowered her window and yelled, "STOP TOUCHING MY CAR!"

The incident neatly epitomizes a culture of teacher blaming in which entitled parents make outrageous demands and fault teachers for not meeting them. "Parents see teachers as a public utility and talk to us as if we're garbage," a Texas high school teacher said. A parent once insisted that when the teacher gave lectures in class, he must simultaneously take handwritten notes on the lecture for her daughter in the student's notebook. "I've made my expectations clear with the principal," the parent said.

"Expectations" is a notable word choice. The public stigmatizes the teaching profession, yet also expects teachers to solve all problems and blames them when they can't. Whereas once educators were expected simply to teach, now they are expected to cater. "The belittling and blaming of teachers, and the lack of parent accountability, need to stop," said an Illinois high school English teacher. "Parents need to ensure that their children are actually active participants in their education and to support their children's teachers."

Too many parents don't. Society's emphasis on teacher blaming as a predominant educational narrative has a trickle-down effect on the ways parents believe they can treat educators. At a candidate forum during the COVID pandemic, a Maryland school board member called students the "customers in our school system," as if teachers existed to satisfy students rather than to educate them. In the following months, a group of parents who supported her tweeted "students are the customers," made multiple calls to "fire" teachers collectively, and posted comments on social media such as "This whole thing is literally making me hate public school teachers" and "teachers are . . . profoundly mentally ill." A doctor in that group posted that he was considering refusing to give teachers' children medical care. Another tweeted in a rant about teachers union members, "I'm so sorry we gave these monsters your vaccines."

Encouraging parents to believe that students are the customers is a slippery slope that leads to attitudes like this one: A father called an Oklahoma high school teacher to berate him after his daughter scored a 53 on a test. When the teacher told the man about assignments she could complete and tests she could retake to pull her grade up to passing, the father interrupted: "I don't give a fuck about that! You fucking work for me because I pay taxes. I need you to change her fucking grade to passing!" The teacher explained that wasn't possible without completed work. "You're insufficient to teach my daughter. I want her out of your class," the father said. He persuaded administrators to switch her to another class the following day.

On a broader level, the student-as-customer attitude has contributed to a growing politicized movement pushing for parents to have authority over what is taught in schools. In just the first six weeks of 2022, state legislatures introduced more than 100 bills aimed at censoring classroom discussions of race, racism, gender, LGBTQ+ issues, and American history—measures akin to what free speech advocacy organization PEN America called "educational gag orders."

In March 2022, Florida governor Ron DeSantis signed into law a bill officially called "Parental Rights in Education." The law, popularly known as "Don't Say Gay," suppressed classroom instruction and discussion of gender identity, gender inclusiveness, and sexual orientation. Several other states have adopted or are considering similar limits on teaching about gender, sexuality, sexism, racism, and race. These policies also "put LGBTQ teachers in a really difficult situation where they're forced, essentially, to disguise their identity or the status of their relationships in order to fend off running afoul of these bills," PEN America researcher Jeffrey Sachs told NPR's Terry Gross.

Even if policies are vaguely worded, they foster "a climate in which some teachers"—and, I'd add, counselors—"worry that if they say the wrong thing, they could lose their job," as *Chalkbeat* reported in 2022. In fact, a New Hampshire chapter of conservative group Moms for Liberty offered a $500 bounty to anyone who caught a public school teacher violating a state law restricting discussions about racism and sexism. The reward offer followed the state department of education's establishment of an online system for parents and students to report educators who disobey the law—and could therefore lose their teaching license.

Similarly, just after Virginia governor Glenn Youngkin signed his first executive order in 2022, which banned the teaching of "inherently divisive concepts, including critical race theory," he launched an email tip line for parents to report on teachers. He encouraged "parents to send us any instances where they feel that their fundamental rights are being violated, where their children are not being respected, where there are inherently divisive practices in their schools. We're going to get critical race theory and other inherently divisive teaching practices out of the schools," he said in a radio interview.

A few months later, Pennsylvania state representative Barbara Gleim suggested that local Moms for Liberty members become substitute teachers specifically so they could monitor educators. "We also need conservative eyes and ears in the schools," she posted on Facebook. "If anyone can substitute even one day a week, the teachers who are activists and indoctrinating children can be revealed." And in July 2022, a Texas chapter of County Citizens Defending Freedom, another conservative group, hosted "volunteer training" on "researching social media of teachers" and other school staff.

Noneducators' attempts to thought- and identity-police teachers and counselors show no signs of abating. More than a dozen states' early 2022 legislative proposals would have allowed parents to vet and veto classroom books, history lessons, and other school materials, activities, and curricula. An Indiana bill passed by the state house but not by the senate originally called for teachers to post all materials and lesson plans for the following school year by June 30, a ludicrous idea demonstrating a complete ignorance of how classroom teaching actually works. The bill also proposed the formation of a curriculum review committee led by parents and a ban on teaching eight race- or religion-related concepts. Likewise, an Iowa bill sought to permit parents to review teachers' "textbooks, books, articles, outlines, handouts, presentations, videos, and any other similar materials."

Though those specific bills did not become law, they illustrated disturbing trends: parents' aggressive mistrust of educators—who are the pedagogical experts trained and certified to select and deliver developmentally appropriate academic content—and lawmakers' indifference toward teacher workloads and historical facts in the name of "parents' rights." Worse, they had only certain parents in mind. As Missouri Equity Education Partnership founder Heather Fleming, who is Black, told *Education Week*, "They're packaging some of these laws as 'parents' bill of rights.' What parents? Because my daughter is entitled to see her culture and her heroes, people who look like her, in the curriculum, too." The majority of public school students are children of color.

The battles over classroom content began ramping up in 2020 and 2021, following mass protests over the murder of George Floyd and a period during which remote learning gave parents an unusual window into their children's classes. Taking advantage of the ensuing backlash to frank discussions about racism, conservatives—like Youngkin—weaponized the term "critical race theory" (CRT). While the NAACP defines CRT as "a framework that denotes that systemic racism is part of American society—from education and housing to employment and healthcare," which is not taught in K–12 schools, politicians and activists intent on galvanizing parents co-opted the term to more broadly refer to teaching about racism, equity, identity, and oppression.

The intensifying attempts to limit conversations about racism and gender identities were accompanied by "unprecedented" efforts to ban books in schools, according to the American Library Association. Between July 2021 and March 2022 alone, 86 districts from 26 states banned nearly 1,600 books. Also new: Rather than removing individual books for specific reasons, lawmakers sought to ban entire book categories. Many of the targeted books featured race, gender, or sexuality themes and/or LGBTQ+ characters or characters of color; a Tennessee district also struck *Maus,* a Pulitzer Prize–winning book about the Holocaust, from the 8th grade curriculum in 2022. While parents have the prerogative to limit what their own children read, to quote the school librarian group #FReadom Fighters, "No one has the right to restrict what ALL children read according to individual ideas and beliefs."

At the same time, parent aggression, including but not limited to verbal and physical abuse, was on the rise. In one of the few pre-pandemic studies on the topic—statistics are scarce—DePaul University psychology professor Susan McMahon and her team found that about a third of teachers had been victimized by parents. A New York 2nd grade teacher told me, "Every year there are 'problem parents' in the classroom who will butt heads regarding our educational philosophy and always blame the teachers first."

Or worse. After a 2017 parent-teacher conference, a Pennsylvania couple followed their child's teacher's car and at a red light threw a brick at her face, knocking out a tooth. They dragged the teacher out of the car and continued to attack her. They were upset that the teacher took their 10-year-old daughter's cell phone during class; the teacher requested a meeting because the student then bit her. The same year in North Carolina, during a parent-teacher meeting, a mother sprayed lighter fluid into a teacher's eyes and threatened to set her on fire.

Between 2020 and 2022, there was a marked increase in parents harassing, intimidating, and threatening school staff; in several states, parents physically assaulted teachers because they were upset about school mask policies even during virus surges. NBC News reported in 2021, "The teacher is now viewed by a small, loud contingent not as a public servant but as a public enemy." The following spring, Fox News host Tucker Carlson said that teachers who discuss gender identity with students should be "beaten up"—and encouraged viewers to "thrash the teacher."

In an October 2021 Justice Department memorandum, Attorney General Merrick Garland warned, "In recent months, there has been a disturbing spike in harassment, intimidation, and threats of violence against school administrators, board members, teachers, and staff who participate in the vital work of running our nation's public schools." He directed the FBI and U.S. attorneys to strategize ways to address these behaviors. In response, Senate minority leader Mitch McConnell minimized the violence and alluded to the parents' rights movement. He wrote to Garland, "Parents absolutely should be telling their local schools what to teach." Which parents was McConnell referring to? Here's a clue: His letter went on to defend, specifically, "parents who opposed the teaching of Critical Race Theory."

⌒

At a local level, some parents go to great lengths to scapegoat educators. An Iowa parent tried to convince a teacher to sign a document for his son to drop her class because he had a B rather than an A. When the teacher refused because the student was doing well in her class, the father lied to the superintendent that the teacher threw a textbook at his son's head and called him lazy. The false accusation led to a disciplinary letter in the teacher's file. "The administration kowtows to parents. If it weren't for the teachers union lawyers going with me to meetings, I would have been suspended or fired for things I didn't do but the parent accused me of doing to take the heat off his kid," she said.

Administrators' tendency to coddle parents only serves to embolden them. An assistant principal made three Texas teachers endure a 27-minute tantrum from a father who insisted that teachers weren't allowed to fail his daughter during softball season, even though she hadn't turned in her work. "We refer to some of these parents as bulldozer parents," said a Texas foreign language teacher. "The digital age has afforded these parents the luxury of being able to email teachers at any time from their phone, and parents become confrontational. We're badgered for higher grades regularly and sometimes the parents want meetings with the teacher and principal to grade-lawyer for higher grades."

Ease of online access to teachers has fueled both parents' aggression and presumption that they can expect instant responses, as Kitty did from Penny. "Email allows parents and students to have a sense of immediacy with teachers that they shouldn't. I've received emails on holidays and over the summer, and when I haven't responded immediately have gotten progressively more abusive emails from the sender," said an Ohio high school English teacher. "Online grades create situations where students obsess over every score. It puts all the focus on the points and none of it on the learning. Email and online grades have created monsters."

Monsters indeed. Parents feel entitled to say things to teachers they wouldn't dare say in other professional settings. A Maryland high school history teacher called a parent because her son was failing his class and acting up. The mother told the teacher, "Punch him." In answer to the teacher's bewildered response that he couldn't do that, the mother yelled, "What kind of man are you? You are no kind of man at all!" A father accused Ali, a Kansas special ed teacher, of child abuse because she helped the school nurse bathe his daughter in the bathroom sink when she came to school covered in dirt and flea bites. He didn't listen to his daughter, who stood beside him crying and explaining Ali helped her because their water had been shut off for a month.

Parents have yelled at Licia, a Tennessee library media specialist, to insist their child turned in a lost book, only to show up at school a few days later, book in hand. One parent threw the book at Licia and walked out without a word. Another mom accused Licia of pocketing the money paid for lost books.

Racism and bigotry can also come into play when parents turn against educators. A prominent Louisiana parent once told an Asian charter school science teacher, "I used to kill people like you in Vietnam." (The U.S.-born teacher, who is Filipino and Chinese, later learned he never served in Vietnam.) When a teacher new to a Missouri Catholic school accidentally threw out students' writing portfolios, a (non-Jewish) parent claimed, "Each piece of writing is like a family member, so essentially what you have done here is re-enact the Holocaust." In 2021, a North Carolina parent reportedly called for two high school teaching assistants to be removed from classrooms because they were Black; a nationwide survey found that approximately 97% of Black math teachers "experienced some form of racial microaggression on a regular basis." The 2022 Kentucky Teacher of the Year left the teaching field because of homophobic discrimination by parents and school administrators. And in a story line that has become so common that it didn't hit national news, an Illinois Catholic school fired a science teacher in 2022 after a parent found her wedding photo online and complained to the school priest that the teacher was gay.

Some parents display a more subtle lack of consideration for school employees: They medicate fevered children to keep them in class. A British survey revealed that seven in 10 parents have knowingly sent sick children to school. Some parents give schools incorrect contact information so that staff can't reach them to come pick up their kids. Little thought is given to the educators, health room staff, or office secretaries who are exposed to contagious students throwing up or coughing as they wait to be picked up. During the 2020–21 and 2021–22 academic years, parents in several states knowingly sent COVID-positive students to school. "I think sometimes parents and students forget that teachers are human," a Hawaii elementary school teacher said. "We have lives outside of school. We love kids and we truly care, but we have things going on in our lives, too: births, deaths, graduations, divorces, health issues."

Parents' mistreatment of teachers has accompanied an increasingly pronounced "us-versus-them" mentality. Instead of welcoming teachers with a cooperative "It takes a village" mindset to educate and nurture their children, many parents view teachers as obstacles to hurdle or barrel through between childhood and graduation. When parents adopt us-versus-them attitudes against teachers, they cut off their nose to spite their face; a parent in the "students are the customers" district announced, "I've refused to participate with the PTA this year precisely because of the 'T.'" An Idaho English teacher said, "There's this crazy dichotomy between parents who are so grateful for you specifically as their child's teacher, and yet teachers as a whole are regarded as the enemy by much of America. Hardly anyone will take a teacher's side. We're accused of 'brainwashing,' being lazy, or whining about money."

Teachers said the most frequent perpetrators are parents in higher socioeconomic strata gunning for top grades or accolades. A New Jersey high school social studies teacher has heard from several parents who demanded meetings to bump their children's 96% to a 97%. A New York high school science teacher was the target of a melodramatically blistering email sent by a C-list TV and film actress who claimed that her son's alleged racism and drug use were false accusations, a teacher "stole" her son's project, a school textbook was pornographic, and the science teacher should be fired.

In addition to managing parents who harass them, teachers

also contend with an opposite problem—parents who are completely uninvolved with their children's education. When a Pennsylvania teacher called a parent to say her child was failing, the parent said, "I have more important things to worry about than my child passing your class. You should just be thankful she's even showing up to school."

"Teachers spend blood, sweat, and tears on many of their students, and parents often don't respond to communication," said a Texas art teacher. "It's pretty freaking hard to fail art class if you have a pulse and pick up your pencil and use it. I can call a kid's parents fifteen times and they don't get concerned until it interferes with graduation."

When teachers leave the profession, it's rarely because of the students. Ali, the Kansas teacher, made the agonizing choice to retire early because parents' unrelenting unrealistic demands wore her down, including a parent who expected her to get a student up to grade-level reading when he began his senior year of high school at a kindergarten level. "I still can't talk about my decision without bawling," Ali told me. "As much as I love my students, I'm so tired of adults."

Miguel Garcia   Middle School Special Ed Teacher

Miguel rushed onto the third bus. "Did you guys do a head count?" he asked a teacher. "One bus is short three kids."

"All my kids are here but I don't know what else is going on," she said.

Miguel found a neglected clipboard on the front seat. "EVERY-ONE SIT DOWN; I'M GOING TO COUNT."

When he counted a three-student surplus, he looked at the teacher in the front seat.

"Oh, they wanted to switch buses," she said. "They said it's okay." Miguel bit his tongue. Keeping students on the same bus both ways was Field Trip Fundamentals 101. He briskly tossed the clipboard to the teacher and returned to his bus.

The next day, Miguel debriefed the trip with his special ed kids. The students chatted about their likes and dislikes.

"How do you think we did with behavior on the buses?" Miguel prodded. "Were we making good choices?"

"I was slapping at Gabe and Gabe was slapping at me," Kavon admitted.

"Yes," Miguel said. He noticed Gabe tense. "Also, I think my behavior wasn't very good on the bus. I messed up, too. I yelled at Gabe and that's not good. The reason I did that was because Gabe's and Kavon's behavior wasn't safe. But the rules apply to everybody, not just the kids. I'll try not to do that again."

The students stared at him in surprise. Gabe relaxed. Miguel turned to him. "Gabe, I'm sorry for yelling at you."

Gabe nodded.

"Great, now what did you think of the museum?" Miguel asked. *I may have just saved this relationship,* he thought. *I can't lose my cool like that again.*

When Dewayne wandered into Miguel's room in the middle of history, Miguel was concerned. Dewayne was supposed to be in Harriet's class.

Last year, when Dewayne was a gen ed student, Miguel had noticed him because he was kind and patient with Miguel's moderately to severely disabled students. At the end of Dewayne's 6th grade year, Western staff had evaluated him and placed him in special ed; academically he was at a 3rd grade level. Upset at being labeled "special ed," Dewayne complained to his mom, who asked the school for help. Western agreed to a compromise: Dewayne would take special ed math and English and gen ed science, history, PE, and electives.

Dewayne needed someone to watch over him, to keep him on task. He wasn't a bad student. He was behind because severe ADHD prevented him from paying attention. With 14 students, Miguel was better able to help Dewayne manage his impulse control issues than gen ed teachers who had classes of 35 kids. In Miguel's smaller, structured class, Dewayne was manageable and even helpful.

But Dewayne's gen ed teachers often complained about him and sent him back to Miguel's room to avoid dealing with him. This was not the right thing to do, Miguel believed, "but I would rather have him in my room than other teachers screaming at him." He had reminded Dewayne repeatedly, "You and your mother chose this, but I'd love to have you in my class full-time."

Miguel knew his coworkers were overwhelmed by their student numbers and the workload dumped on teachers by state officials obsessed with testing and district officials who didn't consider how their constantly changing curriculum requirements affected teachers. Gen ed teachers increasingly had to instruct special ed students without support staff even if they weren't trained to do so, as some districts mainstreamed kids to save money and some charter schools sidelined kids with special needs until they dropped out and enrolled in public school. (Miguel called these students "charter school refugees" because "they're pushed out. Charter schools here are famous for cherry-picking students.") Miguel frequently helped his sister, a teacher in the Midwest, with her questions and concerns about special ed students in her gen ed classes.

Dewayne sat down in his usual spot. Miguel sighed. Did Harriet really have to kick Dewayne out of class on the kid's birthday? Every year, Miguel knew all his special ed students' birthdays and surprised them with celebrations. Before school this morning, Miguel hid cupcakes in the staff refrigerator.

"Hey, what's up?" Miguel said mildly.

"I don't know what I did. She got really upset," Dewayne said, agitated.

"Okay, okay, you've got to work on this," Miguel said. "I'm teaching another class, so you have to be really quiet. You're not allowed to interrupt." Dewayne nodded, seeming both chastened and relieved to be out of Harriet's class. "Anyway, Dewayne, I'm glad you're here. I wanted to ask you—would it be okay if we have a birthday celebration for you later today?"

Dewayne wasn't yet accustomed to Miguel's compartmentalization of discipline. After Miguel talked to Dewayne in his "teacher voice," Miguel always let him know that what was done was done and they could now return to their regularly scheduled program. Miguel never held anything against a kid. He wanted his students to learn that nothing was personal in school.

"What? Yeah, okay!" Dewayne said.

"Okay, good. For now, please do this," Miguel said, handing him a worksheet.

When his students went to PE, Miguel stopped in Harriet's room. "Hey, is everything okay?" he asked.

"About Dewayne: I'm sorry, I just can't do it," she whined. Miguel bit his tongue. Harriet booted Dewayne back to Miguel more often than any other teacher. By contrast, LaShonda, the art teacher, asked Miguel for advice to manage Dewayne rather than giving up on him. "You have to sit him next to you because there's no impulse control," Miguel explained. She'd done that and Dewayne improved in her class.

"I understand," Miguel said carefully to Harriet, "but you have to understand this is a contract the school district signed. When you send him away, we're not fulfilling the minutes we promised him.

You have to have him. We can discuss changing it, but the IEP is a legal document. You can't keep sending him back to me like a punishment."

⤞⤝

Miguel's challenges weren't limited to his special ed students. His gen ed video students alienated Jon, a 6th grader with social issues. And Quiesha, a seemingly aloof 8th grader, and her mouthy friend, the class's two queen bees, were perpetually late to class.

When the girls were late for the third day in a row, Miguel called them out. "You guys are late again."

"Whaatt?" protested the mouthy girl.

"We were in Ms. Dunkel's room," Quiesha said.

"I don't care. You're supposed to be here," Miguel replied, thinking, *Thanks a lot, Harriet.*

Both girls rolled their eyes. Their classmates gawked. Quiesha stared at Miguel defiantly.

Okay, they're challenging me, Miguel thought. "Fine, we can have a staring contest. I can stare at you for as long as it takes," he said, thinking, *Why am I doing this? This is counterproductive.*

The other girl, all bluff and bluster, quickly sat down. Quiesha stared at him for a moment longer, then dismissed him with an apathetic "Pff."

"If you have a problem with it, you can go talk to the counselor," Miguel said.

Quiesha turned around and left.

Ah crap, I didn't handle that very well, Miguel thought. *The last thing you want to do is confront a kid in front of her peers. Then it becomes a status thing.*

Quiesha returned when the class was filming outside. Miguel went to see the counselor, an amiable, perky woman who never seemed fazed. She was an invaluable member of the school community.

"She was upset," the counselor said. "She said, 'I don't want to be in that class. I hate that class.'"

"That's totally not what I want," Miguel said. "I can't have her walking in late all the time, but I think it's the right place for her. She's really good with a camera."

"Well, you should tell her that because she doesn't have a lot of success in her other classes. So this is something she needs to hear from you."

Miguel found Quiesha with her video team. "Can I talk to you alone, please?" he asked.

"Ughh," she said, probably expecting a lecture.

Miguel purposely sat down on a bench so that she was physically taller than he was. That was a psychological filmmaking strategy: Low angles versus high angles changed the emotional perspective of a character. "I'm sorry. Calling you out in front of everyone is wrong. I think you're probably one of the best people in the class at camera-work. I'd like you to consider staying because you're an asset to the class."

"What?" she said, surprised.

"You have a lot of talent. We're at a time where they're trying to find more cinematographers and directors, and I think that could be a future for you. I was talking to you as if I were on a shoot with somebody professionally and I should have talked to you like you're a kid. So I think you should stay. Can we forget this happened?"

She shrugged. "Okay. I'll stay."

The following week, the students presented their first long-term projects of the year. The class unanimously agreed that Quiesha's project was the best.

CHAPTER 3

October

Advance materials parents sent to a Massachusetts high school teacher for her "to review" before a parent-teacher conference: A PowerPoint presentation with more than 20 slides about the history of the student from birth to present day.

A Washington, DC–area private school principal at a faculty meeting: "Students are not to make any noise by using the pencil sharpener. I can hear the sharpeners in my office. Faculty and students are only permitted to use blue pencils with [the school name] embossed on the side, no 'fun' pencils or number two yellow pencils. Also, you are no longer allowed to put stickers on student papers or give students stickers as rewards."

Penny Davis   6th Grade Math Teacher

"I love you guys! Have a great day!" Penny called from her door as she always did at the end of the period, dispersing hugs to students who reached for them. Two years earlier, one of Justin's friends was killed in a car accident after school. Since then, every day, at the end of every period, Penny told her students she loved them. "I want them to know they are loved and protected, and if my students want a hug, I hug them," she told me. "You never know when that might be the child's last hug."

After dismissal, Savannah and Vivian drifted into the room and plopped Penny's missing course textbook on her shelf. They hadn't asked to borrow it and they didn't thank Penny or tell her it was helpful. Instead of offering to create notes for the latest skills the county had added to the curriculum, Savannah said, "We copied all the notes and activities that were in there. So when can you get the rest of the notes done?"

Penny bit her tongue. Sometimes she mused that her reluctance to confront people was a problematic recurring theme in her life. As she'd watched her meager bank account drain, she realized she shouldn't have capitulated when Kent, who made nearly four times her salary, stuck her with the bills. In the past, any extra funds she had she spent on school supplies for students who couldn't afford them. She had nothing to spare now. She was living with her parents while she saved money to rent a small apartment. The twins split their time between Penny and Kent. With only $30 to her name, Penny took on side jobs to supplement her teaching paycheck; she became a skin care consultant and tutored students a few times a week.

When Penny finally made the decision to leave Kent, she'd been mentally prepared for the financial ramifications. However, she had not expected the social consequences. While she didn't broadcast the divorce, Kent did. Penny didn't know how he had characterized her choice to leave him, but their mutual friends dropped Penny, including her maid of honor and two girlfriends Penny had known since high school. Between her loss of friends outside the workplace and lack of friends within it, Penny was lonelier than ever.

Penny told only a few people at school about the divorce: Jan (the 8th grade math teacher), Birdie, and Ed, who'd told Penny, to her surprise, "You're the closest thing to a friend I've had since I got here." Penny figured the divorce news would spread on its own but she didn't feel up to dealing with nosy questions and judgmental looks.

She got the looks anyway. Within days, Blair, Savannah, and Vivian were whispering and pointing at her in the hallways.

Southern had had a vicious clique culture for as long as Penny had worked there. Years ago, in her first weeks at Southern, Penny had volunteered to co-sponsor the student government association with a teacher who she didn't realize led a dominant teacher clique. When the students took to Penny's warm, loving personality, the queen bee angrily turned the clique against Penny and intimidated her into relinquishing her sponsor role. She lost about 10 pounds that quarter because of workplace stress. Scared to try to make friends at Southern because she didn't know which teachers were associated with the clique, she barely spoke to colleagues. Many nights that year she cried herself to sleep.

That teacher had since left Southern, but the culture endured. This year, Blair, who had been friendly with the queen bee, apparently had formed a clique with the new young 6th grade teachers. Because these teachers' classrooms were near Penny's, Penny tried not to interact with people on her hallway so that she could teach in peace. But Blair yelled so loudly and so often at her students that Penny's class could hear her through the wall they shared.

In October, Zach's mom emailed Penny and Blair that a classmate, Asher, had been bullying Zach. Zach had been doing okay in Penny's class. He communicated with Penny with notes or head nods or through classmates. He still had issues with Brentley, the jock, whom Penny had seated farther away.

Asher could be a handful, but Penny hadn't observed him bullying Zach or other students. Zach's mom's said Zach had told Asher repeatedly to leave him alone, but Asher wouldn't stop. Today, he'd supposedly called Zach fat and slow.

Blair didn't respond to the email. Although the incident didn't happen in Penny's classroom, Penny emailed Asher's dad, who had gone to her high school, and asked him to check in with his son.

The next morning, Penny pulled Asher into the hall. "I need y'all to tell me what happened, what you said about Zach," she told him.

"I didn't say anything!"

Penny partly believed him. But still . . . "If you tell me the truth, a lot of times my punishment isn't as severe."

"Mrs. Davis, he's been doing this for years, blaming me for stuff I didn't do." Asher started to cry, which was out of character for him. Nine times out of 10, when a student cried when denying wrongdoing, Penny was inclined to think they were telling the truth.

"Okay, I'll look into it some more. But if you know who said it, who might have said it, or if you might have said it, I just need you to be honest with me."

After school, Asher's father called Penny. If Asher had been involved, his father promised there would be consequences for his son. But Asher tearfully swore he didn't do it. *You know what, Asher might not have*, Penny thought, kicking herself for jumping to conclusions without investigating first. *They are a really nice family. Asher's whiny, but he's not mean.*

When Penny informed Zach's mom that she wasn't so sure Asher had said anything, Zach's mom emailed that upon pressing Zach, he admitted he didn't hear it directly from Asher. A girl had told Zach what he said.

The next day, Penny asked Zach for the girl's name. Zach shrugged.

"What did she look like?" Penny asked.

Another shrug.

"Golly, if you don't know the name of the child and you're not going to tell me what she looks like, how in the world am I going to get to the bottom of this?"

Shrug.

Penny sighed. She already had a headache from a persistent sinus infection. She did not need yet another reason to lose sleep. "Okay, this is what we'll do. I'm going to take you to every sixth grade homeroom and you can look in the classroom and tell me which student it was," Penny said.

They poked their heads into the first room. "Show me the child that you're telling me said those ugly things about you. Is she in here?" Penny asked. Zach shook his head.

Next room. "Here?"

Zach shook his head.

Penny took Zach to every class, but Zach couldn't identify the perpetrator. As they visited room after room, Zach's face grew redder. Later, Penny interviewed the students who sat at Zach's lunch table. None of them had heard the insults.

After math, Penny pulled Zach aside again. "Zach, if you can't tell me who the student was who did this, are you sure it was a sixth grader?"

Zach shrugged. *I don't know.*

"So your story has changed again. Do we need to walk through seventh and eighth and look at all those students?"

He shook his head.

Penny was upset with herself. *Why did I contact Asher's dad before I had all the facts?* Later, Penny would apologize to Asher.

Penny looked at Zach. "I don't know what happened because I wasn't there. I find it very suspicious. But I want you to know that once you have admitted your guilt and made reparations, it's a clean slate with me. We start over if you make changes to your behaviors.

Everybody deserves a second chance. And nothing you do would make me love you less."

Zach only stared flatly at Penny.

At the door of the teachers' lounge, where Penny had to retrieve her lunch from the staff fridge, she paused to check her phone. A text from Kitty: "Can Skylar hang out and do homework in your room for 20 minutes after school until I can pick her up?" Penny sighed. She was about to open the door when she heard Savannah say, "Yeah, why hasn't Penny told anybody? Why hasn't she talked about it?"

"She should have told us she's separated from her husband," Blair said. "We need to know these things if she's on our hall. If personal business affects anybody on our team, we need to know about it in case it affects the way she teaches."

Penny's stomach dropped. *It feels like I'm being picked on by the mean girls in middle school again.* "They don't have a right to know," Penny told me later. "I don't want to advertise it; that's not my style. The way they were talking about me makes me feel like a failure. Will they think I'm a failure at everything? Will they tell parents, 'Oh, she's going through a divorce'? Because there's a stigma here for teachers going through a divorce. Parents don't want those teachers because they think they'll be distracted. But I can keep the two separated."

Penny wanted to turn the other way. *I don't need to eat lunch today. If I go in there, it's going to be painful. No,* said another inner voice, *I am going to walk in that door and make sure they know I heard them.*

Penny steeled herself and barged in, surprising the women. Savannah changed the subject: "Soo about my man saga. I think I might date Tim."

Vivian, Blair, and a new teacher took a beat to catch up, stammering as they tried to restart the new conversation.

"Hii, Penny," Savannah drawled.

Penny gave them a pointed look. As she fetched her lunch, Penny kept her head high until she returned to the hallway and closed the door behind her. She slumped for a moment against the wall, took a deep breath, and went to visit the only free 6th grade teacher she could think of.

"Hey," she asked Ed, who was eating lunch at his desk. "Want some company?"

Over the next several weeks, Penny and Ed chatted when they ran into each other at Southern or the high school. When they had time during lunch, they often talked about their kids; his son was a college sophomore and his daughter a high school senior. Between the two, Ed had taken them on 18 college campus tours by himself and had visited his son at least half a dozen times. The only time his wife had been on a college campus with them was the day their son moved in.

As their friendship progressed, Penny noticed that their conversations meandered beyond the usual Southern small talk. They had wide-ranging discussions about culture, literature, philosophy, and, when Penny could work it in, mathematical mindsets: how to change students' feelings about math and how changing their mindset could span curricula. She hadn't held these kinds of conversations with anyone before.

One day at lunch, Ed asked her, "You're so smart and passionate about your career. Why didn't you ever pursue a master's?"

"I've wanted to for so long," she said. "After helping put Kent through a master's program, I begged him. But every time I asked, he said, 'No, it doesn't make sense for teachers to get a master's degree,' or 'No, you don't get much more money and it's expensive,' or 'No, you have to be here for the boys.'"

Nel, the secretary, came into Ed's classroom. Her eyes widened when she saw Penny sitting across from him. "Hi, Nel," Ed said.

"Hey, Señor. Penny." She put some papers on the desk. "Soo, how's Kent and the twins?"

Penny knew she was digging. "Well, the twins are doing great. Kent and I are getting divorced."

"Wha-at?" Nel was so fake. "How did that happen to y'all?"

Penny gave what had become her standard answer. "Things just change in life. He's a great father and we work together for the boys and get along for their sake."

"I'm soo sorry to hear it," Nel oozed. "I'm always here if you need an ear."

After Nel left, Ed focused his soulful brown eyes on Penny as if she were the only person in the world. Penny continued, "I do everything for the boys. I dedicated my life to my kids, drive them to every practice, every game, every lesson. I work and always did all the cooking and cleaning. A master's is something I really, really wanted, but Kent always told me it's not worth it. I'm sorry, this is painful to talk about," she said, choking up. "But it's a goal I set for myself and it's important to me, yet I still haven't done it. I want to be an expert in the mathematics curriculum. Math is my calling. I've participated in every single opportunity to learn math that has come my way: free math classes at the university, yearlong classes, summer classes, everything. But Kent said it wasn't going to happen for me and I'd just have to accept it."

"You know, you can still do it," Ed murmured.

"I can't afford it."

"You might be able to find grants. I can try to help you find a way to pay for it."

Boy, did I have the wrong impression of him, Penny thought. *He might be the nicest man I've ever met.* She had encouraged plenty of students and former students to search for scholarship opportunities. Why shouldn't she seek opportunities for herself?

Buoyed by Ed's enthusiasm, she found a district grant opportunity, compiled her grad school application package, and applied to a math-related master's program. While she was at it, she also submitted an application for a position as a math resource instructor in the district's central office.

Miguel Garcia   Middle School Special Ed Teacher

In early October, Frank, Western's principal, came into Miguel's room before school. Miguel was always happy to see him. Frank knew the needs of the community and cared about the students and staff. He was pleasant to everyone. He was the kind of guy who told dad jokes even though he wasn't a dad.

Miguel suspected that Chad Tucker and the rest of the school board assumed that because Western had a relatively new principal, the school was a vulnerable target to turn into their academy. The prior evening, Miguel had met with concerned parents and community activists about the looming takeover. Because Tucker's meetings were shrouded in secrecy, Western families, who found out about them only after the fact, didn't have enough information to truly mobilize.

"Miguel," Frank said, "the district said we got enough students that we can hire a math teacher."

Surprise, surprise, Miguel thought. District officials had known the numbers would rise; they'd done this before. They'd remove good teachers, force Western staff to switch subjects and fill in gaps with long-term subs, and authorize new hires only well into the school year. By then, the remaining hirable teachers had to fill gaps across various grades, students had to switch teachers and schedules, and the district eventually would chastise Western for lower test scores. "There isn't stability," Miguel observed later. "They're trying to put up obstacles. They've probably been trying to sabotage the school so it would be easier to take over."

Frank looked sheepish. "The only way we can make this schedule work is if we have another elective," he said. "I know you have a lot going on, but would you teach another elective during your free period?"

Miguel raised an eyebrow. "Free" periods were never truly free. They were necessary time blocks for planning, grading, and meetings. With this fourth schedule change in less than two months, he'd have to start a new class from scratch midsemester. He also would now be planning curricula and teaching the equivalent of 14 different classes spanning three grade levels with zero school-day hours during which to prep. He was already spread too thin. He hardly had time to dash to the bathroom during his workday. At night he prepped for school and mentored his teacher charges. He barely saw his husband or daughter.

"Of course I'll do it," Miguel said, resigned.

"Are you sure?" Frank asked.

"Who else would?"

Miguel's special ed students were about to enter the classroom when Miguel noticed a ruckus in the hall. He was disappointed to see Eli in the middle of it.

When Miguel had worked with moderately to severely disabled students, the gains were slow but significant. With the mildly to moderately disabled students, the gains felt comparatively quick. Since August, Eli had markedly improved his executive functioning skills, stamina and follow-through, and ability to plan ahead. He still had a ways to go, naturally, and he continued to make fun of Laurent, the 6th grader who annoyed him, when he thought Miguel wasn't listening.

Eli's mother was slightly more communicative with Miguel about monitoring her son's progress. In Eli's planner this week, she'd written for the first time. "How's he doing?"

"He's a pleasure to have in class," Miguel responded. "He's challenging and, like all kids, he has a lot of energy and can learn to rein it in, but he's witty. I really enjoy having him in class."

Eli's mom wrote back, "I've never heard him described that way."

When Miguel read aloud a story that included an abusive alcoholic father, Eli said, "My father left us. He drank a *lot*, haha."

"Thanks for sharing that, Eli." Miguel could tell Eli was trying to play this off like a joke as a way to share with the class. Middle schoolers sometimes used dark humor to deal with things that hurt; they wanted to be validated without revealing too much. Expressing any vulnerability was a big step for Eli. If Eli didn't have an adult male role model, Miguel would make every effort to be one for him.

To Miguel's knowledge, the only consistent adults in Eli's life were his mother and the school counselor. Genuine and compassionate, the counselor visited Miguel's class weekly to talk about social-emotional awareness and how the developing brain learns. Her efforts successfully motivated students with learning disabilities. And she somehow could get students to confide in her even if they didn't usually share their emotions. Once a week, Eli visited her office for a counseling session. Sometimes she called Miguel right after Eli left to say, "He's coming upstairs and he's upset after our session. Give him a wide berth."

Now, as Miguel headed toward the doorway to break up the scuffle, he saw Eli shove Gabe to the floor and stomp on him. "Whoa, *whoa*! What are you doing?" Miguel separated the boys.

"It's my fault, it's my fault, I did it," said Gabe, who considered Eli the cool guy in class.

"He's still not supposed to stomp you," Miguel replied. To Eli he said, "You could really hurt him. He's not a bug." He made sure Gabe was uninjured and ushered him with the rest of the students into the classroom.

"What were you thinking?" Miguel asked Eli, now alone in the hall.

"He made me really mad." Eli was unemotional, the still before the storm.

"But is it worth you breaking his ribs? Come on," Miguel said evenly. He needed to show Eli that he wasn't going to explode, as he suspected Eli's father might have. "Eli, you can't do that. You've gotta say you're sorry."

"Are you gonna send me to the office?" Eli geared up to rage.

Miguel visibly took a deep breath, hoping Eli would, too. "I don't know, Eli. First I want to know what happened."

Eli quivered in anger. "He grabbed my pants and he brought them down. He really embarrassed me."

"Ah, that's not cool, that's not a joke. You have every right to be mad. He got into your private space." Miguel wondered if Eli had been triggered. He would not be the first student at Western to have that issue lurking at home.

Eli raised his head, surprised Miguel took his side. "I'm not going to apologize."

"You don't have to apologize. Gabe needs to apologize. But you can't be kicking people. I understand why you felt that way. If anyone ever invades your personal private space, you should protect yourself. But in this case, I am here to take care of this situation and I don't need you to be stomping people."

"So you're not sending me to the office?"

"No, what he did to you was not okay." Eli began to uncoil. "I would've been upset, too," Miguel said. "Remember the assembly about sexual harassment? What Gabe did is like sexual harassment. You can't just grab someone's pants."

Eli wasn't shaking anymore. "Do you need some time?" Miguel asked.

"Yeah."

Back in class, Miguel asked Gabe what happened, then explained that his actions constituted sexual harassment.

"I didn't realize," Gabe said.

"At some point, I'm not saying right now, you should say you're sorry."

A few minutes later, Eli returned.

"I'm sorry," Gabe said immediately.

"It's fine," Eli replied. Both boys looked relieved.

Later that week, when Miguel wrote a compare-and-contrast lesson on the whiteboard, the students squinted helplessly at it. "What does that say?" someone asked.

"I'm so sorry. I have terrible handwriting. I used to get in trouble for it as a kid and the nuns would hit me," Miguel said. Students liked hearing his stories about the nuns. Also, he made a point of broadcasting his mistakes because he wanted kids to know that mistakes weren't a big deal.

"It's okay, I do too!" Eli exclaimed. His guard dipped; he seemed almost excited that his teacher had the same challenge he did.

Miguel turned and smiled at him. "Not as bad as my handwriting!"

"Don't worry about it!" Eli grinned back.

Miguel wondered if Eli's refusal to write was because past teachers had judged him on his poor penmanship, which could be related to his disability. Miguel could make accommodations for him while continuing to nudge him to write. If he could just get Eli to start writing *something*, he could ask him to edit it later with punctuation and capital letters. He guessed that Eli's biggest stumbling block was simply putting words to paper.

Miguel deliberately and obviously wrote more slowly on the board to improve legibility. When he got a chance, he took Eli aside.

"Hey, listen, I understand about your handwriting. When you write for me, I'll give you credit for writing a partial answer instead of a complete sentence for now, okay? But you gotta show me a little writing. As a teacher, they expect me to have students writing, so maybe you can help me out by trying."

"I get it. It's your job. I'll do it," Eli said.

A few minutes later, Miguel noticed Eli deliberately writing slowly.

Over the next several weeks, Miguel observed a shift in Eli. Miguel could now gently admonish him and, because the boy trusted that Miguel wasn't out to get him, he listened. Eli fully bought into Miguel's point system and gradually started to do his homework. While Eli still got in trouble often with his elective teachers, he settled down in Miguel's class.

Miguel's top goal for his special ed students was to develop successful school habits so they'd have a solid foundation to carry them through the rest of their schooling. Frank allowed Miguel the flexibility to teach lifelong lessons and comfort in the classroom. Miguel often let students walk around as a break from sitting at their desks. He'd already noticed that his students were whispering more, now that they knew how. "I'm hoping by the end of the year to train all of them to be able to do their homework, follow through with their work, and advocate for themselves," he told me. This was particularly crucial given the district's plan to force special ed students to mainstream next year. What Miguel did for Eli, Dewayne, and their classmates would be extraordinarily difficult for a gen ed single-subject teacher to manage in a large class.

One of the school board officials spearheading the special ed plan was none other than Chad Tucker. Behind the scenes, Tucker had continued plotting to take over Western. He'd conducted informational meetings with little notice at times that Western parents and teachers couldn't attend because they worked during the day. "If the takeover's such a good idea, why do they always discuss it in the dark and try to bamboozle people?" Miguel wondered.

On a mid-October afternoon, Miguel spotted Frank looking gray and troubled. "You look bad," Miguel said. "What's going on?"

"Uh, I have chest pains," Frank said, wincing. He showed Miguel a handful of emails he'd received that afternoon from Western parents who suddenly were accusing him of cooperating with Tucker to shut down the school. "I thought you were on our side!" said one. "I can't believe you would do this to us!" said another.

"And look what GL just wrote me," Frank said. Miguel privately called the most vocal parent in the school GL, for Grenade Launcher. She and her clique often complained about Frank and others in positions of authority, hunting for crises about which she could be publicly self-righteous. Her email accused Frank of colluding with Chad Tucker to abandon Western, and it got worse from there.

"What is she talking about?" Miguel asked, incredulous.

"I can't believe I'm being accused of this. This is really terrible," Frank said.

The counselor drove Frank to the hospital. He was out for a week.

Meanwhile, Miguel was livid. There was no way Frank had colluded with district officials to eliminate Western. Miguel confronted GL, who showed him a city official's email claiming Tucker said that Western's principal wanted the academy. "That was a lie. The man's not capable of looking me in the eye, knowing what I was going through with my mom, and planning something else," Miguel told me. "It's a kick in the gut."

Miguel's heart went out to Frank. "If a school board member says, 'Do what I want, fall on your sword,' Frank might have to," Miguel said. "The district threw him under the bus. They probably expected him to say okay and they'd reward him with some cushy thing. But he's very invested in this school. And now I'm worried they want to get rid of him. I left the entertainment industry to get away from this type of nastiness. Of all the places, I didn't think I'd have to deal with backstabbing like this in a school. Seeing Frank's reputation maligned really angers me."

Miguel wrote a letter to city officials and a mass email to parents asserting that Frank had said no such thing—and a school principal didn't have the authority to hand over a school anyway. Initially, Miguel asked Quiesha to video the board meeting, but when he learned that Frank's chest pains were related to extreme stress, he opted not to record it.

At the meeting, Frank briefly and politely avowed that he had always backed Western; he did not want the academy taking over his school. Then came Miguel's turn at the mic. Miguel stood up for what he believed in. As a teachers union rep, he had experience amplifying voices. He knew many teachers couldn't speak out because they were "terrified of losing their jobs." He told me, "There's a lot of fear in schools. Teachers don't want to piss anyone off."

Miguel had certainly experienced bad administrators, including a principal who enlisted a staffer as a spy to report back on what teachers said on social media. Frank, by contrast, was a good principal and a good soul. So Miguel went to bat for him. He talked about how Western had stunningly few resources and yet was still successful because of Frank's stewardship. He looked straight at Tucker and affirmed in front of the crowd that Western's principal had never supported the takeover. He advocated for Frank's job and said that if Frank was taken away from the school, he would resign. And he lobbied the district officials to leave Western alone. Frank was moved by Miguel's protectiveness.

When Miguel got home, he told his husband, Jim, about the meeting. "I'm so proud of you! It's so important that you're doing this. You're just like Norma Rae!" Jim exclaimed. "But, Miguel, ultimately it's not going to be good for your health if you keep running at this pace. You've never really even had time to grieve your mother's death."

Miguel paused. Jim was right. Miguel had been so overwhelmed with work and the battle to save Western that he hadn't yet processed the biggest tragedy of his life. He remained convinced that this would be his last year teaching. "Politics, greed, and mismanagement have made this profession incompatible with physical and mental health. I could retire early in a few years, but I don't have the energy to fight this awful district anymore. Most teachers I know have had it," he told me. His sister, who had been teaching for more than three decades, had decided this would be her last year because her school district, too, was trying to mainstream all special ed students without a plan, training, or support staff. She was already struggling with the special needs students her district increasingly placed in her class.

At the end of October, a student asked, "Aren't we going to do spelling quizzes?"

"Do you want to do spelling quizzes?" asked Miguel, who wasn't a fan. Half the class said yes. He opted to give the quizzes on Fridays because he could soften the sting with the doughnut store and his weekly Fun Friday Science Experiments.

Before the first quiz, Miguel explained that every correct word was worth a five-point ticket. He emphasized that the quizzes weren't a big deal. "Do I get upset if you get a wrong answer?" he asked the class.

"Noooo," they answered.

"Is this just an opportunity to get points?"

"Yeess."

After the quiz, Miguel had his students trade papers with partners, whom Miguel carefully assigned. He paired volatile Eli with quiet Isabel, who would be discreet about Eli's score. Spelling was difficult for her because, as a Mexican immigrant, English was not her first language. As he listed the correct answers, Miguel circulated around the room. "You know, when my father first came to this country, he said English was the hardest language," Miguel told Isabel.

"It is!" Isabel agreed.

"Spanish is much easier," he continued. "English has all these weird rules." He made a mental note to teach a "maddening English rule and weird exceptions" every week before the quiz.

"How did your dad learn it?" she asked.

"Practice. And reading a lot."

As he passed her table, he glanced casually at Eli's paper. Every word was illegible. Eli had scored a zero.

Rebecca Abrams   Elementary School Teacher

At the start of a math lesson, Rebecca noticed a group of boys playing with their pencils, waving them around in the air. Rebecca raised an eyebrow. *"Wingardium leviosa?"* she asked.

The boys giggled and waved their pencils more vigorously. Rebecca aimed her Smart Board pointer at them: *"Expelliarmus!"* The boys froze melodramatically and dropped their pencils. Rebecca nodded stoically and returned to the board as the kids cracked up again.

Rebecca and Trixie still laughed about Mia and Luci calling them witches. Last month, Rebecca had left a mug on Trixie's desk featuring a witch on a broom, captioned "Yes, I can drive a stick." Trixie had returned the favor this week with a witch-themed Pop-Socket. Gestures like these could give a teacher a lift for the rest of the day.

JJ, the most advanced student in 4th grade, was still at his desk instead of on the rug with the class. When Rebecca went to talk to him, he showed her he had memorized the algorithm to calculate equivalent fractions.

"Okay, how does it work?" Rebecca asked.

He walked her through the steps of the algorithm, ordering fractions through cross-multiplication, but he didn't explain the logic behind the steps.

"But *how* do you know? What's your proof?" Rebecca asked.

Frustrated, JJ repeated himself louder: "Well, you have to multiply this numerator *here* by that denominator *there*. You just *do* it!"

"But why do you do it?"

"I don't know!" JJ shouted. He had reacted similarly when Rebecca asked him to demonstrate a deep understanding of a story in ELA. Rebecca suspected that he wasn't accustomed to explaining himself because he answered questions correctly.

Rebecca could fix that oversight, but she worried about finding time to provide him enrichment when she taught 37 other students throughout the day with different, varied needs—she had 26 homeroom students and 12 others who came to her for gifted math, ELA, or both. At a teacher planning meeting earlier in the week, Rebecca said to Camille, the math specialist, "I've never had a student who was so far ahead of the rest of class that there's no need for him to come to half the lessons." Camille, similarly stumped, searched for advanced tasks for JJ.

Now Rebecca returned to her Smart Board. "Since you're not really sure why that strategy works, come to the rug—"

"Why?" JJ interrupted.

"I want to show you another strategy that might make more sense to you."

"But I can already make equivalent fractions!"

"You do know how to follow the steps, but you don't know *why* it works, and that's what I want you to learn, which you will. Humor the teacher."

JJ grudgingly sat at the back of the rug and sulked.

Rebecca turned to the class. "Blindly following steps isn't the same as *learning*. If you don't understand *why* something works, you haven't actually learned the math. You've just memorized steps. If you don't know why something works, ask me, and I'll help you understand it—and it's okay if it takes a while for you to understand it. We'll keep practicing as we go!"

Just five minutes into the lesson, JJ perked up. Midway through, he declared, *"Now I get it!"*

Afterward, Rebecca worked with him individually for a few minutes. "Okay, let's go back to that problem from before. Talk me through it, and now tell me *why* you do each step."

And he did. But those were the only moments she could carve out to work one-on-one with him all week.

Oliver presented a completely different set of challenges. While he excelled at academics, he struggled socially and emotionally. When he got stuck on a complex math task or couldn't decide what to write about for an assignment (even "What did you like about the book you read?"), he burst into hysterical tears.

Rebecca held individual conferences with Oliver about resiliency and growth mindset, a theme in her classroom. One of her bulletin boards defined fixed and growth mindsets and gave examples of things people with each mindset say ("I can't do it" versus "I can't do it YET," "I made a mistake, so I'm a failure" versus "I made a mistake. What happened so I can change it next time?"). Rebecca taught the mindsets at the beginning of the year and regularly referenced them. She congratulated kids when they used growth mindset words and helped them reframe their fixed mindset comments with growth mindset language. She rewarded risk-taking and mistake-making with high fives. Oliver, she knew, would need more work on these skills than his peers.

Later that week, Rebecca lay in bed, reviewing her day. She did that a lot, ruminating over everything she needed to do. Almost every night, sleep would bring what she called "schoolmares," school-based nightmares featuring students, coworkers, or the school building, typically starring Rebecca standing in front of the class inexplicably lacking lesson plans. During the day she maintained her buoyant "I got this" façade to everyone but Trixie, with whom she commiserated regularly. But inside she was a mess.

Rebecca kept having to push off her work/life balance goals. Last month had brought the usual September workload: creating, administering, and grading writing samples and spelling inventories, figuring out a new schedule, ice-breakers, community building. Even grading took much more time than non-teachers assumed. Rebecca explained why all incorrect answers were wrong and how they could be corrected, and she gave writing assignments careful attention and specific feedback. This year Rebecca also had to rein in students who'd been in Fiona's 3rd grade class, where there was evidently little behavioral management.

In September, Rebecca had also graded preassessments, analyzed the data of her class's first social studies test results, created sub plans for two days of Rosh Hashanah and one day of Yom Kippur, and graded all the classwork and homework from those days, answered an inordinate number of emails, participated in planning meetings, got recaps of planning meetings that were inconsiderately scheduled on the Jewish holidays, and started her continuing ed course to teach gifted students, a yearlong class that counted toward her license renewal and would earn her certificate to teach enrichment classes in the long term.

Now, in October, she was still working straight through weekends except for meals. She often worked past 11 p.m. "So much for trying to have a work/life balance this year. I'm trying to not lose hope and to convince myself that soon I'll be able to balance things better," she told me.

Rebecca's school system perpetrated what she called "passive discrimination" against non-Christian teachers. Teachers were allotted only two days of religious leave per year, but Christian teachers didn't need them because school was closed on their holidays. To take days off for religious reasons, teachers had to fill out a lengthy form detailing plans for making up those days, get their principal's approval, and mail it to the district's central office 30 days in advance, even during the summer if the Jewish High Holidays fell in early to mid-September, as they did this year. District officials also scheduled principals', staff, and leadership meetings, mandatory PD days, and trainings on non-Christian holidays. Last year Rebecca had to miss a meeting she was supposed to lead because it was scheduled on Yom Kippur, the most sacred day of the Jewish year. Rebecca's Muslim colleagues faced similar hurdles.

In ELA this week, Rebecca was required to begin teaching several small group lessons every day based on kids' needs and the books she could find for them, which was time-consuming to prep. The following weekend she'd have to write interims—mid-quarter progress reports—for her homeroom students and memos for the teachers of the gifted ELA and math students who weren't in her homeroom. She also had to create a parent-teacher conference schedule to send to English-speaking parents and work with a liaison to set up conferences for Spanish-speaking parents who needed translators.

All of this was on top of daily planning and grading, not to mention grocery shopping, cleaning, and cooking; sometimes she had time to cook only one meal to last the week. "My house is disgusting, my dishes are unwashed, my lawn isn't mown, I haven't gone to the gym or dancing since mid-August," she told me. She was so frazzled that she kept losing small items from her desk that she'd sworn she hadn't moved.

Upset that she wasn't meeting all her students' needs, Rebecca called her mother. "I feel like a failure. I'm working so damn hard, but they're so far behind that I don't have enough time for all those groups! How can I ever differentiate enough? And freakin' Fiona didn't follow the third grade pacing guide! It specifically says *don't* teach them cross-multiplication! The kids are actually *below* grade level on some things because I'm having to reteach them things from scratch!"

Rebecca had to redo her math lesson plans because they were too wordy and complex for most of her current students. "So the highest kids will keep getting shafted, the lowest kids will be rushed and pushed beyond what they can comprehend so far, the middle kids still won't get as much time with a teacher as they should have, and I'll continue to be completely crazed and frustrated about the subject that I was anticipating would be the calm in the storm this year."

"You're not a failure, Rebecca. You can only do so much," her mom said.

"I develop so many things, and revise them up and down, and search out resources, but without having more time to work with the kids to fill the holes of what they didn't get last year, there isn't enough time to get all of them where they need to be." Now Rebecca was weeping. "We take our first major math unit test this week, and a few kids will fail. They're not ready. The gifted pacing guide rushes us through too many units."

"I think it would help if you got more sleep and did things for yourself, like getting back to dancing."

"I'm lucky if I get five and a half hours of sleep on a school night. I've been at school for between eleven and thirteen and a half hours almost every school day, and when I finally collapse into bed, my brain is still so wired that I can't sleep for thirty minutes or more, which means I teach on four to four and a half hours of sleep," Rebecca said. "Working with the kids is generally great, but the prep is killing me. I just can't do this anymore. Emotionally and physically, I'm already burning out. I'm just *tired*. And it's only October."

"Well, do what you can do with what you have in the time you have," her mom advised. "Think how much they've learned already from you. What can they do now?"

That was a helpful perspective. Thinking about the successes, even if the class hadn't gotten as far as she would have liked, helped Rebecca to calm down.

Rebecca called herself a recovering overachiever and pushed herself to perfectionism. "I'm trying to get better, but I could always do more," she told me. "So I push myself and push myself and stay up late and don't do other things I should be doing because I'm working, and then I finally get to the point where I melt down. I feel desperate that there's nothing else I can do." She wanted to do more for Oliver. She wanted to help Mia get past her test anxiety. Every time Mia finished a computer test and her score flashed onscreen, her face fell and she lamented "how bad I am at taking tests." Rebecca wanted to foster a safe-space classroom in which kids felt comfortable opening up, like Illyse, a student from Grace's homeroom who wrote a heartfelt, detailed personal ELA essay about how difficult it was to be the child of divorced parents because she was always missing one. And the child Rebecca most felt she was letting down was JJ. "I feel really helpless. He must be so bored and I don't have the time or resources to give him what he needs."

Rebecca desperately wanted to do right by all her students. They were creative and fun and made Rebecca laugh every day. One student's response to an "About Me" homework assignment was "I am really good at: breathing and drawing platypuses." Another student suggested Rebecca prank Evangeline by sticking googly eyes on some of the music room instruments, then gamely helped Rebecca execute their mission.

At indoor recess one afternoon, a group of kids played monkey in the middle along a classroom wall. One of Rebecca's students decided it was more fun to watch than play. She folded a piece of scrap paper into a cylinder, wrote "POPCORN" on it in red marker, then pulled up a chair and "ate popcorn" while she watched the game. Every time Rebecca rotated to monitor the room, she couldn't help laughing as the student catcalled the participants and pretended to munch away.

Moments like these carried Rebecca through her days.

"I Would Have Done It for Any Child": Teachers Are Heroes—but They Shouldn't Have to Be

Alabama 5th grade teacher Ms. Maiden was part of an army of school staff who looked out for Jamie, a sweet, quiet student who belonged to the school's 2% racial minority. When Jamie was in 2nd grade, her mother severed parental rights and the grandmother who took her in died. The elementary school staff helped Jamie's grandfather gain custody and fixed up his ramshackle rental house, providing furniture and partnering with carpenters to bring it up to code. Maiden bonded further with Jamie when the 4th grader was placed in her after-school-care classroom, where Maiden helped her with homework. When Maiden got to know Jamie, as a tutor and the following year as her 5th grade teacher, "the bond really grew." Maiden told me, "Jamie didn't have that many women in her life, so I wanted to help out and fill the void."

One day when Jamie was absent, a distant relative informed administrators that Jamie's grandfather had died and that Jamie would enter the foster care system. Knowing immediately that she would volunteer to foster the girl, Maiden went to family court that day. In 2020, she officially adopted her former student. Their school staff celebrated them with an exuberant "Gotcha Day" drive-by parade. "She is such a blessing," Maiden said. "We're learning and growing together as a family, and the biggest thing for us is family is not just blood related. Family is those who love and take care of you."

Maiden never thought twice about shifting from being Jamie's teacher to being Jamie's mom. "She was born for me," she said. "But I would have done it for any child that had the same difficulties."

Reports abound of teachers doing everything in their power to help students. Many teachers have donated kidneys to students or students' parents. A Kansas special ed teacher fostered, then adopted one of her students who had severe special needs. She also donated respite care, babysitting students with severe disabilities so their families could go to weddings or take vacations. Rose, a Missouri middle school teacher, welcomed a former student and his young son into her home for two summers as he struggled to emerge from systemic poverty. "People thought I was out of my mind. All I could say was if you're good at teaching, you have to have an open heart," she told me, "and sometimes, if they need it badly enough, kids crawl right inside."

Teachers are this country's silent, constant superheroes. And that's a big problem.

Somewhere along the line, as the expectations and responsibilities foisted on teachers expanded beyond educating, being good at teaching wasn't enough for the public or school districts to consider someone a good teacher. Exhaustive, relentless selflessness became part of the unspoken job description. A Maryland district's April 2021 press release about Teacher of the Year finalists included these words in one finalist's short bio: "[She] has continued to teach with joy and expertise despite running a temperature for more than 200 consecutive days due to COVID-19." The same district's June 2021 press release about its Counselor of the Year highlighted, "Although she is in a higher risk category for dangerous symptoms from COVID-19, she brushed her fears aside to recognize the extreme community needs during the pandemic."

The descriptions represented a dangerous normalization of societal expectations that educators must sacrifice their health and well-being. Teachers are rhapsodized when they're martyrs, demonized when they're not—and the narrative is quick to flip. As Pennsylvania language arts teacher Steven Singer astutely wrote in a blog for advocacy organization Badass Teachers Association, "I don't love being called a hero if I put my life on the line to keep children safe during a shooting or emergency but vilified if I ask for reforms to make sure it doesn't happen (again)."

Pigeonholing teachers as heroes doesn't just dehumanize them, it also deflects focus from the lack of a social safety net preventing students from falling into circumstances that require "saving" in the first place. The COVID pandemic exposed the vast unrealistic roles schools were expected to fulfill as social service providers even as federal, state, and local governments failed to supply the funding and resources necessary for schools to satisfy their academic purpose alone, turning an already critical problem into an even more urgent one. (Chapter 4 discusses education during the pandemic in more detail.)

Portraying teachers as martyrs also slights their professionalism. A widely circulated 2020s meme announced, "Teachers don't teach for the income, they teach for the outcome." Educators were not amused. While the students are the draw, teachers shouldn't have to choose between the pay and the kids. Teachers are skilled professionals who choose the career for varied reasons, "none of which are reasons to pay us anything less than a professional salary that reflects our skills," said a Washington, DC, humanities teacher. "I've found myself being sucked into the teacher martyrdom mentality such that I took pride in how little time I could take for myself because it was a sign of how dedicated I was to my job and my students. I embraced the idea that teaching was such a huge responsibility that there was no way to truly repay my dedication. This is unhealthy and ridiculous, but it's propagated everywhere, even by well-meaning people."

Including the entertainment industry. "Teachers are constantly portrayed poorly in movies unless the point of the movie is the amazing teacher," said a California private school math teacher. "But even those usually carry a savior narrative that's not awesome to 'regular' teachers. It creates a situation where you have to be the savior teacher to be considered a 'good' teacher."

The savior narrative "exoticizes youth and positions them as automatically broken. It falsely positions the teacher, oftentimes a white teacher, as hero," Columbia University Teachers College professor Christopher Emdin told *PBS NewsHour*. "Not only are we setting the kids up to fail and the educators up to fail, but most importantly, we are creating a societal model that positions young people as unable to be saved." Emdin's illuminating book, *For White Folks Who Teach in the Hood . . . and the Rest of Y'all Too,* recommends how teachers can work and learn along with students as unique individuals "wholly visible to each other and to the teacher," rather than see them as people who need saving.

The cinematic savior trope also commonly carries racial undertones; consider the many films in which a white teacher comes to the rescue of students of color: *Dangerous Minds, Music of the Heart, Freedom Writers, The Principal.* The majority of the teacher workforce may be white women, but assumptions about who helps whom and why can be insulting and biased.

Recall the story about Jamie's adoption and the picture you formed in your mind's eye. If you envisioned a white teacher as savior, you were mistaken. Valencia Maiden is Black. Jamie is white. There aren't many movies like that.

～

Teachers may be heroes, but they shouldn't be expected to be heroic, as if heroism is a job requirement and anything less than martyrdom is a failure to meet the standards of the position. They are humans "rendered superhumanly responsible for the current and future state of the whole country," as University of Wisconsin education professor Alan Block has said. It is impossible for teachers to constantly measure up to an unsustainable bar of self-sacrifice—and when they don't, some administrators are disappointed, the public becomes disenchanted, and teachers like Rebecca can feel guilty, as if they've done something wrong.

They have not.

While the grand gestures make the headlines, the truth is that most teachers do something extra for students, from working after hours to simply being accessible as a trusted adult, seemingly little things with big impacts that the public and sometimes even their own administrators don't know about.

Teachers I talked to bought eyeglasses, furniture, mattresses, clothes, winter gear, books, holiday presents, and food for students whose families couldn't afford them—and also for some students who could. Many, like Miguel, anonymously paid for students' field trips or school spirit wear. A middle school teacher in an impoverished West Virginia district enlisted a local Walmart to help her set up an in-school closet of free toiletries for students. All of this is on top of the nearly $500 per year the average teacher pays out of pocket for classroom supplies; at least 94% of public school teachers spend their own money on supplies.

A California special ed teacher gives his personal cell phone number to students and graduates "even though that's not recommended, because many of my students don't have that stability outside of school to have someone to turn to. I want them to know that someone cares and is thinking about them."

Teachers are often the people who recognize an undiagnosed condition and have difficult discussions with parents to get children tested so they can get the services they need. Rose, the Missouri teacher, taught a 6th grader whose older brothers were smart, athletic, self-aware big men on campus. The youngest brother, who had ADHD, was awkward, easily frustrated, a B/C student, and tired of living in his brothers' shadows. "As I got to know him, I totally fell for this kid. I noted his poor handwriting, lack of fine motor control, terrible spelling, and occasional reading errors. I started collecting evidence: He wrote 'fracture' instead of 'fraction' but read it back correctly. He left off the ends of long words, like silent 'e' and plural 's.' He sometimes misspelled his own last name," Rose said. "I had a long, gentle conversation with his mom. She got him tested and found out he was severely dyslexic and dysgraphic."

At the end of the year, the boy gave Rose a gift: the book *Fish in a Tree*, which draws its title from the quote "If you judge a fish on its ability to climb a tree, it will spend its whole life thinking that it's stupid." This experience convinced Rose to get a master's in special education and switch from gen ed to special ed.

The extraordinary moments are rewarding, but not what keep teachers going day to day. The vast majority of educators mentioned two things when I asked them what is wonderful about being a teacher: the "aha moment" when students understand a concept or make a connection with the material, and when former students contact them. At a Georgia school's graduation, minutes before seniors lined up to march in, the valedictorian sought out her former English teacher. "I just wanted to thank you," she said. "You taught me how to write a conclusion and I appreciate it." The teacher told me, "This brilliant young woman was about to deliver a valedictory speech to a thousand people, and she took the time to find me and say thanks. I have never received a greater teaching prize and I doubt I ever will."

Recently a graduated student contacted the teacher who had sponsored their Texas high school's Gay/Straight Alliance. After undergoing gender reassignment, he adopted his teacher's first name to honor him for being the first person to support him and make him feel comfortable with his identity. "I just felt so honored that he adopted my name while becoming the person he aspired to be," the teacher said.

Teachers also mentioned "that moment when the bell rings and a class collectively cries out in surprise, 'Already?' because the lesson made the class go so quickly. It's like everything clicks and it feels like magic," said Jaqui, a Pennsylvania high school English teacher. "Also, when you teach a lesson you love and wrap up a book—for me, it's *Gatsby*—and the whole class applauds. (This is usually followed by a class where a student curses at you or throws a desk or something, so the feeling never lasts long, but it's a good one when it does)."

Even just a heartfelt thank-you can brighten a teacher's week. A New Jersey English teacher choked up when she read an email from a student she'd taught junior year. The student wrote, "You told me once that you wrote your Common App essay about a teacher in your life who you wanted to be like someday. Well, you are the teacher I hope to be like someday. Thank you for constantly inspiring me and pushing me to reach higher." The teacher told me that what she admired most about her favorite teacher was "how loved he made every student feel, to the point where former students, even grown adults, were so excited to see him. For this student to say I was that teacher for her really hit home."

⁓

Teachers aren't generous only to their students; they also often take care of one another. Many teachers donate their sick days to union sick banks so that teachers who run out can extend their leave without losing their salary or health insurance. In the fall of 2020, when a California teacher took disability leave following a stroke, his wife, who had been laid off, posted their plight on Facebook. Teachers who were complete strangers offered an outpouring of support and their sick days, even though the COVID vaccine was not yet available and they could need those days themselves if they contracted the virus.

Like Miguel, many teachers serve as mentors. Mentorship is crucial: More than 44% of new teachers leave the field within their first five years. A study of seven districts using Peer Assistance and Review, an expanded mentoring program that supports new and struggling experienced teachers, found that first-year teacher retention averaged 90%, high above the national average in urban districts. An Illinois high school English teacher new to her school told me about mentors and teammates who "made an effort to check in, had lunch with me, helped me move into my apartment, and delivered snacks. This school has an amazingly supportive faculty and administration." She pays it forward by assisting coworkers with technology tools and troubleshooting.

Mentors, too, benefit from the relationship. Mentoring a student teacher helped Jaqui "see my career through new eyes. She was energetic, creative, and thoughtful about teaching in ways that hadn't occurred to me. She's now a full-time teacher in another district. We've stayed close, shared many materials, and collaborated a ton over the years."

Administrators have the power to foster a collaborative, considerate environment, as well. A Hawaii school principal "is great about providing fun bonding activities and outlets for us," a 4th grade teacher said. "We've gone to escape rooms together, had a silent disco, trivia contests, beach days. Sometimes, we'll show up at a meeting and there will be wine and snacks. Our administration really tries to find ways to make us feel valued and provide opportunities to have fun."

At a faculty meeting, a midwestern psychologist administered the Adverse Childhood Experiences (ACE) test to teachers and support staff. ACE, scored from 0 to 10, tallies abuse, neglect, and other traumatic childhood experiences; the higher the score, the higher one's risk for future health problems. The psychologist shared the results. "Our team averaged [a high] 6.4," a teacher there told me. "The psychologist said studies show that people who survive bad childhoods and are able to turn their lives around often reach back to places where they feel they can make a difference. But the burdens of a place like that actually make them struggle even more. It was a revelatory meeting, looking around the room and realizing how wounded everyone was around me. It made us want to make things less hard on each other."

After two coworkers visited a temporarily hospitalized Washington, DC, history teacher at the same time as a college friend, the friend expressed amazement that in only seven months the teacher's coworkers had become "like lifelong friends." "He said I was lucky to have found them in my school. But, honestly, I've left every school I've ever worked in with lifelong friends," she told me. "The friendships you make with teaching colleagues are deep because the experience of teaching is so intense and this field draws people who value relationships and know how to show up."

Some teachers find this supportive sense of community with educators outside their own school. A Pennsylvania teacher joined the

AP Language and Composition Teachers Facebook group and enthusiastically attends AP Reading, an annual weeklong event where teachers attend professional development sessions and score 1.5 million AP exam essays. "It's a built-in support system and fabulous group of cheerleaders," she said. "Within a single school building, sometimes teachers can be catty because you're around each other so much and dealing with day-to-day frustrations. But online, you seek out your tribe and find your people who are the ones who keep you going day after day when you think you've had all you can take."

Grateful for those connections, she co-founded Twitter's now-lapsed #aplangchat, which for years hosted hour-long discussions and Zooms. Now, in various subgroups, "we talk about school and life in general. We help each other with ideas and provide moral support when one of us is dealing with frustrating issues at school. It's nice to have someone outside our district for a sounding board, a fresh perspective," she said. "Events like the AP Reading and these groups are really important in forging connections among teachers, especially when you're teaching something specialized. Most of my department members would laugh if I suggested we get together online and talk shop in the evenings; so many teachers want to keep their work brain at school. But this amazing network of AP teachers has shown me that I'm not crazy for volunteering to brainstorm and share awesome classroom ideas in my free time. They are really positive online environments because the teachers participating are equally passionate and eager to connect."

When a California middle school math teacher received no training on a new curriculum, she searched online for help and found the #MTBoS: the Math Twitter Blog-o-Sphere, a welcoming community of math teachers who blog, tweet, and attend conferences, often on their own dime, to work and learn together. "These conferences have filled both my person heart and my teacher heart more than anything I've done," she said. "My online community has taught me all the best things I know about being a teacher and most of the best things I know about being a person."

She annually attends state and national math conferences specifically to spend time with the #MTBoS crew. "In my classroom I have a bulletin board of pictures from the conferences. My students 'know' the people on the board. When we do an activity, they ask if the person who made it is on the board. They ask questions all the time that start out, 'Can we ask your Twitter friends . . .'" They're desperate for them to visit our class. One of them did this year—a person who has become my best friend just because of this amazing #MTBoS community in which I have found my home."

The shared mission and uniqueness of the profession lend educators a feeling of solidarity. Teachers don't consider it heroic to do good for fellow educators, as Miguel did for Frank, just as they don't consider it heroic to step up for students. When a colleague's house burned down, Pennsylvania teachers rallied to raise thousands of dollars, provide temporary housing, food, and class coverage—"all in a night," said a teacher who worked at that school. "The kids change every year, but the teachers? We are the home team. And even if we have our differences, we always band together in times of strife. It's a big part of what keeps me in the field."

CHAPTER 4

November

At a Maryland district-organized elementary school staff meeting about active shooter situations:

Police officer: "Do any of you teach in that building over there?"

The 5th grade team raised their hands.

Police officer: "Well, you guys are pretty much screwed, because bullets go right through those walls, so good luck."

Rebecca Abrams   Elementary School Teacher

In ELA, Rebecca worked with a small group of students on short essays. When Mia had trouble finding adjectives to describe cats, Rebecca pretended to be one. She mimed licking her paw, crawled languidly on desks, nuzzled her head against her arm, and purred. As a student reached out to "pet" her, she hissed and pretended to claw at him, to his and his neighbors' amusement. The students on the other side of the classroom watched bug-eyed, wondering what was going on as the small group laughed and cheered. Once those students explained to the rest, the class played along.

"Good kitty!" JJ said.

Rebecca stretched and meowed while students comedically narrated her inner cat monologue.

Only Oliver continued to look confused. "Why are you acting it out, though?" he asked.

Rebecca was now certain that Oliver was on the autism spectrum. Oliver's combination of academic strengths and difficulty with social understanding fit patterns the 4th grade teachers had observed in diagnosed students. When Oliver got stuck on assignments, he still engaged in negative self-talk, cried, or shut down and stared. He didn't recognize personal space, which annoyed his peers, and he kicked, pushed, or insulted classmates if someone took "his" seat in the lunchroom or "his" first spot in line. He flipped out if he lost a game at recess and couldn't fathom why his classmates thought it was gross if he picked his nose or his pants slid down his backside.

When Rebecca discussed her concerns with Yvonne, Eastern's instructional coordinator, Yvonne asked her to gather data on Oliver so they could determine the best teaching strategies and placements for him. Every day, Rebecca would have to document whether Oliver had done his work promptly, stalled out, or needed Rebecca's one-on-one support to pull him back from distraction. "He's practically twins with a boy on the spectrum I taught a few years ago. And I'll bet that every Eastern teacher except Fiona knows it," Rebecca told me. "Yvonne knows it, but she's too conflict averse to tell parents, 'I think your child may be on the ASD.' So guess who's probably going to have to do it after a month of documenting his behaviors and having another meeting with them? Aarrgghh."

Rebecca felt like she was winging it without a special ed background, but she tried her best to connect with Oliver. She focused on getting to know him more fully and emphasizing his strengths. When kids didn't want to play with him at recess after he'd thrown a fit because he wasn't first in the lunch line, Rebecca spent recess with him, swapping wordplay jokes. When he didn't react to the drippings swaying from his nose, Rebecca quietly handed him a tissue and five minutes later asked him to share with the class his impressive self-made strategy for adding fractions so as to divert his peers' attention from his personal hygiene to his smarts.

Rebecca tried to remind herself that she couldn't "take on everything for everyone at school, that depending on the day, depending on the time, there are some things I can't control." But she continuously monitored her students' socio-emotional states. One afternoon, Illyse, who'd written the powerful essay about her divorced parents, told Rebecca she was worried about her friend Rory. At recess, she said, Rory was crying and talking about cutting herself.

When Rebecca saw Rory for ELA, Rory seemed happy and playful. After school, Rebecca talked to the guidance counselor and assistant principal. The administrators explained that Illyse and Rory could be melodramatic attention-seekers and that they shouldn't worry. Rebecca took them at their word.

To introduce a social studies lesson the week before Thanksgiving, Rebecca did her rewind schtick: "Okay, guys, we're going back in time!" she said. From their desks, the kids windmilled their arms along with her in a "rewind" movement. "Woop woop woop! Brllp brllp brllp!" they chirruped together.

Rebecca casually sauntered over to a cluster of desks. She smiled at the students, sat on the edge of a desk, and moved the kids' materials out of the way. To the students' surprise, Rebecca sprawled her body across the desks. She picked up a pencil box. "Nice pencil box!" she said and put it in her pocket. "Heeyy, that's a really cool eraser!"— she took it—"Thaannkks." She flopped over like a beached whale, spreading across the desks and gathering as many items as she could. The students at the other end of the cluster started frantically clutching their things.

Rebecca explained that she represented the Europeans invading indigenous people's land in America.

A boy made a fence with half a dozen pencils. Rebecca reached over and plucked one. "There's a wall in your way, there's a wall in your way! You can't get by that!" he protested.

"Wanna bet?" Rebecca countered, swiping all the pencils.

She knew from teaching this lesson in the past that for the rest of the year, anytime she mentioned a European invasion and approached their desks, students would hurriedly guard their stuff.

Perhaps Rebecca should have been doing the same. When a dog-shaped eraser disappeared from her supply closet, she began to suspect that the items that had gone missing from her desk disappeared not because she'd misplaced them but because a student had a case of sticky fingers. But which student?

Miguel Garcia   Middle School Special Ed Teacher

During science, Dewayne sidled uneasily into Miguel's classroom to retrieve something. "How are you doing in class today?" Miguel asked.

Dewayne's behavior had significantly improved over the last few weeks. He seemed able to focus in ways that he had not before, perhaps, Miguel guessed, because he'd finally started taking ADHD medication sometime back in October. When Miguel sat with him one-on-one, Dewayne understood concepts, had good handwriting, read well, and retained facts. His gen ed teachers still complained about his lack of focus, but in Miguel's class, he was solid.

The long-term substitute science teacher, installed at the last minute at the start of the year, was generally a patient man whom students liked. Initially he'd complained often to Miguel about Dewayne. "He has an IEP. He's gotta go to you," Miguel had reminded him. Dewayne's IEP specified that he attend gen ed history, science, and elective classes.

"This kid, he can't stay in his chair."

"Yeah, that's part of his disability. It's part of his IEP. Here are some strategies," Miguel offered.

The sub hadn't complained recently. Today, however, he was absent—the long-term sub had a short-term sub.

"Are you okay?" Miguel asked Dewayne.

He looked uncomfortable. "The new sub said somethin'."

Miguel peered into Dewayne's eyes. "What did he say?"

"He said a bad word."

"What word? It's okay to tell me."

"I don't wanna get in trouble."

"You won't get in trouble for this, I promise you."

"He called us stupid assholes."

Miguel tensed. "That's not okay."

"Yeah."

"No, really, Dewayne, that's not okay because that's not the way a teacher's supposed to act," Miguel said. "What he did was wrong and I'm going to make sure he doesn't do it again. Thanks for telling me. You can stay here for the rest of the period. It's going to be okay."

Miguel called Frank, who relayed that the substitute denied Dewayne's claims. "Dewayne," Miguel asked, "did anyone else hear what the sub said?"

Dewayne lifted his chin. "I can give you names."

With Miguel shepherding the process, Dewayne and other students reported the sub's behavior to Western administrators. Frank removed the sub from school.

A student in Miguel's new video elective was so spoiled and negative that Miguel and the counselor privately called her Veruca Salt, after the Willy Wonka character. One day, as Miguel assigned new student groups, Veruca objected loudly. "I don't like this group," she huffed. "I don't like this class!"

"Well, you have to be in this group until the next project," Miguel said, continuing to move students around.

"You know what?" Veruca erupted. "I fucking hate you."

Miguel calmly gestured her to the doorway, out of earshot of the other students. "First, don't ever swear in my class. Second, I don't care if you hate me. I have enough friends. I don't need more."

"Well, I hate your class."

"That's fine. Please go talk to the counselor."

Veruca strode down the hall.

The counselor told Miguel later that she instructed Veruca to stay in the class because it was good for her. Miguel was unbothered; he knew he could teach any student.

Students didn't usually curse at Miguel. As a teacher, he encountered more disrespect from adults than students. Even some acquaintances unintentionally conveyed disdain for his career choice. "It is so disheartening to have been asked by people on many occasions, 'Why are you a teacher? You should have gone to law school or business school,'" he told me. "Basically, people think my career choice is some sort of waste, especially when they realize I teach disabled kids. It's insulting. It also proves how little regard the general public has for teachers. There is no respect for the teaching profession."

Parents' Visiting Night was the following week. After Miguel gave his video class presentation, Veruca's parents introduced themselves. Veruca was mostly hiding behind them. "How's she doing?" Veruca's mother asked.

"She's creative and has a lot of potential. She's got a very strong attitude about certain things. We're working through it," Miguel said.

"This is great. You're learning a lot of good stuff," Veruca's father said to her.

"Are you having any trouble with her?" Veruca's mother asked.

"Nothing out of the ordinary for this age-group," Miguel lied. He made eye contact with Veruca. "She's a pleasure to have in class. I look forward to continuing to work with her. I think we're going to have a good year."

Veruca did not erupt in class again.

⁓

Miguel's special ed class was just getting into a rhythm when an administrator informed him he would have a new student "starting tomorrow." Miguel barely had time to prepare. Hakeem, who had depression and other disabilities, was transferring because he was being bullied at his charter school, where his gen ed classmates laughed at him whenever he participated. The work required for an extra student was not insignificant considering Miguel's already saturated caseload and his ongoing battle to keep the district from taking over Western. But he had spent so many weeks working hard to create an inclusive class culture that he thought his kids could handle one more student.

When Miguel showed Hakeem to his seat, he said in front of the class, "If anyone gives you a hard time, please let me know, because that's not allowed here." He was glad to see his kids included Hakeem without issue. *Okay, we have someone else in our family*, he thought. *Now we just have to work on his academics.*

The next day, the counselor came to Miguel's second period with a girl in tow. She ushered the girl to a seat, then spoke quietly to Miguel. "You have this kid now," she said.

"I do?" Miguel had heard nothing about this development.

"Her name is Trinity. The district sent her here with no information."

"Do we know what her needs are?"

"We have no information except that she mainstreams science and history."

More work, more prep, more differentiation. Now Miguel had two more students, six full classes with no prep period, and a wider range of students whom he couldn't teach in small groups because he had no assistant. He would have to conduct hours of extra testing because Trinity had come from another state. "Western has a reputation for being a bleeding heart. We want to help the kids. So they keep sending us difficult cases," Miguel said later. "You get penalized for showing even a little bit of compassion. That's why we have such a large special ed population."

On her first day, Trinity presented as neurotypical. Her reading and spelling were far above average. Miguel wondered why she was in special ed. Perhaps, he thought, she had only a learning disability. When he took her aside to chat, she said she was doing okay. Miguel asked Dewayne to make sure she got to history in the morning and science in the afternoon.

After school, Miguel saw the counselor running down the hall. He'd never seen her shaken before.

"What's going on?" he asked.

"Oh my god, we have to call the police," she said.

"What happened?"

The counselor explained that no one could find Trinity. When her parents came to pick her up, they told the office staff, "She's not here."

The district had neglected to inform Western that Trinity was autistic and had many other hidden challenges. Without her file, teachers and administrators didn't know that she couldn't be left alone after school. Her parents explained that Trinity's IEP, which wasn't sent to Western, repeatedly mentioned that she should be placed at another, specific school. But the district had inexplicably assigned her to Western instead.

Now there was no sign of Trinity. She didn't pick up her phone. Next to Western was an unsafe area frequented by drug addicts. Miguel was wracked with guilt. *Should I have picked her up from her last class?* he wondered. The counselor called 911.

"To Teach Your Kids, I Have to Leave Mine": COVID-19, the Disrespect for Teachers' Work, and the Disregard for Their Lives

First, in the 2000s, school districts piled so much extra work on teachers that they had to spend evenings, weekends, and lunch periods working overtime for free: Not only were they teachers, then, but they were also unpaid tutors and parent liaisons. When school systems didn't provide teachers with the budget to properly stock their classrooms, teachers spent hundreds of their own dollars annually on books, learning tools, classroom decor, educational software, math manipulatives, school supplies, and snacks for students who forgot or couldn't afford their own. Now they were teachers and also unpaid tutors, parent liaisons, book buyers, charity workers, and benefactors. Even cash-strapped teachers took on these roles—because they loved their students, and if they didn't do it, no one would.

Next came a rise in social-emotional learning: Teachers were expected to fit in instruction for students on how to be considerate, resilient people because these lessons weren't necessarily sinking in at home. Additionally, an increase in mandated compliance trainings obliged educators to learn how to monitor for and report child neglect and abuse. Now teachers were also unpaid tutors, parent liaisons, book buyers, charity workers, benefactors, therapists, social workers, and crisis managers. Teachers shouldered all of these time-consuming requirements, despite low wages and unjust disrespect for the profession, because they loved their students, and if they didn't do it, no one would.

The 2010s' sharp surge in school shootings increased the frequency of lockdown drills. Some districts insisted on arming their teachers, adding security enforcement to their list of duties. School systems trained teachers to put their body between a shooter and their students, expecting educators to take a bullet as part of the job. Now teachers were also unpaid tutors, parent liaisons, book buyers, charity workers, benefactors, therapists, social workers, crisis managers, security staff, and human shields. With heavy hearts, teachers accepted this horrific reality, too, because they loved their students, and if they didn't do it, no one would.

But in 2020 their districts told them to risk their loved ones' lives. And that was a step too far.

⟝⟞

Disrespect for teachers has been a longtime problem from certain parents, district office personnel, school boards, government officials, and superintendents. But nowhere was the clash between society's mounting expansion of teachers' roles and its callous disregard for their well-being more evident than during the COVID-19 pandemic.

When schools initially shifted to virtual learning in the spring of 2020 and parents at home caught the slightest glimmer of educators' hardships, they gushed and memed about their newfound appreciation for teachers, who, they quipped, were saints who deserved enormous raises and fancy cars. But by summer, antsy parents clamored for in-person instruction, teachers' health be damned, and many decision-makers re-envisioned schools and ordered buildings opened without consulting teachers or considering the dangers to educators and their families.

Politicians followed suit. President Trump announced he would "pressure" governors and threatened to withhold funding from schools that didn't reopen in person even as virus cases spiked. Secretary of Education Betsy DeVos, who had never been an educator herself, demanded that schools must open "fully operational," inadvertently referencing a fitting Sith-like indifference to people's lives. The Trump administration and congressional Republicans refused to provide schools with the resources needed to get buildings up to baseline safety levels, with then Senate majority leader Mitch McConnell calling a House-approved relief bill including money for K–12 schools "dead on arrival."

In-person schooling in 2020 forced educators into cramped, poorly ventilated buildings and/or classrooms lacking openable windows to supervise crowds of children, whose ability to follow health and distancing guidelines was questionable and whose hygiene habits were often deficient even before the threat of a contagious deadly virus. Some districts tried to paint rosy pictures in mass communications proclaiming, "We're all in this together," but in practice they excluded school staff from their definition of "all." Rather than enforce a mask-or-leave student rule, teachers in many districts were told not to discipline students who refused to wear a mask, but to consider noncompliance a "teachable moment." Days before a Maryland county began hybrid instruction, its school nurses didn't have properly fitting masks, building service workers received no guidance in the event of a positive infection, and some schools' "new" PPE was several months expired. In addition, Maryland governor Larry Hogan announced that school boards should listen to parents and "stakeholders" regarding in-person schools rather than teachers unions, whom he referred to as just one "personal interest group."

Because closed indoor spaces fell into the highest-risk category for COVID transmission, state and local correctional departments released thousands of inmates from prisons and jails to protect them. By contrast, some school boards voted to force educators to teach in person even as their own board meetings were conducted online for their safety. While employees in some other sectors continued to work in person, they had more safeguards than teachers: Doctors and grocery store workers, for example, could attend to one patient or patron at a time, and managers of those and other workplaces could remove people who refused to abide by COVID protocols.

Not so teachers, many of whom understandably balked at endangering themselves or their loved ones by spending hours each day without proper protection, squarely in the kind of high-risk environment that, at the time, the country's top scientists warned people to avoid. As the 2020–21 school year loomed, the Kaiser Family Foundation reported that one in four teachers, which it estimated to be 1.47 million educators, had preexisting conditions that increased their risk of serious illness from COVID. This calculation did not include high-risk loved ones or the potential for fatal and/or seriously debilitating long-term effects on otherwise healthy people. Teachers told the media they were afraid for their lives. Even young educators said they were preparing their wills.

Many districts told medically high-risk teachers to report to their classrooms anyway. In July 2020 the president of the Delaware School Boards Association emailed fellow school board members: "The standard was bend the curve, not prevent any death . . . teachers are first responders to our future, if they cannot handle the risk, seek a new career." His cavalier attitude toward potential teacher fatalities was distressingly common.

As school systems in many areas of the country chose to begin the year safely online, sentiment toward teachers nose-dived among certain vehemently one-track-minded parents who heaped vitriol on educators on social media. Some news media outlets didn't necessarily appear unbiased, either. A *Washington Post* headline read, "Teachers in Fairfax Revolt Against Fall Plans, Refusing to Teach In-Person," using language painting teachers as against the greater good. Just five days later, a *Post* headline characterized professional athletes' in-person refusals differently: "For Athletes, Decision to Opt Out Is Fraught with Health Concerns and Pull of Social Activism." The newspaper positively portrayed athletes, including MLB and NBA players—who could afford to take off work, were paid millions of dollars, and got free virus testing—as concerned and contemplative, while teachers with the same rationale, paid mid–five figures to work in schools with no provided PPE or testing, and forced to choose between risking their and their loved ones' lives or leaving a job many of them couldn't afford to lose, were in "revolt."

Teachers would have strongly preferred to instruct their students in person, had classrooms been confirmed safe. Virtual teaching took much more time to prepare, execute, and evaluate. A Michigan English teacher who had 207 AP Literature and AP Language students worked from 6 a.m. to 11 p.m. every day, including weekends, when she taught remotely. "It was brutal," she said. "There weren't hours in the day to move all my materials to an online format, teach my Google Meet class sessions, respond to students via email and Remind, and grade all their essays as I prepped my students for their AP exams." Many districts adopted hybrid or "concurrent" teaching methods, euphemisms for the cockamamie idea that teachers should instruct two classes, online and in person, at the same time, a process that teachers said was exhausting, disheartening, and difficult to conduct equitably.

In-person learning is a far better mode of instruction for most students, too, in terms of academic progress, social-emotional development, and physical activity. Remote schooling is particularly difficult for students without reliable internet access, many children with special needs, and parents who depend on schools to supervise their kids while they work. In-person school also provides ready access to free and reduced-price meals, mental health services, and other social supports. Furthermore, during face-to-face instruction, staff can more easily watch for signs of child abuse or neglect to report to authorities when they believe children's safety is at risk.

But "safety" is the operative word. Many school districts required educators to teach in person, though they weren't providing adequate respiratory protections or testing services, vaccinations weren't yet available, and school ventilation systems hadn't been upgraded. Teachers were "absolutely right" to be wary of in-person instruction "because this was an infectious disease that was killing people. I know a number of teachers who died," epidemiologist Michael Osterholm told me in 2022. Osterholm, director of the Center for Infectious Disease Research and Policy at the University of Minnesota, was a member of President Joe Biden's COVID-19 Advisory Board during the presidential transition. "No school has really gotten through unscathed. We have to have a tremendous amount of humility about this virus. None of us really knows for certain how to most effectively handle schools. We have so much to learn about learning that we haven't learned yet." Teachers, as experts in learning, understood that there were inevitable knowledge gaps about the new virus—and that districts were obligating them to be the guinea pigs.

As the United States repeatedly set new records in the 2020–21 school year with more than 200,000 daily COVID cases, some parents' calls for remote learning schools to "reopen" (they were not closed) and teachers to "get back to work" (they never stopped) remained thunderous, even as in-person school outbreaks and staff deaths surged. Countless teachers lost loved ones, such as an Alabama teacher who said her mother died after she contracted the virus at school, where at lunch, students were "sitting on top of each other without their masks." Her county had not supplied school staff with adequate PPE, or the training on protective measures it had promised.

Meanwhile, some decision-makers enacted policies that increased educators' exposure to the virus. Trump's designation of teachers as "critical infrastructure workers" allowed districts to keep virus-exposed teachers in schools, ignoring public health agencies' 14-day quarantine requirement. Tennessee and Georgia school districts quickly adopted the quarantine exemption despite the heightened risk that contagious teachers could spread the virus among students and staff.

Penny's district did the same. When Penny was notified that Birdie had COVID, Southern required her and the other exposed educators to continue teaching in person unless or until they tested positive, at a time when test results took a week or more. She told me then, "It's awful here, our cases are rising, teachers are sick, and [the district] says just deal with it. I am in tears with *no* PPE and students are not required to wear masks. They actually tell kids that when they sit down, they don't have to wear a mask." Southern parents like Kitty lobbied to keep schools in person because, as Kitty announced, "I need my me time." By the end of what would have been a 14-day quarantine period, two additional Southern teachers contracted the virus—and this was in 2020, pre-vaccine. Eventually, a district staff member died of COVID, and nearly 40% of Southern teachers were infected, including a teacher who was hospitalized and passed the virus to his wife, who sustained permanent severe health damage. During that time, Penny's sons contracted COVID and a close relative died from it. (When the Omicron variant surfaced a year later, a much higher percentage of staff tested positive.)

Nationwide, less than three months into the 2020–21 school year, nearly 22% of educators surveyed by Horace Mann Educators Corporation reported that they or a close family member tested positive for COVID. At least 6.5% required hospitalization, a significantly higher rate than the general population's 0.2% hospitalization rate. During a 10-day stretch in September 2021, 15 Florida teachers died of the virus. By 2022, one in five educators said they had long COVID, according to an *Education Week* survey.

The pandemic mistreatment drove teachers—genuinely wonderful, effective teachers—out of the workforce. "Teachers are working themselves to the bone, often at the expense of ourselves and our families. Social media posts about teachers from people who have no idea what they're talking about have taken a toll on every educator I know. When I see posts from parents in our school, it's that much more crushing," a Maryland elementary school special ed teacher told me. "I have been teaching for almost thirty years. I wanted to be a teacher from the time I was six years old. As a very strong student growing up, my parents fostered going into education and celebrated it as a noble profession. I've gone above and beyond my entire career. I've won awards, mentored many teachers, and continue to have a strong reputation in the county and school community. This being said, it breaks my heart to say that I can't wait to get out. These last two years have broken me and many of my colleagues."

By the fall of 2021, schools across the country had lost a staggering number of teachers, paraeducators, substitutes, bus drivers, and other staff who quit, retired early, got sick, or died because of the pandemic. In September 2021, 30,000 public school teachers gave notice. Florida had 67% more teacher vacancies than the previous year. California's largest school district had five times the number of teacher vacancies as in prior years; Fort Worth, Texas, was close behind with four and a half times the number of vacancies. A small Michigan district lost a quarter of its teaching staff, while statewide there was a 44% increase in midyear teacher retirements. Lacking enough staff to operate, some schools across the country temporarily closed; hired students to serve lunch during school hours; grouped classes together in the cafeteria, where building services workers or untrained parent volunteers supervised hundreds of students; and/or asked the National Guard to fill in as bus drivers and substitute teachers.

Notably, the United States could have enacted mitigating policies in summer 2020, as other countries did, so that more school buildings could open that fall. But instead of slowing COVID transmission by hunkering down for the summer, the Trump White House encouraged Americans to be out and about. This was a societal failure: The country did not prioritize schools. When cases jumped in the run-up to back-to-school season, the government demanded that educators bear the weight of its dereliction. As usual, society leaned hard on teachers to clean up its mess. "We cannot be everything to everyone," said a West Virginia middle school teacher. "Society wants us to cure their ills but treats us like crap."

～∽～

Disrespect for teachers has entrenched historical roots. "The disregard of teachers' shared professional expertise and practical knowledge is no accident. It reflects the way that, instead of treating teachers like other American professionals, society has long blamed them for the failings of schools and worked to constrain them through bureaucracy and regulations," wrote education reform historian Diana D'Amico Pawlewicz in *The Washington Post*. In the 1800s, "informed by deep-seated gendered stereotypes of women as nurturing, submissive and intellectually inferior to men, education leaders and policymakers ignored the problems that plagued schools—organizational chaos, a lack of funding, adequate school sites and curricular materials and rising social inequality. Instead, they blamed teachers for the schools' shortcomings. According to one early critic, the legions of women standing at the front of public school classrooms were the 'anchor . . . that drags on the bottom,' impeding the promise of education."

A teacher wrote in a 1946 op-ed that she quit teaching because "the teacher is considered community property. Everyone has a right to speak sharply to her, criticize her and tell her wherein she is not doing her job right." A 1957 article in education journal *The Clearing House* claimed, "Unfortunately, not a few teachers look upon themselves as despised underlings who labor 'unwept, unhonored, and unsung.' They exhibit a martyr complex that could conceivably engender in students an aversion to teaching." Even the journal's editor weighed in; an editor's note remarked, "Counterparts of melodrama characters occasionally land on high-school faculties and, as you would expect, they ask to be pitied in true martyr fashion."

Globally, a 2014 study that spanned 34 countries reported that fewer than a third of teachers believed society valued their work. In the U.S. the same year, a Gallup poll found that teachers ranked last among surveyed professional groups in believing that their opinions at work were heard. A 2015 survey found that 55% of education employees identified the "negative portrayal of teachers and school employees in the media" as a major source of stress. In 2018, a successful series of "Red for Ed" and grassroots teacher protests and walkouts, accompanied by major media coverage of teachers' insufficient pay, briefly swayed public sympathy toward educators. Parents largely supported the teacher strikes, which aimed to increase school funding and resources.

But the support waned by late 2020, thanks in part to a hostile White House administration that portrayed teachers as the enemy. "When I started teaching in the late 1990s, teachers were not seen as idiots who couldn't be trusted. We weren't viewed as evil and lazy like we are now," a midwestern special ed teacher told me then. "It's exhausting to face what I face every day and then have my profession mocked."

Yet, despite the continuing contempt and escalating hardships, despite more responsibilities divided among rapidly thinning ranks, despite the risks to their and their families' lives and long-term health—even during the COVID pandemic, most teachers showed up: because they loved their students, and if they didn't do it, no one would.

In March 2020, a California 3rd grade teacher reported to work in a school district that kept buildings open even as neighboring districts had closed and nearby cities had ordered citizens to shelter in place. The teacher, who took medication for high blood pressure, was so stressed that a vessel in her eye burst. When I asked her the following day during her lunch period why she came in, she began to cry. "I come in anyway because they're my kids. I'm not going to leave my kids. This is a safe place for them and I don't want to take that away."

An Idaho high school English teacher also worked in person despite having a chronic health condition and weak immune system. District officials said they wanted buildings open so that health-care personnel and other parents could work, she told me at the time, "but teachers aren't babysitters and schools aren't daycares. Every teacher I know would do everything in their power for their students. But I feel like we're expected to make these sacrifices, constantly guilted into situations 'for the kids.' When is it enough? When are we allowed to care for ourselves and our families? To teach your kids, I have to leave mine. He has asthma, so this situation is scary. But putting my family first is almost treated like selfishness and doesn't fulfill the picture of the martyr teacher."

This crucial point renders the disrespect of teachers especially galling. The public has forgotten that educators take on extraordinary risks and sacrifices, unpaid work and undue stress, and put their lives on the line—all for other people's children. Illinois English teacher and author Jason Fisk publicly posted the following (abridged here) on social media in October 2020:

This is the second time in my professional career where my personal health and welfare has been taken out of my hands, out of my control, and an actual value had been placed on my life and worth by others, by the community I serve.

I distinctly remember feeling the same thing when we were doing a live-shooter drill at school, and police officers were shooting Nerf guns at a gym full of teachers. We then went to our classrooms and had to decide between running to safety or barricading our classrooms while the police officers marched through the hallways, again with Nerf guns, shooting at everyone. I remember standing in my classroom, thinking: If this were a real-life scenario, I would have to decide between staying alive for my family or saving the 25 students who have been placed in my care. I decided that I would have to save the 25 kids in my care. It was a crushing and overwhelming thought.

And now I'm back to that feeling of dread. I'm reading community message boards filled with vitriol, watching video clips where I hear people saying things like, "We should put LoJack anklets on teachers, so they don't leave their houses during school hours," and reading articles about the battles between school boards and teacher unions. . . . The next time you feel like attacking teachers, please envision me standing in the middle of my classroom during a live-shooter drill, having to decide between my family and your child, and remember that I chose your child.

Penny Davis   6th Grade Math Teacher

Late afternoon on a day Penny had stayed home from school with a lingering bad cough, Kent texted her, "Why weren't you at school today?" Penny didn't respond. The boys were with Kent and didn't know she wasn't at work. *Who is feeding him information?* she wondered. She had a hard time sleeping that night.

Before class the next morning, Zach came to Penny looking

sheepish, a departure from his usual poker face. Since Penny's "clean slate talk," Zach had communicated better with her. Instead of quick nods or curt notes, he was more facially expressive and wordier on paper. His math skills, Penny noticed, improved.

"Good morning, Zach," Penny said.

Zach shyly held out a gift bag.

"Oh! Is this for me?" Penny asked.

Zach nodded.

Inside the bag were treats and trinkets Zach had picked out for her: chocolates, Post-it notes, a picture frame, a mug. A Post-it read, "Your class is fun. Thank you for making me feel included."

"This means so much to me, Zach," Penny said, hugging him.

Zach smiled at her and went to his seat.

After school, Penny roamed the hallways as she always did, collecting all the discarded pencils from the floor. James, one of the custodians, emerged from a classroom.

"What are you doing?" James asked.

"You're going to throw these away, right?" Penny asked.

"Yes."

"I have kids who don't have school supplies, so I keep them and hand a child a pencil when they need it."

From then on, every day after school, James left a large bag of pencils in Penny's classroom. "I wish people understood that it's not just the teachers or principal who influence students' lives," she told me.

At nine o'clock one night, Ed called Penny. "Hi, what are you up to?" he asked.

"Not much, just grading while the boys do homework. What's up?"

"I've got a problem," he said.

This is interesting. "What's the problem?"

"Well, Claudia and I went out to dinner, and she locked the keys in the car," he said.

"Oh, everyone's done that before," Penny reassured him.

"Well, it gets worse," he said. "The car's still running."

Penny laughed. "Okay, where are y'all?"

Thirty minutes later, Penny was driving Ed home through some backcountry roads, making fun of him while their kids goofed around in the back seat (Penny's boys did not pass up the chance to hang out with a senior cheerleader). A balmy autumn breeze wafted through the open windows. Penny looked over at Ed, who was laughing at one of her jokes. The moonlight was hitting him just right and his dimples were awfully cute. *Boy, he's a really good person, nice, fun, funny, and pretty much raised his kids by himself and did a great job*, she thought. *He does everything for his kids like I do everything for mine.* When he smiled at her   she must've been doing her awkward toothy grin again, she thought—it hit her that she was attracted to a man for the first time since high school. *It's too bad we work together. Southern girls shouldn't date where they work.*

In the middle of last period, one of Penny's students asked to go to the bathroom. At dismissal, she whispered to Penny that she'd seen several 6th and 7th graders, including one from Penny's class, meet up in the bathroom to vape.

"Love you!" Penny called to her class as they filed out. She asked the girl some questions and typed up a discipline report to give the principal. In the hall on her way to the office, Penny overheard one of those students say to the others, "We need to have our stories straight about the vaping."

When Penny shared the report, the principal said, "I can't do anything about it unless a teacher actually saw them."

Penny was surprised. That hadn't prevented past principals from disciplining students doing dangerous things. "I heard them say they needed to have their 'stories straight' about vaping," Penny said. "Couldn't you tell them they were seen?"

"If the kids admit to it, I can do something, but let's face it: They're not going to," the principal said.

Penny recognized the real issue. The principal had already sent more than the average number of students to the alternative school for students at risk of long-term suspension or expulsion. She was avoiding sending more students because she didn't "want her reputation to be ruined her first year here. It's all about the smoke and mirrors," Penny told me.

Disciplinary issues were on the rise because the principal didn't hold people accountable for them. In prior years, staff had weekly leadership and monthly behavior meetings, but this year there were no monthlies. The administrators didn't attend the weekly meetings or encourage teachers to schedule them. "The principal only cares about whether her school looks good," Penny told me, not unlike the principal's response when Penny again complained about the mold in her classroom: The principal had it painted over. "It's all about perception. She is covering up so much this year."

Penny later learned the principal had also doctored teachers' discipline reports. Students were caught drinking and chewing tobacco and a teacher saw a student sexually grab a classmate, infractions that were supposed to merit mandatory 10-day suspension, a disciplinary hearing with the school board, and, often, a transfer to the alternative school. But the principal said these offenses didn't "need to be punished at the office level." The students returned to their classes as if nothing had happened.

As these incidents increased, staff morale dropped. As morale dropped, some teachers became frostier. Frequently when Penny walked past colleagues in her hall, they stopped talking and furtively eyed Penny as if they'd been talking about her. Nel, the administrative secretary, did the same in the office.

Birdie came in early one morning looking troubled. "Penny, I don't know what to do about something."

Penny gave Birdie her full attention. "What's up?"

"Blair keeps making derogatory comments about special ed kids. I've never heard anything like it before and I've been teaching special ed a long time. She calls them lazy instead of recognizing their disabilities."

Birdie relayed how Blair screamed at special ed students: "If you can't keep up, you need to be in a separate class by yourself!" Birdie was horrified that Blair was yelling at the kids as if they were misbehaving, when they were only working more slowly than their classmates. Also, Blair refused to provide accommodations for special ed students. When they couldn't work at her pace, she gave them detention during PE, art, or music, classes that were often their refuge from the rigors of Southern academics.

"Oh no, these kids have weak self-esteem already," Penny said. "They feel they can't learn like everyone else and this is just reinforcing the idea in their head that they can't do it."

"Do I need to talk to the principal?" Birdie asked.

Yes, Penny said. Blair wasn't adhering to the children's IEPs. "She's breaking the law."

Penny invented a math game she played each year with her classes that she called Empire Versus Rebellion. The class was divided into four teams, each represented by a Star Wars character on the Promethean board. Students clicked on a card to reveal a problem to solve. If they answered correctly, their team earned 10 points and they could choose whether to click a Darth Vader card. The Vader card randomly doubled or tripled their points, gave two of their points to another team, or asked students to choose another team to give some of their points to. (Another clickable button emitted a Chewbacca yowl.)

The game was a perennial class favorite. One day in late November, Penny had her classes play it for a test review. When it was Zach's team's turn, Penny asked Zach if he wanted to come up to the board. He'd always declined before.

This time, Zach nodded uncertainly. *Yes.* His team was behind. If he got the problem wrong, it would be difficult to catch up. As he hesitantly approached the board, his team cheered: "You got this, Zach!" "You can do it!" Penny had faith. Zach was now earning As on homework and tests. He clicked his team's card, tackled the problem quickly and efficiently, and clicked submit.

Zach nailed it. The game made a celebratory *beep-boop* and Zach's team cheered. They inched closer to first place.

"Zach, do you choose to risk the Vader card?" Penny asked.

Zach grinned and clicked on Vader. "Impressive," Promethean Vader said. The card flipped: "Double points." Zach's team erupted; they had taken the lead. Zach looked up at Penny, his eyes shining, his smile proud.

Penny went home on a high. "Home" was now an apartment outside the school district that was a fraction of the size of her former house. But it was all hers, it was tension-free, and "there's nobody to yell at me anymore."

She was just settling into bed when her phone dinged with a new email from the school counselor. Darren's mom, the sunshine nurse bearing extra school supplies at Open House, had passed away unexpectedly from a brain aneurysm. Penny was heartsick. Just as their students' joys caused teachers joy, students' tragedies were also teachers' to bear. It was nearly impossible for teachers to truly compartmentalize the workday because their connections to their students ran so deep.

Miguel Garcia   Middle School Special Ed Teacher

The counselor called Miguel from Frank's car as they searched the neighborhood for Trinity.

Should it have been any surprise that Trinity slipped through the cracks? The district had "a total lack of respect and consideration for teachers, principals, and special ed students," Miguel told me. "Administrators are supposed to do observations, but they don't. You're in crisis mode because a new kid just blew up the class dynamics. The district's always creating these situations that shouldn't happen and our school becomes the place that fixes them. Then if we don't hit one of their many goals, the district complains we're not doing our job. They drop the ball, like assigning a student to a school that's not on her IEP, and we're supposed to look the other way. I'm stretched nearly to my breaking point."

The district's lack of consideration for its educators was the number one reason Miguel expected to leave teaching at the end of the year. It wasn't just the obvious things that grated on him—destroying a school, eliminating special ed, endangering a student. "This isn't a healthy work environment anymore, so it's time for me to go. I don't have time to work out at the gym. I'm eating on the go. The only way to do the job right is to have no other life. Who can do that?" Miguel said. "Districts keep on loading more and more. So everyone feels like they're behind, no one's caught up, and people have to take shortcuts, which makes them feel less professional."

One of Miguel's former student teachers, whom he had continued to mentor informally, had just told him she was leaving the district because teachers weren't getting any support. Miguel knew too many struggling educators who were scared to speak up against a system rigged against them. One teacher friend lived in a small two-bedroom apartment with her retired father, ailing mother, college freshman daughter, and elderly grandmother, who slept on a hospital bed in the living room. She couldn't afford to lose her job because she supported her entire family. Miguel knew several teachers who were similarly stuck, unhappy with how they were treated but unable to leave the district because they needed their pension and lifetime medical coverage.

The counselor filled Miguel in: After more than an hour, the police had found Trinity wandering three miles away.

"Oh my god," Miguel said. "Is there something I should have done?"

"No! None of us knew she needed extra support. The district didn't give us her file. They weren't even supposed to send her to Western!"

"Some random dude could have picked her up somewhere!" Miguel fumed.

The next morning, Miguel asked Dewayne to escort Trinity back to him after science. Daily, Miguel would walk her to the office, where staff could watch her until her parents arrived.

Eli now came to school on time more often than not, but he was conspicuously absent on Fridays, which at first surprised Miguel because Eli liked the doughnut store. Miguel got the feeling Eli wanted to be at school and that when he wasn't punctual, he'd been thwarted by the logistics of his homelessness.

When Eli was present, he was engaged. He had even started writing legibly by hand more often, which Miguel considered a big win; he'd progressed from one-word answers in August to full phrases in

November. Because Eli was verbally eloquent, Miguel wondered if perhaps he had a processing disorder that impeded his writing.

When Eli was absent the day of the Book Fair, which he'd been looking forward to, Miguel realized he was purposely missing Fridays to avoid the weekly spelling quizzes. At the fair preview, Eli had been drawn to a journal with a lock. Miguel bought the journal, thinking it would motivate Eli to practice writing.

When Eli returned to school on Monday, he discovered the journal in his cubby. "Oh wow, I got the book I wanted!" he exclaimed in a rare show of excitement.

Miguel knew Eli wouldn't want him to make a big deal out of it. "Oh, look at that," Miguel said lightly. "See what happens when people do a good job? You must have gotten it because you deserve it." Miguel saw Eli grin as he stowed the journal in his backpack.

CHAPTER 5

December

A holiday present a Maryland 1st grader gave his teacher: a card reading "Have an extra Merry Christmas!"—accompanying a sexy red negligee and matching thong.

Mother of a 16-year-old to a New Jersey high school librarian who called her from the hotel while chaperoning an overnight field trip: "My daughter is not drunk! I know what my daughter sounds like when she's drunk! She is not drunk!"

Mother at a meeting with administrators and a Maryland AP Art teacher regarding the teacher's approved AP College Board syllabus: "I am here today to inform you that my daughter will not be working from your syllabus. I have prepared another syllabus with anticipated works and anticipated dates that my daughter will create for your AP Art class."

Miguel Garcia   Middle School Special Ed Teacher

In December, Dewayne's behavior began to slide. He was less able to concentrate on his work and frustrated because he wasn't earning the reward points he had in the past. His gen ed teachers had ramped up their complaints about him. The science teacher said he frequently swore in class.

In Miguel's class, too, Dewayne acted up, but Miguel could handle him. When he tried to give Miguel attitude, Miguel shut it down: "Stop it. We don't do this mess in my class. Do what I asked you to do." Dewayne listened.

Miguel suspected that Dewayne had stopped taking his medication; he could practically pinpoint the day when Dewayne lost his ability to focus. Miguel knew that some parents felt guilty medicating their kids. Or perhaps Dewayne's behavior had improved so much that his mother thought he didn't need medication anymore. "The sad thing is, I don't even think he needs special ed services if he's medicated. I'm not a big fan of medication. I think it's overused. But for some kids it's necessary," Miguel told me. "Dewayne was doing his assignments last month, but now he's off the rails again."

He was increasingly worried that Dewayne's tipping point loomed. "We're in this window now. There are a couple gen ed kids he's been hanging out with who are bad news. He's a sweet, happy go-lucky kid. I could see him getting in trouble because he's just following along."

Later that week, Miguel showed his first period video class a silent movie from the 1920s and asked them to choose a partner to create a documentary in the same style. To his surprise, Quiesha walked straight over to Jon, the ostracized 6th grader, and asked him to work with her.

For the next several classes, Quiesha and Jon worked quietly. They were an unlikely pair: a stoic, tough 8th grade cool girl and a socially challenged 6th grade boy. The other students called Miguel over every five minutes—"Come look at this!" "Mr. Garcia, you have to see this!"—but Quiesha and Jon never summoned him.

On the project due date, Quiesha was absent from school. Miguel went to their computer station, where Jon was sitting, to check on their progress. Not only were they finished, but their film was exemplary. Jon's editing was precise and the pacing, use of music and effects, and particularly Quiesha's camerawork were striking compared to the other students' projects.

"Hey, Jon, this is really good. Well done," Miguel said.

"Can I play video games now?" Jon replied.

She was so smart to choose a partner who she recognized had a unique perspective, Miguel thought. Of all Miguel's students, Quiesha intrigued him the most.

When the room emptied after Miguel's other video class, Veruca Salt awkwardly held out a gift bag and a card. "Here, this is for you," she told Miguel. "It's not a Christmas present. It's just a present."

"Okay, thank you!" Miguel said. The bag contained a goofy mug, plush sleep socks, and candy. "Thanks for a really good class," Veruca had written in her card. "I think you're an amazing teacher."

Later, Miguel brought the card to the counselor. "Look at this!" he said.

"Ohh! Veruca Salt turned around!" she said.

It was one of the highlights of Miguel's month.

⌇

"Your math scores have gone down this year," a district representative announced at a Western staff meeting. Sounding smug and accusatory, she pointed to the schoolwide data she projected on the board. "Your students are far below basic and are not meeting expectations."

"Excuse me," Miguel said to the rep, "but perhaps if the district didn't take away our great math teacher and didn't move things around so we had to change our schedule four times at the beginning of the school year, we wouldn't be having these troubles." LaShonda turned around, smiled at him, and quietly clapped. Other teachers nodded in agreement. Miguel continued, "Maybe if the district showed us a little support, we could actually show gains instead of always trying to catch up from all these curveballs you throw at us. I'm not trying to shoot the messenger, but this is the reality and probably why we're not 'meeting expectations.'"

Flustered, the rep did not know how to respond.

If the rep had visited Miguel's classroom right after lunch and seen Miguel at his desk while the kids played Uno, she probably would have written him up. She'd have only seen kids playing a game. But Miguel saw the class dynamics improving and the kids' socio-emotional skills expanding. Last week, Miguel had partnered his students during game time so that Eli and Laurent, the thorn in Eli's side, were the last two students left. Eli, who could have chosen to play alone, for the first time invited Laurent to play with him. Following Eli's lead, kids who never used to tolerate Laurent included him now without prompting. They were learning how to deal with a kid despite his annoying behaviors—and Laurent was learning how to monitor those behaviors because he felt valuable when his classmates included him.

When Miguel started teaching two decades ago, educators had more autonomy to be flexible and creative. Now, however, the district seemed to care about only data and money. Staff meetings like today's were continually overrun by district-mandated data review. But "data" didn't explain why Miguel's special ed students could be involuntarily mainstreamed next year when they needed small classes with accommodations. "Data" wouldn't help Western's underprivileged student body if the district succeeded in displacing them with an academy for wealthy white kids.

Now that Chad Tucker knew, from Miguel's impassioned speech at October's meeting, that the Western community wouldn't passively accept the takeover, he held a meeting in nearby Citywest High School's library about the academy. He suggested that the academy could instead take over the Citywest wing that housed a public high school special ed program. Again, he'd given little advance notice and held the meeting when parents and teachers were at work. But the difference this time was that the Citywest school librarian observed the entire meeting like a ninja and related everything she heard to a group of activists, including Miguel.

"We could do the academy here. We'd find adequate replacement space for the people who are here now," Tucker said.

Parents exploded: "This isn't fair." "What happened to Western? You promised us Western!" "We don't want Citywest." "We don't want our kids near high school students. We want Western." Several people stormed out of the meeting.

Because of the librarian, the activists now had the information and the ammunition to increase their numbers and amplify their voices. They shared the librarian's report with the Citywest and Central Middle School communities. Citywest and Central joined Western's fight.

"Safe Harbor": The Most Underestimated Teacher in the Building

Why didn't anyone notice the Citywest school librarian observing the takeover meeting? Too many school librarians are overlooked and underestimated, their image stereotyped, their roles misread.

"People think librarians just check out books. Some teachers think I'm below them, even though I'm a leader at school," said a Nebraska elementary school librarian. Many schools celebrate National Assistant Principals Week without acknowledging National Library Week, which overlap in April. "I've gotten over this, but our elementary buildings give Christmas gifts to the cooks, janitors, secretaries. They honor Boss's Day, Administrative Assistant Day, and School Nurse Day. Never Library Week or School Librarian Day," said Kathy, an Iowa librarian who works at multiple elementary schools.

December

Some administrators make a habit of treating school librarians like floating subs and close the library or cancel library classes to plunk librarians in other rooms for free coverage. This practice markedly increased during the COVID pandemic. Administrators put a New Jersey elementary school librarian on 90-minute lunch duty and canceled her classes at least once a week to assign her as a bathroom monitor and classroom sub. "They would never do this to a math teacher. The math specialist is never pulled to sub," she said. "It sends the message that what I do is not important." When she asked an administrator to include her on emails about students' IEPs and 504s,* the admin said, "Well, you don't teach them anything."

Many school librarians told me they feel underrated in their workplace although their years of training often eclipse their colleagues': 15 states require school librarians to have master's degrees and plenty of librarians in other states choose to earn them. "As a librarian, my team and I receive lots of blatant disrespect from classroom teachers. It's very frustrating to be treated as less when we are just as important to our students," said Licia, the Tennessee library media specialist. "The flip side is students tend to love our classes as we offer fun content. One of my favorite things to do if I'm feeling stressed at school is to walk through the cafeteria during kindergarten lunchtime. You walk out of that room feeling like Beyoncé must feel after a concert."

Positive associations with school librarians run much deeper than the general public is aware. For more than 30 years, impact studies have linked strong school library programs and student achievement. Students are more likely to graduate, master academic

---

* IEPs cover 13 qualifying disability categories and developmental delays (the latter for students up to age seven). Students with other physical or mental disabilities that "limit a major life function" may receive accommodations under a 504 plan that help them learn in general ed classrooms.

standards, and score higher on standardized tests if their school has a high-quality library program. One might guess that these results dovetail with affluence—richer schools might have more books and better tech—community demographics, overall staffing, or teacher qualifications. But researchers controlled for these circumstances.

Simply having a school library doesn't necessarily increase student achievement. In study after study, the factor that improved students' test results, writing scores, and academic skills wasn't the books, the bucks, or the building. The game changer was the presence of a full-time qualified school librarian. What's more, student scores were higher in schools where staff considered librarians to be teachers and school leaders, and where librarians spent more time instructing students, collaborating with and providing professional development and tech support to teachers, and meeting with the principal.

But many schools don't view their librarians this way. More than 90% of principals get no formal training about school librarians, and administrators have high turnover rates; even if they develop an appreciation for and understanding of what librarians can do, their successors might not be on the same page.

"My previous principal was not open to meeting with me to discuss the role of the librarian in school, including ways I might be able to support teachers, students, and families," an Alabama elementary school librarian said. A Nebraska district curriculum specialist made a point of telling teachers on a number of occasions that sending middle school students to the library for a mini-lesson and a group book checkout was a "waste of time." Zoe, the librarian at that school, said, "This is unfortunate: Some students won't choose to come on their own because they've decided or been told they aren't good at reading. If they come as a group, they have more opportunities to be introduced to something that will speak to them and ignite their love of reading."

Several teachers at two Iowa elementary schools hold back their students from library class to make up missed work, as if "their work is more important than mine," Kathy said. Some colleagues have told her, "You really don't teach, you just read books."

Librarians battle old-school stereotypes that people seem reluctant to shelve—and that contribute to the problem that "often, staff don't see us as 'real teachers,'" Zoe said. "I hate when librarians in books are mean and always 'shhhh' children. I love the sound of a busy working library. The other day I had kids filming at all four green screens, another set working on finding books, and another group playing a game because they couldn't go to PE. Most librarians I know don't like downtime; we want the hustle and bustle of helping kids."

Leading library research experts Keith Curry Lance and Debra E. Kachel observed in one of their many important studies on librarians, "Unfortunately, school leaders seldom recognize librarians as essential technology leaders, and often they perpetuate stereotypical views of the librarian as the 'keeper of books.'" It's possible that some people cling to the stereotypes they know because the job title hasn't been consistent. In the 1980s, the American Association of School Librarians (AASL) updated the standardized position title to "school library media specialist." In 2010, the AASL initiated a return to the title of "school librarian," but not every school followed its lead.

Today a school librarian might be called a media specialist, teacher librarian, library interventionist, library media specialist, or library and instructional technology teacher. As the position names drift from the term "library," administrators might be more inclined to hire non-librarians, which adds to the public's confusion. "I hold a BA in elementary education, an endorsement in reading, and a master's in library and information science, but some schools fill these positions with people who have only a high school degree," Kathy said. Other schools staff their libraries with only parent volunteers or call the aide who checks out books a librarian, which a librarian compared to calling a doctor's office receptionist a doctor.

Some school librarians I contacted dislike the title "media specialist" because students, parents, and staff don't always understand what it means; it's easier to drum up community support for "librarians," a term people can relate to. "Media specialist" sounds "mechanical and industrial," said a Maryland private school librarian. "We are book people."

Yet "book people" doesn't nearly cover all that school librarians do. School librarians are up-to-date on educational technology and can provide training to teachers on online programs and platforms. They are familiar with the best resources and literature for every grade level at their school. They also manage the library, which entails tireless behind-the-scenes work on collection development and organization: poring over review journals, attending conferences and meetings about various aspects of librarianship, selecting books and other materials to order, and training volunteers or library staff to process and catalog new materials. They conduct much of this work on their own time, unpaid, outside of school. They support other teachers and offer outreach to families, providing book lists, reading advice, and support for individual students. "All of that is a big joy for me, but I think a lot of it is invisible to most people," said Fern, a Massachusetts elementary school librarian.

School librarians are teachers. They plan lessons, lead classes, instruct students in literacy, research, and ethical use of information skills. They can design, implement, and teach curricula and also teach students and teachers subjects such as coding and animation. Yet "classroom teachers not only don't get what we do, but don't understand what we could do—and by striving to collaborate, we're not threatening their turf but want to support them and alleviate some of their planning burdens," said a South Carolina school librarian. (Jane, an upstate New York librarian, added, "Once we convince them to let us come into their classroom, they're hooked and continue to use us.")

When admins include librarians as part of leadership and planning teams, classroom teachers are more likely to think of them as teaching partners. But librarians whose classes are in the "specials"* rotation often can't participate in designated grade-level co-planning time because "the teachers have planning meetings while I have their kids," said an Indiana elementary school librarian frustrated by this schedule. "Ideally, I would not be 'break time' and would have a flexible schedule so I can meet with teachers during regular grade level meetings when a lot of the discussion happens."

Vermont elementary school librarian Kelly Ahlfeld noted in a *Journal of Library Administration* column that a fixed rather than flexible library schedule puts school librarians at a disadvantage: "You can't understand what a library professional offers your students when they simply disappear for 30–60 minutes once a week and are returned after you've tried to accomplish every task you can during a precious prep period. 'Library' is a mystery to most teachers."

Which may be why many schools wrongly view librarians as expendable. In just six years, U.S. schools eliminated more than 9,000 full-time school librarian positions. Schools have lost approximately 20% of full-time librarians since 2009 and 45% of library support staff positions since 2000. At last count, nearly 40% of public and independent K–12 schools don't have full-time librarians and 31% of school districts don't have any librarians at all. About 8,830 public schools and more than half of charter schools don't even have a library.

---

* While "specials" is a commonly used term for library, music, art, PE, drama, and other classes, some people might misinterpret the designation as a signal that these classes are extra. These classes are just as important as academic classes and should not be deprioritized.

Hiring practices vary by state and district. Spokane, Washington, eliminated all school librarian positions in 2020. One of the worst state offenders is Michigan, where 92% of schools do not have a full-time certified librarian. During the period when Michigan dropped nearly three-quarters of its school librarians, the state had the worst 4th grade reading scores in the Midwest. Michigan, Massachusetts, Minnesota, Pennsylvania, and Rhode Island require prisons to employ librarians but not schools.

A new school position may have contributed to schools' undervaluation of librarians. When instructional technology specialists entered schools, librarians were no longer the only staff responsible for integrating technology into the curriculum, although they're specifically trained to do so. The overlap has caused power struggles. In many schools that employ both positions, instructional technologists have excluded librarians when working with teachers and students, reported University of West Georgia library and information studies professor Melissa Johnston.

Meanwhile, when school librarians retire, administrators may be more likely to eliminate the position. At the same time, training programs for new school librarians have dwindled; as universities cut school library degree and certification programs, the number of people earning master's degrees in library science fell by more than 30% in five years.

These disturbing trends are especially shortsighted because hiring a full-time qualified librarian helps close the achievement gap. The American Library Association reported that students in high-poverty schools are almost twice as likely to graduate if their school has a certified school librarian. Lance and Kachel have written, "The benefits associated with good library programs are strongest for the most vulnerable and at-risk learners, including students of color, low-income students, and students with disabilities." But districts with high percentages of Black and Latino students have eliminated more school librarian positions than districts with high percentages of white students.

School librarians provide equitable access to literature and technology and a safe, quiet space to study, learn, and dream both during and outside of designated library class hours. Low-income students might rely more on school libraries than wealthier peers do if they have fewer books and/or older, slower, or no technology at home. A comprehensive Washington State study found that "a key factor distinguishing high-performing high-poverty schools from low-performing high-poverty schools is a quality library program."

Librarians also have the unique opportunity and know how to create extensive book collections and displays that make all students feel seen and welcomed and that expose them to diverse perspectives. A Maryland elementary school librarian tries to focus lessons on books with characters from marginalized groups. Recently her weekly lessons during Women's History Month revolved around women in the space program. At the end of March, a 3rd grade boy asked her, "Can boys be astronauts?"

School librarians' impact can be immediate. When a Black student excitedly showed Arya, a New York City high school librarian, a book with a Black girl on the cover and said she'd read more if books looked like that, Arya showed her all the books in the library with Black teens on the cover and compiled a list of additional books to purchase. Fern, the Massachusetts librarian, applies for grants to host presentations by children's book creators of color. After Fern brought in a Chinese American author to present, a quiet 6th grader said he'd never seen himself represented in a guest speaker, and the experience made him feel connected.

Several students have come to Zoe's Nebraska library to ask for books with LGBTQ+ characters; a trans student once said to her, "I bet you don't have any books about trans people." "They're always surprised and pleased that we do have books with characters like them, then they recommend those titles to ally friends," Zoe said. "I don't shy away from talking about race or LGBTQ issues. Everyone should be able to see themselves in a book."

When an 8th grader wanted to write an essay arguing that gay main characters in YA books are usually male and more YA books should feature lesbian characters, Zoe helped her find articles supporting her thesis. Zoe also applied for a grant to acquire a button maker for her library, then made a button with the student's pronouns to signal her acceptance. As a result, students created pronoun buttons, too. "This is another great use of our library resources. The kids I love to see are the ones who don't think they 'fit.' I love giving them a safe harbor, even if it's just during recess or before school for the three years I get to have them," she said.

The books librarians can provide access to are safe harbors as well, which is why a group of school librarians mobilized to battle a wave of book bans and challenges they called "a war on books." In October 2021, Texas state representative Matt Krause sent a letter to school districts targeting the removal of 850 books about race, sexuality, or oppression that he claimed "might make students feel discomfort." In response, four librarians created the marvelous #FReadom Fighters social media campaign to champion diverse and inclusive books; support readers, books, school libraries, and librarians; and defend intellectual freedom, students' right to read, and access to information.

The next chapter for school librarians should be straightforward: Districts should hire more school librarians, prioritize them, give them a seat at the table as school leadership, and empower them with the platform to utilize their specialized skills and with the support to encourage their collaboration in classrooms. Schools could recruit volunteers to handle tasks like shelving and checking out books so librarians have more time for in-depth projects. Districts could offer paid extended library and staff hours, more frequent student library visits, and flexible scheduling. And parents could advocate for increased library staffing and funding both to expand the librarians' role and to ensure equitable student access. School librarians are integral and, as Jane said, "The library is really the heart of the school."

Some school librarians have had success advocating for their position. In 2021, Washington, DC, school librarians convinced DC legislators to place at least one librarian in every public school. Zoe presents at PTA meetings to show parents the library's online resources and how she teaches students to verify and fact-check information. When Arya worked at schools that didn't understand her role, she knew that some "teachers are very protective of their students and time, so building these relationships takes time and effort on my part. I had to be flexible to get my foot in their classrooms and show them that the things I and the library had to offer were important to students' education." She kept administrators apprised of library activities and invited them to all culminating events. Classroom teachers and administrators have acknowledged her work at faculty, school leadership, and PTA meetings.

School librarians are magical not just because they open books but because they open worlds. They are information wizards who stand at the ready to escort students through portals via which they can find identity, connection, acceptance, escape, validation, passions, purpose, and peace. Librarians shouldn't be invisible; they should be the most sought-after specialists in the building. They are collaborative professionals who, with literature, technology, and other educational resources, potentially could enhance lessons for every teacher and student. Yet they're often the most underestimated teacher in school—and recognition of their essentiality is long overdue.

In truth, the Citywest librarian could not have been more suited to the role of ninja observer and covert school reporter. Librarians aren't antiquated; they are cutting-edge. Lance and Kachel equate school librarians to the chief information officer of a school: They receive more training in selection, evaluation, and integration of educational resources than any other educators.

There is so much more to librarians than reading, so much more to libraries than books. And while nomenclature like "keeper of books" rings noble and inspirational to those of us who are book lovers, antagonists who adhere to stereotypes to diminish librarians, or who consider library time a "waste" or "not important" compared to other classes, might be surprised to learn that school librarians' involvement can also increase students' learning gains in science; and in at least one statewide study, the subject in which the librarians' impact was most significant—across the board in elementary, middle, and high schools—was math.

Rebecca Abrams   Elementary School Teacher

Rebecca pointed at the schedule on the wall. "As we get toward Winter Break, we'll continue to work on our colonial life projects in social studies, or if you're in my ELA class, you can work on it during independent writing time. That way, we can kill two birds with one stone." Rebecca heard a squeak and looked up.

Mia and Luci were staring stricken at her. Rebecca surveyed the room. Most of the kids were baffled and others gaped at her in dismay. For a moment, Rebecca thought they were looking at her sweater. Today was the staff's Ugly Sweater Day. She and Trixie always worked together to uglify each other's sweaters. This year, Trixie had bedazzled Rebecca's sweater in heinous shades of brown.

With a small half smile, JJ raised his hand. "Miss Abrams, what you just said, I'm guessing, I mean, well, you've talked to us sometimes about figurative language and idioms and how things don't always mean the words. I think I know you. We're not really going to be killing birds, are we?"

Rebecca guffawed. "JJ, thank you so much. I couldn't figure out why everyone in the room looked horrified! No, we are not killing birds. I used a figure of speech. Mia and Luci, is that why you're looking at me like this?"

"Uh-huh," Mia mumbled.

"YES! That's why!" Luci said.

"Guys! I carry spiders outside when we find them in the classroom!" Rebecca said. She could see some of the other students were still processing: *Okay, good, sounds like we're not killing birds.*

"Well, what does it mean?" JJ asked.

JJ's classroom attitude had improved, but Rebecca still had to cajole him to learn alongside his peers. Later that week, when she began a multi-digit-division unit, she pulled him aside. "I saw in the preassessment that you already know the algorithm," she said.

At his defensive look, she reminded him, "I just want to make sure you know why this works. Blindly doing things without knowing why they work won't make you a stronger learner or thinker."

"I *know* this, though. I can do it *fast.*"

"Can I please teach you other strategies to see if they make sense to you?"

"I already know the division algorithm. I can just use that."

"Remember, I don't want you to use the algorithm you memorized until you understand *why* it works. Eventually, I can show you why it works, but I'd like you to know other strategies, too, so why don't you come join us. Humor the teacher."

JJ slunk to the rug.

In one week, five mechanical pencils, three 3-D erasers, and a slap bracelet went missing from Rebecca's classroom. Rebecca held a class meeting. "Things have been disappearing from people's desks," she said, listing the items.

Rebecca pointed to the Class Constitution on the wall that every student had signed. She read Article III aloud: "'Ask before using something that's not yours.' You came up with these rules for yourselves because you thought they were important to keep everyone safe and learning in our room. But now somebody is breaking the laws coded in our constitution, so we don't feel safe and our property isn't respected anymore. While it might be a mistake or things might have gotten knocked off desks and kicked under furniture—it's happened!—there might be someone stealing in our classroom, which is not acceptable."

She pointed to Article II: "Tell the truth." "If anybody knows anything about what happened, please tell me. It can be in an anonymous note. If the items that disappeared magically reappear on my desk, I'll be happy to get them back to the people who lost them, announce to the whole class that the stuff came back, and we'll all feel safe again. That doesn't necessarily mean that someone stole them. It might be that someone picked something up by accident and forgot to give it back but now it could *look* like they'd stolen something and are afraid to give it back publicly. So they can just quietly sidle past my desk and drop it there en route to the Word Study folders. And, of course, I expect that nothing else will disappear."

Heads nodded.

"Does anyone have any questions or other thoughts?"

Mia raised her hand. "It makes people sad when they lose stuff they love."

The items didn't reappear. Rebecca met with the principal and the AP to explain the situation, how she'd addressed it, and how guilty she felt that items had almost certainly been stolen from under her nose. The administrators were helpful and supportive.

"It's definitely not your fault," the principal assured her. "It would be impossible for you to monitor every student at every second."

"You're doing everything you should have done so far," the AP said. The administrators said they'd talk to the class about respecting others' property.

Rebecca was grateful to have administrators who strongly supported the staff. The principal was "unfailingly supportive of teachers, actually listens to what we have to say, gives us responsibilities and opportunities, likes coming to see what we're doing in our classrooms and interacting with the kids, provides food for meetings, and just works her *butt* off," Rebecca told me.

The missing objects, however, remained missing. Rebecca mulled over how to word a letter to parents. "How do you send a letter saying, 'I Icy, do you know for sure that your child isn't the thief?'" she asked me. Eventually she sent a casual email requesting that parents not "send your kids to school with cool things because they might be taken," and if they noticed new or unusual items at home, to please ask their children about them.

None of the parents responded—or mentioned the letter at parent-teacher conferences the following week.

Conferences were a lot of work for teachers, from prepping to scheduling (and, at parents' requests or for no-shows, rescheduling and rescheduling). Many teachers also had to coordinate with team mates regarding students who left homeroom for classes like gifted math or remedial reading so they could fully inform the parents about all subject areas.

In Rebecca's case, that meant instead of conferencing with, for example, Illyse's parents, she sent a memo to Grace, Illyse's homeroom teacher, about Illyse's math and ELA work. During a team meeting, Grace mentioned in passing that Illyse was having issues with her social circle. Rebecca hadn't seen any problems from Illyse or her friends, who were well behaved in the classroom.

"In groups, she always has a partner and there's always a group of people who want to work with her," Rebecca said.

"Classes are one thing. But recess, lunch, arrival, and dismissal—

that's where the drama's happening," Grace said. "Illyse is the queen bee of her clique of five girls. When I talk to them, they acknowledge she's being horrible to them. But when I'm like, 'Why are you friends then?' they just shrug."

Some past conferences had revealed red flags: parents who became overly angry about grades or behavior such that teachers detected hints of violence, or cared so little about school that teachers might suspect neglect. Early in Rebecca's career, she sent a draft of a behavior plan home with a student before the conference. By conference time, his father had changed "If he gets 3 smiley faces each day, he'll earn a reward" to "If he doesn't get 3 smiley faces each day, I hit him with the belt." On the spot, Rebecca cited several imaginary examples of specific research and personal experiences to convince the father to stick with the positive incentive plan.

This year, conferences started out well. The first four sets of parents were the kind of involved parents who showed up with notepads and thanked Rebecca for challenging their children and making them "really think" or "really work" for the first time at school. Holly's mom was elated that Holly loved her new school and especially Rebecca's class, where she felt free to be what Rebecca called her "bouncy weird goofball" self.

Rebecca's heart beat faster when Oliver's mother, who'd requested a gifted math and ELA conference, walked in. She was nervous about discussing the possibility that Oliver might be on the spectrum with a mom who other teachers said could be prickly. It had helped that Yvonne and Grace, Oliver's homeroom teacher, had conferenced with her last week. Rebecca had pestered Yvonne until she'd agreed to raise the prospect of recommending Oliver for a special needs evaluation and autism testing. Yvonne gave Rebecca a heads-up that Oliver's parents were not on the same page: His father wanted testing, his mother did not. Testing required both parents' approval.

Rebecca felt bad for Oliver, though he didn't seem to care what his classmates thought of him. She had conditioned them to tone down their disgust with his nose and pants issues. But finding a place for him to sit in a desk team was hard because there weren't enough classmates who played it cool. The few times Rebecca sat him with less tolerant kids, she had to give serious stink eye to deter them from protesting.

Oliver's mom was respectful and willing to listen. She told Rebecca she tried to get Oliver to do some writing at home, where she saw some of the issues that arose in school. "I see how much he struggles to come up with ideas and write legibly," she said.

"Those are challenges, but they're two totally different ideas that we can tackle in two different ways," Rebecca said. "For instance, for the ideas, he could type instead of write. For handwriting, he could use larger-lined paper and spacers."

Oliver's mom said she was hesitant to get her son observed and considered for testing and special services, which she believed carried a stigma.

Rebecca had practiced and refined her answer to this concern every night in bed for a week. "The testing would be for information. We wouldn't have to decide immediately what to do with the results, if there even were conclusive results. We wouldn't need to actually *do* anything with the results if we didn't want to. But testing would help us figure out how Oliver's brain works, how he learns best, and, if he needs any sort of additional help, what sort of help might be most useful. The help wouldn't replace anything he already has. He would still get gifted services. But there's not a stigma with testing. It's simply a way to get more information that we can't get any other way."

Oliver's mom, seeming comforted, took a moment to process Rebecca's words. Rebecca let the silence linger. "I just wish he could be normal," Oliver's mom said.

Rebecca thought about that conference for a long time afterward. "Conflicts between the parents definitely complicate helping my student," Rebecca told me later. "I also wonder if Oliver's aware of his parents' opinions of him: the father who thinks he's 'off,' but at least wants to help him, and the mother who mostly works with him on things like handwriting and blowing his nose because she wants a 'normal' child. If he's aware of his parents' different opinions, it's even more reason for him to be so paralyzed by choices and afraid of making mistakes."

The remaining conferences were pleasant, except they each ran more than 40 minutes, the longest conferences Rebecca had ever had. Only one family was "a little pushy about their son's wonderfulness," as Rebecca put it, but that happened every year. These parents mentioned that their son didn't always finish his work or put in his best effort.

"It could be because he's bored," Rebecca suggested diplomatically. Actually, he chose to mess around instead of work.

"He might be a little bored," the mother said, "but it's more because he's so busy thinking about his more complex interpretations, which are more interesting to him, that he runs out of time to write down his assignment."

Rebecca's last conference was a doozy. Through a Spanish interpreter, Rebecca discussed Mia's academics and test anxiety with her mother for about 20 minutes. Then Mia's mother and the interpreter struck up an unrelated conversation. Rebecca caught bits and pieces about the mother's boyfriend and the women's clothes as she kept a polite smile plastered on her face because she couldn't get a word in edgewise in any language. The women shared family photos on their phones while Rebecca thought, *Oh my god, I have been at work for twelve hours and I want to go home and eat dinner already*. After 70 minutes, Rebecca "ran out of politeness" (her words) and organized papers around the room. The other women gossiped for 10 more minutes before they stopped looking at their phones and apparently remembered they were at a parent-teacher conference.

"Do you have any final questions for me?" Rebecca asked.

Mia's mom did not. She and the interpreter resumed their conversation and continued to chatter until Rebecca walked out the door.

◦◦◦

When Rebecca's best friend reminded her about their online dating pact, Rebecca cringed. "No way! Too many horror stories, too many options."

"If you actually want to enter the dating scene and meet someone, this is the way to do it now," Aiko said. "You can't expect that you'll just happen to meet people you want to date. Also, you made a pact and you have to honor it."

Rebecca face-palmed. Aiko knew Rebecca had a powerful sense of responsibility. She kept her promises.

"The way I stay sane is by thinking about it as a sociological experiment," Aiko advised.

"I guess I could try that. Maybe then I'd be less horrified by the crazies and take it less personally when I inevitably get burned," Rebecca said. "I just want to dip my toes in the water. I don't have time for a major commitment, and I move slowly romantically even at the best of times." She agreed to set up a profile.

Sunday night, hopped up on caffeine for a marathon grading session, Rebecca realized that if she put off online dating until she had the time, it was never going to happen. *Now's as good a time as any*, she resolved, and she set up her profile with an overly wordy bio because overly wordy was how she rolled. Two nights later, she had 356 likes and a message from a 45-year-old man looking for 21- to 35-year-old women for "short-term dating, hookups, and non-monogamy."

"NOPE. NOPITY NOPE NOPE NOPE," Rebecca texted Aiko. She did not have high hopes for dating.

Penny Davis   6th Grade Math Teacher

During her planning period, Penny received an email from the master's program to which she had applied. "Congratulations . . ."

"Oh my gosh!" Penny shrieked. She had been selected to receive a full scholarship and yearly stipend and could start as soon as January. "Oh my gosh oh my gosh oh my gosh!" She raced to Ed's classroom. "I got it!" she exclaimed, bouncing with excitement. "I'm going to get my master's degree! For free!"

Ed's smile spread ear to ear. "That's exactly right," he said.

When Blair emailed the team about joining a parent-teacher behavior conference, Penny groaned. Typically, when a parent had an issue with a teacher or a teacher with a student, the parent met with that teacher alone or with an administrator. Blair had more behavioral meetings than any other 6th grade teacher at Southern. As grade leader, she used her authority to pressure every teacher on her team to join her meetings. In November, Penny had attended so many of Blair's behavior conferences that she missed both her planning and lunch periods every day for a week. The other teachers never missed a meeting. Penny worried that if she skipped one, Blair would report her to the principal, who seemed to be in Blair's corner; she hadn't even disciplined Blair for berating her special ed students.

Today's meeting was about Kendra, a slightly mischievous girl who sometimes made sarcastic cracks or asked non sequiturs, common 6th grade behaviors. Penny had only a few issues with her this semester, little things she took care of in the classroom by giving a look or putting her finger to her lips with a wink to signal that Kendra's timing was inappropriate. Penny thought Kendra was a "funny little firecracker who I'd take home in a heartbeat."

As soon as the door closed, Blair and Kendra's mom began yelling at each other.

"This is not the way a teacher should be! You pick on Kendra!"

"I expect my students to behave! Your daughter does not!" Blair shouted.

Baloney, Penny thought.

"Other kids are saying you target her just because she doesn't sit there and be quiet all the time!"

"I do not target your child! I treat them all equally!" Blair shrieked.

As the two women continued to feud, Penny tried to catch the other teachers' eyes; she wanted to ask wordlessly if she should find an administrator. But everyone was uncomfortably looking down.

"Y'all want to tell me why Kendra doesn't have any problems in any other classes but yours?" Kendra's mom pressed. "Ms. Davis never tells me about any problems. Kendra loves Ms. Davis."

Blair shot dagger eyes at Penny, who flinched. Blair retorted, "Well, I can't help it if Princess Perfect over there never has any problems with behavior. I discipline my students."

The next day was worse.

Blair called the team to "a quick meeting" during planning period. It was not a quick meeting. Apparently, Kendra's mom had reported Blair's behavior to administrators, and an assistant principal had spoken with Blair. When the team was gathered in the conference room, Blair lashed out: "I felt so unsupported in that meeting! Y'all were saying you didn't have any problems with her. Penny, she was talking about how perfect Kendra is in your class."

Penny put up a hand. "Hold up, just because I don't have problems with her during that portion of the day—" She interrupted herself with a coughing fit; she still hadn't been able to shake her cough. "I handle it, but I can put up with a lot." *Because I know these are kids doing normal kid things*, Penny thought. Penny saw in Blair's behavior write-ups that Kendra's transgressions usually involved simply chatting with classmates. Blair reported the majority of 6th grade incidents, which all seemed trivial. She had written up Zach, for example, for "talking out of turn" to classmates. Zach never talked out of turn in Penny's class. In fact, in Penny's class, Zach was now an active class participant who came to the board whenever Penny called on him. His mother had told Penny that Zach had never done that before. In team meetings, the other teachers complained that Zach was not participating at all.

Penny did have behavior issues in her classes, but they were insignificant. She didn't send write-ups to the office unless a student's behavior was dangerous. She kept her students so busy with math games, group work, and class discussions that they barely had time to misbehave anyway.

Penny used several techniques with Robert, her autistic student, for example. She never disciplined him publicly. When he blurted out in class, she whispered in his ear, firmly but quietly, "When you interrupt me, you make me feel frustrated because I'm trying to teach." He'd calm down. When he was agitated about a difficult assignment or generally fidgety, Penny gave him a stapled piece of paper and asked him to deliver it to another teacher. He didn't know the note he carried alerted the recipient, "Robert just needs five minutes. Can you please talk to him for a second and send him back to me?" When he returned to Penny, he was usually fine because leaving the room had broken his tension.

Blair, though, had no patience for anyone who didn't fit her narrow vision of her ideal student. "If Zach so much as looks around the room while Blair's teaching, she writes him up. She writes kids up for every teeny tiny behavior, which as a teacher sometimes you ignore when they don't interfere with the flow of the class," Penny told me. Blair had actually said more than once in staff meetings, "If I could just take these children over my knee, they would behave."

She seemed to believe that education was about forcing children to sit at a desk and do paper and pencil work. "But it's not. It's messy discourse, creativity, letting kids be themselves. It's like a game of Jumanji except a little more under control," Penny said. "Traditional education ideas don't work for these kids nowadays. But with Blair it's 'Bookwork, bookwork, yes ma'am, no ma'am, sit ramrod straight in your seat.'"

Blair refused to believe that she was the problem. She turned to Penny. "I can't help it that you think you're so perfect and you never have discipline problems. But you don't need to sit there during the meeting and say you don't have any problems with Kendra."

"I can't make up something that's not there. And I never said I didn't have problems, but I'm just not seeing the same things you do," Penny said. "Maybe Kendra doesn't like science. Maybe she loves math."

"You're just not recording discipline because you want to make yourself look good."

Penny shook her head in disgust. She saw Birdie staring at Blair in disbelief. *Poor Birdie, she left her last school because of a toxic environment and now look where she landed, Penny thought.*

"Well, I don't have problems with Kendra either," Celia interjected. "I can't make up problems."

"Even if there is a tiny problem with the child, you need to state it," Blair said. "I expect to be supported. You need to not make me look bad. You're supposed to have my back no matter what."

No, I'm not, Penny thought. Trying to balance post-divorce survival with rising workplace tensions was difficult enough. "I feel like I'm on the team that has all the problems," she told Ed afterward. "And then I get attacked because my classes don't have problems."

"When you're good at what you do and passionate about it, and your students have a positive relationship with you, people get jealous," he said. "They want to attack your character because they aren't respected by their students. They're insecure about their teaching abilities."

~~◦~~

By the week before Winter Break, the administration hadn't said a word about the annual staff Christmas party. Teachers grumbled about the new principal's budget tightening when morale was already low, then decided to meet anyway at a local hotel's outdoor bar/restaurant. They didn't need the principal's permission to party.

Penny arrived late, after picking up the boys from basketball practice. Following dinner, as teachers mingled or left, Penny scooted over to Ed's table. They watched Savannah stumble out the door with Southern's instructional technology specialist.

They were chatting with Jan when the waiter set a drink on the table in front of Penny. Penny nudged it to Ed. "Excuse me, ma'am, this drink is for you," the waiter said. "That gentleman over there wants to know if he can have your number." He gestured to a man in a business suit who winked when he caught her eye.

Penny looked at him incredulously. "Me?" The waiter nodded.

"Tell him she's married," Jan said.

"No, ma'am, I'm not telling him that," the waiter said. The group laughed and the conversation resumed.

Fifteen minutes later, the waiter brought another drink to the table. "For you again, ma'am."

"Please tell him thank you but don't send any more drinks," Penny said. She didn't touch the drink this time. She was three drinks in already. Jan said, "Okay, I'm leaving. You, Señor"—she pointed to Ed—"take care of Penny. Do not let anything happen to her."

"You know I'll take care of her," Ed said.

Penny and Ed continued to talk late into the night, long past the time when Penny had sobered up. "The conversation flowed so naturally and smoothly, it felt like I'd known him forever," Penny told me later. "The friendship is just so easy and he's so much fun in a social setting."

When he saw Penny safely to her car, Ed thanked her for "the most fun night I've had in a long time."

The day before Winter Break, Blair came to Penny. "I know you see a counselor," she said, almost deferential.

"Yes, I do see a counselor. It helps me. I need someone to talk to every now and then." In truth, Penny hadn't been able to see her therapist as often because Kent had dropped her from his health insurance coverage and her school district's insurance plan had exorbitant copays.

"I think I need some counseling," Blair said. "I think this job is getting to me. Would you mind telling me who you see?"

Penny knew Blair had some health issues. *Maybe they're stress related*, Penny thought. *If she talks to somebody, it really might help her.* She gave Blair her therapist's name.

"Thank you," Blair said. Later, she stopped by to say that she had made an appointment, though it would take several weeks to get into the practice.

Penny was pleased Blair had made the effort to get help. *Maybe Blair's turning over a new leaf,* Penny thought. *Maybe we can be friends.*

"Fluff Subject": Subject Misconceptions and the Marginalization of Specialist Teachers

School librarians aren't the only educators who feel misunderstood at work. Some music, PE, art, drama, and other teachers commonly known as "specialists" also said that districts, coworkers, or parents minimized or ignored their contributions at school.

When Barb worked at a Michigan elementary school, her co-workers "treated me like garbage and never included me in anything because I'm a PE teacher," she said. They regularly were rude to her, she said, didn't talk to her in the staff lounge, and treated her more like a temporary babysitter than a professional teammate. "I loved what I did, but I hated coming to work. Teachers looked at me not like a colleague but as someone lower than them, even though I teach physical life lessons. They never talked to me, invited me, or sat with me," she said. On one occasion, "I was one of the first people in the lounge for lunch. As everyone came in, they sat at other tables and moved chairs from my table to different tables. I was so offended and hurt that I ate lunch in my office the rest of the year and left the school."

Barb moved to a middle school where colleagues socially included the two PE teachers. But some staff still treated them like inferiors. Other teachers took over the gym without telling the PE teachers until the morning of, sending them scrambling for space to teach outside or, inexplicably, in the library. Staff sometimes forgot to give the PE teachers advance notice of assemblies held in the gym. When administrators asked the PE teachers to proctor a state standardized test, a science teacher said, "Gym teachers can't administer tests."

Barb told me, "My colleague and I were like, 'We can both read. We went to the same college you guys did.' We were not capable in her head of doing a standardized test. That made us feel stupid, as if only core teachers could administer these important tests because they're smarter and more trustworthy with students and tests."

Many studies have shown that "PE teachers often struggle for the legitimacy of their subject and may feel as if they are not treated like 'real' teachers," according to University of Alabama kinesiology professor K. Andrew Richards. School communities may be more likely to view PE as a peripheral or "low status" subject because, experts say, it requires more physicality than cognition. As a result, "PE teachers receive both explicit and implicit messages that their subject is less important than others." The science teacher's message was also ignorant because PE teachers teach physical education, not gym; the gym is the site of a class, not the subject itself. It's no more appropriate to call a PE teacher a gym teacher than to call a music teacher an auditorium teacher.

Music teachers, too, said they're misjudged because of their specialty. "Music is considered a 'fluff subject' and I hate that," said an Ohio charter school music teacher. "We should be taken seriously! We are real musicians who play real music on real instruments. I can connect this 'fluff subject' to any other subject taught. Some music teachers justify their place based on the cross-curricular nature of music, but I believe the best part of music is making music, not how it better informs social studies or math."

Specialists are "often treated differently by classroom teachers; some think we don't teach 'a real curriculum' and are just a placeholder for their kids when they have plan time," said Jesse, a Nebraska computer science teacher. "We work hard to support their curriculum when we can, but we do have strict curriculum guidelines and goals to meet, and what we do is important in a well-rounded education."

Some specialists don't feel excluded, but rather that their needs and working conditions go unnoticed. A New York art teacher said that as administrators cram more students into her middle school classes, the larger numbers increase the risks of behavior issues with sharp, dangerous, and messy materials. When a California public school added more daily classes to a dance teacher's already full schedule, she tore her meniscus; her administrators didn't consider the wear and tear on dance teachers' bodies.

An interesting thing happened when I asked a variety of teachers if they believed there was a prejudice against their subject: All kinds of teachers said yes. Some kindergarten teachers said high school teachers think their job is easier because their classes might be more play based. Special ed teachers told me about coworkers who treat them as if they are special ed students. A Virginia elementary ESOL teacher said staff often exclude ESOL teachers generally and sometimes forget to invite them to their students' IEP meetings.

A midwestern Latin teacher's coworker told her that Latin shouldn't count as a foreign language credit "because it's not spoken and you really just teach history." (She was proud that when a physics teacher told one of her students that the class was a "colossal waste of time," the student retorted with a list of scientific terminology rooted in Latin.) "The focus on STEM is concerning," the Latin teacher told me. "It devalues other areas of study which promote broad-based, imaginative, and innovative thinking. It puts language, music, art, and other programs in danger. No matter the career path students take, they still must be able to communicate clearly and have other skills supported by the humanities."

A New Jersey high school English teacher said that for students, her class is "always last on the hierarchy. Math, science, history—all those come before us in terms of time dedicated. Even those who love literature spend time on math homework or even reviewing for the SATs instead of reading or writing. We simply cannot convince most of our students that English class matters."

Private and public school social studies teachers in Pennsylvania said that because the subject isn't frequently tested on state assessments, districts and schools tend to neglect the department, such as when ordering new books or necessary supplies. "Social studies is like the ugly stepchild of core subjects," a public school teacher said.

"Some administrators at my school are pushing to make social studies classes practice for the state literature tests and take out requirements for students to know any social studies content."

Guidance counselors, too, can get short shrift in schools even as both their caseload numbers and student mental health issues rise. "There's very little professional development at schools directly for ancillary staff or student services faculty," said an Illinois high school counselor. "So often, counselors and like areas are lumped into teacher professional development, shoehorning us into trying to make it applicable to our jobs. It rarely fits. We're a forgotten bunch in education. Everything is about teaching, but we provide an essential and vital support that schools wouldn't survive without."

Many staff members, it seems, are frustrated by stereotypes and prejudgments about their roles. It would be glib to call these similar feelings unifying, but schools could use them to do a better job of fostering understanding and appreciation among departments. Not everyone considers how English teachers spend extra time grading because they evaluate and refine students' writing, or how kindergarten teachers oversee one of the most comprehensive periods of student growth as they teach children to read, write, do basic math, develop social skills, and adjust to the routines, standards, and socioemotional realities of school. Likewise, it's offensive to presume a hierarchy of subjects and to rank "specials" at the bottom.

But specialists, like the Citywest librarian, seem to be particularly unseen. This invisibility could be because specialists are more often psychologically and physically isolated than generalists, particularly in elementary schools and rural schools, where specialists are likely the only teacher of their subject, or in districts where they travel to multiple schools. The lack of time for collaboration, guidance, peer support, and interaction with coworkers can make specialists feel emotionally detached from the rest of the school. "Emotional isolation is experienced when arts teachers feel like they have no one to talk to, no one to bounce ideas around with, no one who is teaching in the same area and so who understands the issues that affect an arts teacher the most," Australian researchers observed.

Specialists' physical distance can also contribute to their sense of being stranded. The general tendency toward closed-door classrooms is known in the field as "egg-crate isolation" because teachers are separated from one another. "In other professions I was in, we had opportunities to see how others did the job on a daily basis, learned from and taught each other, were able to see successes and mistakes in others that we could replicate or steer clear of, and had constant discussions with each other throughout our days about our job," Jesse said. "Teachers are typically siloed in our own classrooms. We rarely, if ever, get to see what works in each other's classrooms, because we're all teaching at the same time. This is more extreme for specialists."

The disconnectedness can be even more pronounced for PE teachers whose gyms are located at the end of the building, and music, arts, and other teachers whose rooms are tucked away from other classrooms. The physical separation reduces specialists' opportunities to interact with coworkers and impedes their ability to navigate staff micropolitics.

Some experts recommend online professional learning communities or informal PDs to give specialists a sense of belonging and peer support. When Concordia University education professor Catherine Bell-Robertson formed and studied an online community for new middle and high school instrumental music teachers, she observed that the camaraderie and feedback satisfied participants' need for emotional support.

Districts or school clusters could also form interscholastic professional learning communities. A South Carolina school librarian said, "I'd appreciate more time with school librarians in similar situations so we could support each other emotionally and exchange new ideas.

There isn't a good supportive cohort network in my district." Researchers additionally suggest that specialists address isolation by watching videos of other teachers' classes, "visiting and observing fellow teachers," participating in mentoring programs, teaching outside the isolated classroom (such as leading PE on a field), and proactively reaching out "to work collaboratively and cross-curricularly to develop professional and personal relationships with their colleagues."

Many of these approaches, of course, are much easier said than done, in terms of practicality, resources, and time. But districts can help. In Brevard County, Florida, the teachers union invested a $600,000 grant from the NEA Great Public Schools Fund in an orientation and mentorship program. The grant funds substitute teachers who cover the mentor-mentee teams' classes when they observe other teachers' classrooms together, as well as iPads the pairs use to record their lessons and analyze them. Through this program, two music teachers who worked at different schools were able to collaborate on music lesson plans and provide feedback on classroom strategies. The mentor benefited as much as the mentee. "I honestly learned so much through the process," the mentor told NEA Today, "It's one of the most profound things I've ever done."

Mostly, teachers I interviewed wanted connections with their colleagues. After all, "teaching is a socio-emotional practice," as education professor Alfredo Bautista, co-director of the Centre for Educational and Developmental Sciences in Hong Kong, has said. "Teacher growth also requires improving the quality of teachers' socio-emotional experiences, reducing their stress, and establishing communities of practice and social networks to alleviate psychological and emotional isolation." By making staff members aware of all that their coworkers actually do, and how they can collaborate, schools can help them shatter false impressions and make one another feel seen. Administrators can fold specialists into informal staff groups and publicly highlight to staff and parents the ways library, PE, arts, music, and other specials classes play critical roles at school.

A few years after Barb switched schools, one of her former elementary school colleagues joined the middle school staff. During a meeting, the colleague said to Barb from across the table, "You look familiar. Do I know you?"

Barb replied, "Yes, I was the PE teacher who worked with you for two years."

Barb told me later, "I didn't realize how much anger I still had. She was like, 'Oh. Sorry.' I wanted to say so much more, but my colleagues were busy remarking, 'Whoa, Barb spoke up.' Because I usually don't."

Administrators, school leadership, and teachers should speak up for their specialists. By making specialist teachers feel like recognized, valuable staff members, schools would benefit—and these professionals could better focus on the unique joys of being specialists that few other staff members get to experience. "As a specialist, I get to see the kids grow. I have the same kids from kindergarten through fifth grade, and I get to see the changes," said Jesse, who got emotional when he told me about some of his beloved students. "I feel fortunate to be a part of their lives for so long. The broader, deeper relationships with students are truly 'special.'"

CHAPTER 6

January

A principal, putting her finger in the air when a Maryland special education teacher and a colleague were in the middle of asking her a question: "Do you hear that? That's God telling me I don't have time for you."

Email from an Oklahoma high school administrator to teachers in which she repeatedly pressured them to bump report card Ds to Cs: "Grading is never truly objective."

A student's mother to a New Jersey 2nd grade teacher: "Are you pregnant?"
    Teacher: "No, I'm not."
    Parent: "Are you sure?"

Rebecca Abrams   Elementary School Teacher

The first day after Winter Break, Rebecca walked into her classroom after a team meeting to find that the morning message she'd written on her whiteboard had been changed to: "Good morning, class. It's Hammer Time." Rebecca laughed and plotted her Prank War revenge against Evangeline.

In ELA, students dawdled when they were supposed to be

retrieving their guided reading lesson books. "Come on, shake a leg, people!" Rebecca said.

The class stared blankly at her. "Is this a killing birds thing?" JJ asked.

Rebecca snorted and stopped to recall what she'd said. "Yes, yes, this is a killing birds thing. It's a figure of speech. Let me explain it."

Guided reading lessons were one of Rebecca's favorite class activities because she loved to see the kids get to the good parts. Today, Rebecca watched gleefully as her students independently read a chapter in which a character was so wicked that Rebecca knew her class, a sweet group, would be scandalized. Sure enough, a student screeched, "OH MY GOD!" furiously diving back into the story as the next student reached that passage with the same reaction. The slower readers frantically tried to catch up to understand the commotion. Rebecca watched the kids as if she were watching a movie, laughing when Mia shouted "WHAT?" and the whole class jumped because for once, Mia didn't mumble.

Rebecca was still working with Mia on her test anxiety. She often reminded Mia about growth mindset messages and reviewed study tips with her. But even when Mia got a decent score, her face still fell because it was lower than her friends'.

After school, a group of Rebecca's former students, now in middle school, stopped by to visit. They weren't at all surprised to see that a student had made Rebecca an intricate paper snowflake, or that Rebecca was wearing it on her nose throughout dismissal.

Rebecca was so happy to see them that, she said, "my heart grew four sizes." Rebecca never tired of seeing former students. These four in particular were especially endearing: They had told Rebecca for years, even now, that she was their favorite teacher. "Considering how much time and energy we pour into teaching each individual student, knowing that they remember you fondly enough to take time out of their day to have a conversation with you, to see if your room looks the same, or if you're still as funny as they remember— it's powerful, and it's humbling, and it just makes your week, if not longer. It just makes it all feel worthwhile," she told me. "Thinking back on how you made students happy helps you keep going when those really tough days happen, and there are a lot more tough days than there are old student visits."

Seeing Sara, one of the students, reminded her what the girl had said when Rebecca taught her 1st grade class. Rebecca thought elementary schoolers were hilarious; they blabbed whatever came to mind. Once, a student informed her that he wished he had sound-proof underpants. During a 4th grade group project about the benefits of bodies of water, a student gobsmacked his group by announcing, "They're a good place to hide the dead bodies!"

When Sara was in Rebecca's class, Rebecca and another teacher salsa danced for her students one afternoon. During dismissal, Sara exclaimed, "I really loved that dance you and Mr. P. did!"

"Thank you!"

"It looked like you were really having fun."

"You're right, we were! Salsa is really fun."

"My mommy dances, too. But I don't know if it's as fun as yours. She dances on a *pole*!"

Sara's mother was a prim high-powered attorney. Rebecca did everything she possibly could to keep a straight face as the child continued blithely, "And she has to wear super-high heels when she does it! They're *red*. They don't look very comfortable at all, I don't know how she dances in them."

When Rebecca was able to regain her composure, she said, to divert the conversation until Sara's bus was called, "Wow! Well, I'm glad I get to wear low heels when I salsa. I don't like wearing heels very much. But you know who'd probably like those shoes? Ms. B.!"

"Yeah! She always wears *crazy* high heels! I don't know how she does it!"

"Did you see the heels she's wearing today?" Rebecca asked.

After dismissal, Rebecca went to tell Trixie, through snorting laughter, what prompted a kid to lean into the hall at dismissal and yell, "Ms. B., can I see your shoes?"

"How do you look a parent in the eye after their kid gives you the mental picture of them pole dancing?" Rebecca asked Trixie. "And now she's going to go home and tell her mom all about my dancing and probably say, 'And I told her that *you* dance, too, on a pole in your super-high red shoes!' Because that's totally the sort of thing a first grader would do and in that case her mom would rather eat live scorpions than look at *me* afterwards, either!"

On a crisp winter night, as a light snow began to fall, Rebecca and her colleagues were still at school doing extra work. Every teacher at Eastern was required to work two after-school events throughout the school year and strongly encouraged to attend concerts, plays, and other evening functions. Sometimes teachers secretly thought these duties were a chore, especially when they involved extra prep work, or boring when they were surrounded by students with whom they'd just spent the entire day. But the events could also be fun opportunities to chat with students and families they hadn't spent time with before. The Book Fair was one of Rebecca's favorite Eastern functions. One year, a questionable book jacket had led Rebecca, three students, and their mothers to have an in-depth discussion about how advertisers influenced girls' beauty standards and expectations.

Teachers had to stay late to set up Book Fair books and activity stations for students, families, and alums. Half an hour before start time, the teachers were hanging bulletin boards in the hallway and arranging books in the all-purpose room when a 2nd grade teacher hollered from down the hall, "OH MY GOD, WE HAVE A DELAY!"

The teachers froze and stared at her. She held up her phone like the Olympic torch. "IT'S ALREADY BEEN ANNOUNCED! DELAY TOMORROW DUE TO WEATHER! WE GET TO SLEEP IN!"

Everyone in the hall clapped and cheered. "After having to stay late for this?" "Thank god!" The teacher who made the announcement sang, "Ceeeelebrate good times, COME ON!" and danced down the hall, waving her phone over her head. Rebecca and other teachers joined in, laughing and singing.

"You know how excited kids get when there's a two-hour delay or snow day?" Rebecca told me later. "It doesn't hold a candle to how excited teachers get."

Later that evening at the Book Fair, JJ's mom approached Rebecca. "I just have to tell you what happened," she said. "JJ came home asking me to show him the standard algorithm for division, so I did. But then he said he wasn't sure he really understood it and asked me to go through the steps and why it works again, because 'Miss Abrams will only let me use it if I truly *understand* it.'"

Rebecca did a happy dance and fist pumped.

JJ's mom laughed and continued. "He kept asking for more problems and practice. We ended up working on division for forty-five minutes. He likes math, sure, but he's never done this before. It was amazing—and it's all because of you!"

Rebecca cackled dramatically and tallied a point on an invisible scoreboard as she announced, "Miss Abrams, one!"

After that, JJ seemed to trust Rebecca enough to think more deeply about the ways she challenged him. He even came to Rebecca's classroom during recess occasionally to share with her something new and interesting he'd learned or to tell her what he thought about a book he'd read.

Oliver was also progressing, thanks to Rebecca's frequent one-on-one efforts. When he got worked up because he didn't know what to write about, for example, Rebecca asked if he could tackle a previous assignment's topic through another lens. She often reminded him why taking deep breaths would help calm his brain, rather than simply suggesting it would help him; his analytical side understood explanations more easily than his emotional side accepted that he needed coping strategies. His mother still declined to get him evaluated.

~⊱~

Two students complained that items had been taken from their backpacks: a key chain and a Pop-It. To address this new wave of thefts, Rebecca held a class meeting to discuss ways to stop the behavior.

The next day, after teaching an ELA lesson, Rebecca returned to her desk to find that the PopGrip was missing from her phone. Rebecca was staggered by the deliberate calculation: Despite the prior day's discussion, a student somehow sneaked over to Rebecca's desk while she was teaching a lesson, removed the PopGrip from its base, and returned to their seat without anyone noticing. Rebecca wasn't sure whether to make a big deal of the theft or to address it quietly, in case the attention encouraged the student to steal again.

Rebecca sought guidance from the principal. The next morning, the principal and assistant principal watched every student in Rebecca's homeroom empty their backpacks, jacket pockets, and desks. The stolen items didn't surface.

On the wall, Rebecca taped a list of missing items, with the hope that students could cross them off as they were returned. One student crossed off a marker that he'd found on the floor, assumed was up for grabs, and returned as soon as he saw it on the list. The other objects remained unaccounted for.

As the mystery of the class thief continued to perturb Rebecca, her efforts to "get a life" (her words) were a welcome distraction. She had more wiggle room in her schedule, after having spent part of Winter Break figuring out which ELA strategies and lessons to prioritize. By now, she also knew her students so well that she didn't have to prep various motivational methods. She already knew what worked best for whom.

First, she signed up for two musicals. For a community show, she asked to be on the crew, a smaller commitment than cast, even though the director, who remembered Rebecca's past performances, pushed her to audition for a lead role, too. As a compromise, she agreed to sing one short solo. For her synagogue's show, the director cast her as the lead. Rebecca was thrilled to be part of musical theater communities again. Dancers, singers, theater nerds—these were "my people," quirky, warm, and accepting, she told me. "While I have many nerdy friends with whom I can bust out random movie quotes, deliver soliloquies about why *Labyrinth* is one of my favorite movies of all time, and generally talk about things that aren't mainstream, musical theater people are the ones who not only don't bat an eyelash when I spontaneously burst into song or start dancing in place when I'm too fidgety to stand still, but will also join in. Because we don't have to worry about looking cool for each other or being judged, musical theater geeks can all just be ridiculous together. This crosses ages and backgrounds, and it goes from the actors to the production crew to the stage crew to the pit."

Rebecca was also finding online dating more entertaining than she'd expected, both her own experiences and Aiko's recounting of her self-titled "Adventures with Bozos." At first, Rebecca had treated every profile page as if she were meeting the men in real life, which led to overthinking. Once she treated the search as more a casual hobby, the process became easier.

Rebecca had messaged with several people so far. Some conversations died quickly. One guy asked her out after two weeks of messaging, but when she wanted to talk some more first, he ghosted her. She turned down a man who asked her out instantly and remained in good humor when others rejected her. She had an ongoing conversation with Pete, a friendly guy who was fun to talk to. "Overall, I'm proud of myself for not taking this too seriously. I usually overanalyze everything related to boys, so I think this is a very positive step for me," she told me. "I've found a good balance of how much time I spend on it. I feel desirable for the first time in a long time, which is a nice change. And I got my butt in gear and *did* something during the school year. Go me!"

Penny Davis   6th Grade Math Teacher

Penny was sick again with a sinus infection and bronchitis. Because her doctor said she wasn't contagious—this was not COVID, not this time—she kept going to work. She gave herself nebulizer treatments during her lunch and planning periods. She felt awful, but subs were hard to find. The district gave teachers few sick days and docked their pay if they exceeded their allotment.

Other teachers in the hallway were experiencing similar health issues. When Penny again suggested to the principal that the mold on the walls could be causing their symptoms, the principal said that if there was something wrong, fixing it would require a roof repair that neither the school nor the district could afford. Other administrators also dismissed the teachers' concerns, insisting they were constantly sick only because "kids are germ factories."

During a lunchtime conversation in Ed's classroom, Ed told Penny that he and his daughter were going to visit his son at college for the weekend. "Their mom hasn't been to see him at all," Ed said, dejected for his children. "She's always chosen her job over the kids and me. We moved here for her. When she decided over the summer she didn't like her coworkers, she could have gotten a job thirty minutes away after already uprooting her family. But she chose a job two hours away because she was chasing prestige. How could a mother not want to be with her children?"

Penny was quiet for a few moments. "I don't get it and it's not fair to you. But you've been an incredible father. Look at all you've done. You took them on college visits, you were at every game, you coached their sports . . ."

"We got married young and quickly because she was pregnant. We were never even friends."

"Why did you finally separate?" Penny asked.

"It was after I told my brother some things she had done. He's a psychologist. He told me that what was going on with Ellen wasn't right, and I needed to think about the message I was sending to my kids about staying in an abusive relationship."

"Wait, what do you mean 'abusive'?"

Ed took a breath. "Well, she hit me."

Penny was speechless. "Oh, Ed. I'm sorry."

"Things weren't good for me for a while. I haven't told anybody here that. A few times a year, she'd fly into a rage. She'd get drunk and scream that she hated me, accuse me of things I didn't do, throw things at me. Sometimes she'd sneak up and hit me." He nudged his phone across his desk. "One time I got it on video."

Penny watched the events unfold on video as Ed had described. "I'm sorry. I'm so sorry. I don't have the words," she said.

"I just wanted to be with my kids. I couldn't leave."

"I understand exactly what you mean," she said, thinking, *We've both been dealing with tough personal situations in terrible marriages, yet we came to school every day with smiles on our faces like everything was fine.*

About half an hour after lunch, Penny got a text from Kent: "Who you eating lunch with Penny?"

Penny shivered. Who was keeping tabs on her? "Someone's definitely watching us," Penny told me. "It makes us mad because other people eat lunch together, males and females, and no one ever says a word to them."

When the grad school semester began, Penny told her classes about it. She wanted her students to see how excited she was about math and about learning, and she hoped to emphasize that she had a goal and was working toward it. She told them her assignments would be hard, but she would do the best she could. She didn't mention that she was also glad to have the extra work to occupy her on the lonely nights when the boys were with Kent.

Penny's professors wanted the teachers to put what they learned into practice immediately in their own classrooms. Rather than beginning her lessons with students taking notes while Penny gave examples and explanations, Penny shifted her teaching methods. She asked open-ended questions that pushed students to come up with the answers on their own. Her classes now had even more discourse, hands-on math tasks, games, and group work. Penny quickly saw an improvement in her students' test scores, which already were good. Some of her inclusion students' scores had the biggest jumps.

The new principal's lack of guidance continued to create trouble for teachers. The 6th grade teachers' meeting at the end of the semester was running much longer than usual. The teachers couldn't agree on the content of the letter informing parents that their child was failing a subject and might have to attend summer school. Each teacher was responsible for the letters sent to students in their homeroom. They argued for more than an hour about whether to send the letter only to students who were failing a class, as Southern had traditionally done, or also to students receiving Ds.

"But why can't we do it the way it's been done? The way admin last year handed it down?" Penny asked. Without direction from the principal or central office, 24 teachers with 24 different personalities each had their own ideas about how the letter should read.

"If they are getting Ds, they are at risk of failing sixth grade," Blair said. "Parents need to know that Ds are unacceptable."

"We should just follow the same rules we've used for years, because they work," said Celia. "For Ds, we have a parent conference, but we don't send them the failure letter."

The teachers spent another hour debating the wording of the letter. "We need to be in-your-face with the parents," Savannah said. "Their child is failing because of them. If your child doesn't come to school, doesn't do their homework, I don't care what's going on at home, sorry. That's on y'all." Her clique loudly agreed.

"Well, but in reality many parents have limited time or a poor mindset when it comes to tackling math," Penny objected. "And some families might not have the means to have the materials at home."

"Southern is the best. If they come to Southern, parents should be on their kids at home to do the work," Vivian said.

Savannah and Vivian just want their students to have perfect grades and standardized test scores, and if they don't, they can blame the parents, Penny thought. An acquaintance told Penny that at Vivian's old school, Vivian tried to move special ed students out of her classes because she didn't want them to affect her classes' test scores.

The discussion broke up further among the 6th grade teams. Penny's team argued in circles. Confused about what she was expected to write, Penny leaned over to a teacher on another team and whispered, "What are y'all writing on yours? Because I don't understand the back-and-forth."

"We're going to specify the class or classes and keep it matter-of-fact. The letter will be for Fs, but if the student is also getting a D in another class, we're going to say which class it is in a line at the bottom. I think all the teams are doing that."

"Okay, that's what I'll write, too. Thanks," Penny said.

After school, she stuck the letters in the principal's mailbox so the principal could return them to her with a signature, and thought nothing more of it.

Until Blair called an emergency team meeting a few days later.

"What is this!" Blair screamed at Penny when the door closed. She brandished Penny's stack of signed failure letters.

"Wait, did you take those out of my mailbox?" Penny asked, aghast. There was no other way Blair could have gotten them.

Blair ignored the question. "Why did you write this on here?" she bellowed, pointing to the line that read, "Your child is also getting a D in science."

Penny wondered why Blair had called a meeting about this rather than simply coming directly to her for a conversation. Most of the team's failure letters specified Blair's class. She was the harshest grader at Southern.

"How could you do that to Blair?" Wilma said. "You were horrible to write that on there."

Penny was perplexed. In all the time they had worked together, Penny had never been in Wilma's crosshairs. "What do you mean? I didn't do anything intentional. Our team wasn't coming up with a solution, so I asked another team and wrote what they wrote."

"You did? You just used their language?" Now Wilma was confused.

Blair exploded. "You are not as perfect as everyone thinks and one day your sins will catch up to you!" she yelled at Penny. "If you actually were a good person, maybe you wouldn't be getting divorced! And you know what else? Everybody thinks you're trash because you hang out with Ed all the time. Everybody thinks you're having an affair with him because you're trash!"

Some of the other teachers looked stunned. No one came to Penny's defense. Savannah smirked and shared a look with Vivian.

Penny knew Blair was mean, but for her grade leader to call her trash in front of the entire team, and to betray her after she'd shared her therapist, pierced her to the core.

"First, let me tell you about my divorce," Penny started.

Blair's voice dripped with sarcasm: "Ooh, I'm *so* sorry you're going through a divorce."

"I'm going through a hard time," Penny said, to explain her friendship with Ed. As much as she willed them not to, tears streamed down her face. "I'm at a difficult point in my life. I have very few friends—"

"If you weren't such a liar, maybe you'd actually *have* friends," Blair interrupted.

"You can't attack her," Celia said. "Please stop."

"Yeah, you stepped over the bounds," Wilma said. "I don't believe she intended to harm you."

"Do you understand that I lost all my friends when I left my husband?" Penny said, now openly bawling. "I lost everybody." *I'm a good person,* she thought. *Why do they hate me?*

"You think you're so perfect because your kids never have any behavior problems," Blair snarled.

Oh. That's why.

Later, the principal called Penny and Blair separately into her office. "You need to work it out between yourselves," she said.

"I did nothing wrong. I asked another team how they worded the letter and she got upset," Penny said.

"Well, you need to learn to trust your peers, because if you want to be in administration, you need to know how to manage people," the principal said. A district official had apparently told her that Penny had applied for a central office math resource instructor job.

The assistant principal added, "Penny, all I have to say is y'all need to learn to suck up the tears. You'd better get a stronger back than you've got."

After school, Penny went to Ed's room, where she wept as she recounted the story. "Blair's known for her outbursts, but your heart is pure, Penny. You are an amazing teacher and there's a lot of jealousy toward you because students adore you," he said.

"I'm sorry. I don't mean to cry," Penny said. "But it was just awful."

"You need to go to HR and file a complaint," Ed said, angry on her behalf.

"What good would that do?" Penny asked. Blair had been reported to Southern administrators before, but her behavior didn't change. "If I complain, central office will never hire me."

"It's workplace bullying. You could file a grievance against her," Ed said.

"No, that would just piss everyone off. You don't do things like that at our school. Southern has a reputation. They just cover everything up."

"Well, make sure you eat something. You need to take care of yourself," Ed said. He handed her an orange.

Penny told me later, "In the school system, you shut up and you don't become a whistleblower. That's why I'm telling you every bit of my story even though it hurts so bad. That made me feel like everything I worked toward for almost twenty years was worth nothing. I don't want another teacher to go through this, ever."

That night, Penny's phone dinged at 10 p.m. when she was in bed grading papers. "Look in your mailbox," Ed texted. Penny put on a robe and went outside. She pulled out a container of Frogmore stew, her favorite takeout dish. Ed had driven to a restaurant 45 minutes away just to pick up something he knew would cheer her.

At school Penny tried to avoid Blair and walked on eggshells when she couldn't. When she saw Blair's name on emails, Penny automatically felt nauseous, even if the emails had nothing to do with her. Penny was so distraught by the incident that, after consulting with her doctor, she started taking anti-anxiety medication. "I need something to get me through this school year," she told me. "I've read enough articles on workplace bullying to know that's what this is."

The "Dirty Little Secret" in Schools

When the high school bell rings, a group of slender, fashion-conscious young women race from their classrooms to grab seats at the prime lunch table. They plunk their bags on chairs to mark their territory before retrieving their lunches while one clique member remains at the table to ensure no "losers" join them. If people they don't like—peers who don't dress like they do, for example, or are socially awkward—try to enter their conversation, they ignore them, talk over them, or "look at them like, 'Why are you talking to us?'" said Ana, among the outcasts. "They'll be really rude. They pretend you don't exist, or they whisper about you or make sarcastic comments, and the others snicker like, 'Oh my god, she didn't even realize we were being obnoxious.'"

The scenario might be business as usual for students in a school cafeteria. Except that when it actually happened daily in New York, the dozen or so clique members were teachers in their late twenties, and the table was the only one in the staff lounge.

Expert Jo Blase, a University of Georgia research professor emerita, calls it "the terrible, dark, dirty little secret" of education: Clique hostilities and bullying among educators exist in schools, even at schools that spend money on programs to combat these behaviors among students, even when student anti-bullying posters line the halls. Nearly three-quarters of teachers report that they've observed workplace bullying. A 2019 study even reported that one year in Michigan, about the same percentage of surveyed K–12 staff were bullied by adults as K–12 students were bullied by peers.

Approximately a quarter of all calls to the Workplace Bullying Institute come from educators, second in frequency only to health-care professionals. In Europe, too, education is one of the fields with the highest frequency of workplace bullying, particularly verbal abuse. This behavior does not characterize the majority of educators, many of whom are drawn to teaching because they are compassionate, caring people. But there is something about being back in school buildings, surrounded by student social hierarchies, that seems to cause some adults to regress.

The American Federation of Teachers (AFT) defines workplace bullying as "repeated, unreasonable actions of individuals (or a group) directed toward an employee (or a group of employees), which are intended to intimidate, degrade, humiliate or undermine, or which create a risk to the health or safety of the employee(s)." Administrators and staff have engaged in a wide range of behaviors that fall under this umbrella, including socially isolating teachers from peers or communication loops; spreading rumors, false information, or malicious gossip; publicly humiliating coworkers in front of colleagues and/or students; setting colleagues up to fail; attempting to ruin a reputation, failing to correct false information, or making personal character attacks; unfairly criticizing; name-calling, yelling, and other forms of verbal abuse; showing favoritism or nepotism; making threats; administrators setting rules about the friends teachers can have and the clothes they wear; using physical violence; and other attempts to frustrate, wear down, pressure, or provoke a target. Bullying can also include eye-rolling, headshaking, and other rude gestures. Blair's treatment of Penny qualified as bullying. So did Nel's.

The Michigan study reported that 65% of teachers, paraprofessionals, and support staff were made to feel ignored or excluded, and 65% experienced a decline in performance because someone withheld information. Nearly half of participants were targets of rumors or gossip; 40% were humiliated, ridiculed, ignored, or faced hostility when approaching; and 40% were pressured not to use sick days or claim expenses. More than one-third of respondents were "the target of spontaneous anger" and a fifth of participants received hints or signals from others that they should quit.

The clique at the New York school, which Ana eventually left, gossiped viciously, used nasty nicknames for outsiders, spread untruths, and openly discussed parties and happy hours to which they invited only certain colleagues. "They talk about everyone behind their backs as soon as they walk out of the room," Ana said. "It's toxic."

Workplace bullying is toxic, which makes it all the more perplexing that while student bullying issues plaster the mainstream media, teacher bullying remains largely unaddressed. Bullying among educators is "extraordinarily destructive," Blase said. "Teachers feel trapped, angry, stressed, traumatized, guilty, and humiliated, and their self-esteem plummets." A small UK study found that 100% of the 39 surveyed bullied teachers became ill as a result, mostly with anxiety, stress, and depression. Symptoms included heart palpitations, raised blood pressure, uncontrollable shaking, frequent crying, drinking too much, and taking multiple medications. Teachers were so upset "they were crying in their cupboards, while still on the job. This was due to an atmosphere of fear within their schools, and the extreme nervousness and stress it created for them."

This atmosphere can affect students, too. An underperforming North Carolina elementary school hired Nora because her students at her previous school had exceeded the state's expected reading growth for the year. The three veteran teachers on the 2nd grade team, whose students had not met standards, targeted Nora and the other new 2nd grade teacher. They "had it out for us, making rude comments, lying about us in front of administrators to make us look bad, like saying we chose not to attend team meetings, when really they never told us about them," Nora said.

By the time the school held its midyear standardized reading assessment, the veterans knew that Nora's students were outperforming theirs. Nora said the group falsely bumped up their own students' scores and deliberately gave her and the other new teacher's students lower scores than they deserved, in at least one case testing a student on a more difficult level than she should have been tested. Nora was too intimidated to report them. Nervous about further retaliation, for many months Nora didn't even go to the computer lab when she needed to print something because walking past those teachers' rooms made her uncomfortable.

When we spoke, Nora wasn't sure if she would return to this school. "I know how good it can be in a good school. None of my teams have been perfect; you're not always going to like everyone or agree, and that's okay. But if this had been my first experience, I don't know that I would have stayed in teaching. It's disappointing. I'm too old for this. They're too old for this."

As Nora suggested, educator bullying may be driving teachers from the profession. National Institute for Occupational Safety and Health (NIOSH) research fellow Srinivas Konda found that staff who experienced at least one workplace bullying event in a school year were five times more likely to say they would probably leave the education field.

~∽~

Many researchers have concluded that principals are the most frequent workplace bullies in schools. In this situation, bullied teachers can have a difficult time finding allies. "They lack peer support, possibly more than in other professions, because teachers are afraid of being retaliated against if they help the victim out. So these people are left alone, which makes it worse," said Blase, who found that 70% to 80% of teachers had witnessed a principal bullying staff.

Meg, a music teacher at a Texas Catholic school, was repeatedly targeted by her principal, whose "MO was to turn people against each other." The principal allowed teachers to harass Meg for making a minor script change to the annual Christmas program. One teacher sent a mass email that "said I was conspiring against her and leading us all to hell," Meg recalled. "I tried to talk to the principal, get things sorted out, and she refused to speak with me." The teacher continued to spread rumors, leaving Meg feeling "completely isolated."

During a full-ensemble rehearsal, another teacher yelled at Meg in front of more than 200 students and staff. "She screamed that I didn't know what I was doing and said I was a terrible person. I had to keep it together to conduct my students and run the rest of the rehearsal with tears coming down my face. I was a wreck that entire week, I lost my voice, I had teachers yelling at me, teachers plotting against me, a batshit principal, a deacon on my ass, and I had to make this program work. My boyfriend and parents were stressed because of what I was going through. It was absolutely awful."

Ultimately, Meg's program went smoothly and parents were pleased. Although the principal and offending teachers left the school, Meg said, "what they did to me has not healed."

When the boss is a bully, the arsenal can expand to include giving teachers unfair evaluations, stealing their materials, chastising them unfairly, unilaterally transferring them, or excluding them from choice assignments. A New Jersey high school administration rewards only what a teacher calls its "boys club." They annually select the same teachers, often coaches, to chaperone prom, the senior trip, and graduation. "The division between those who are in the club and those who are out is always an underlying concern for many staff members," the teacher said.

Compared with other occupations, bullying may be worse in education because principals are "more direct in their bullying," Blase said. "That could be because of the power distance. Principals are not to be challenged. Bullying can be rewarded because districts think you're being a tough boss." She found that 77% of teachers who were bullied by their principal wanted to leave their job, 50% wanted to leave teaching altogether, and 50% "can't cope."

Jada, a Maryland elementary school teacher, experienced two of those effects during a school year that "was the worst and most emotionally trying time of my life." A principal targeted Jada after learning that she had a mental health challenge (one that didn't affect her teaching). The principal called Jada into her office weekly with unwarranted reprimands. She wrote Jada up for petty non-issues such as not seeking her out in her office to say hello, though when Jada greeted her in the hallway, the principal often ignored her. She fought against Jada's district-approved Americans with Disabilities Act accommodations. "She treated me in ways she didn't treat anyone else. I couldn't stand it emotionally. I was afraid of her because she had so much power over me. It made me sick, I cried all the time. I had never in my life doubted my ability to teach until then," said Jada, who had won national and local teaching awards.

Jada tried to file complaints, but the principal technically wasn't breaking contract rules. When she set up a mediation, the principal refused to call the mediation program back. And when Jada filed an administrative complaint, the principal denied it, blocking it from escalation to the community superintendent.

Suffering from anxiety, depression, and stomach problems, Jada said the emotional abuse led her to become suicidal. "It was relentless harassment. I felt trapped. I tried my hardest to leave, but she sabotaged me at every turn. Other principals told me she said negative things about me, that she didn't trust me, that I was unprofessional and hardheaded. I'm like, if you don't like me, let me go! She was in control and there was nothing I could do." Eventually, Jada returned to a previous school that appreciated her.

The mental health toll on bullied targets can be devastating. A Minnesota science teacher told me that a principal bullied her so mercilessly for a year that after she left the school she was treated for PTSD. Many of Blase's study subjects became clinically depressed when they were bullied at work. "People become suicidal for less than this kind of long-term, soul-crushing, career-annihilating, family-destroying abuse," Blase said.

How can these hostile climates pervade a profession known for its nurturing and selflessness? Education could be a hot spot for workplace bullying for a variety of reasons:

Oppression

Disrespect for teachers has deep roots, as discussed in chapter 4, and the profession has been marred by gender inequality. In 1892, influential education leader Joseph Mayer Rice declared, "The professional weakness of the American teacher is the greatest sore spot of the American schools . . . The truth is that as a rule our teachers are too weak to stand alone, and therefore need constantly to be propped up by the supervisory staff." He called for reforms that would "teacher-proof the schools," education reform historian Diana D'Amico Pawlewicz wrote in *The Washington Post*. "Rather than bolster teachers' expertise, autonomy and authority, the reforms subverted teachers' professional legitimacy by limiting their voice and placing teachers on the lowest rungs of a growing educational bureaucracy. In practice, teacher professionalization bolstered the bureaucratic order of schools—dominated by men—and hamstrung teachers. Standardized curriculums, high-stakes tests and teacher evaluation practices all emerged thanks to this warped conception of professionalization."

This legacy continues. Female educators earn less than male educators; in Illinois, they earn an average of nearly $8,000 per year less than men. More than three-quarters of K–12 public school teachers are women but 73% of superintendents are not. A midwestern teacher told me about a football coach who won Teacher of the Year even though he didn't teach a single class.

Brazilian educator and philosopher Paulo Freire theorized that when a dominant group forces its own values and norms upon a less influential group, the oppressed group develops low self-esteem and becomes angry and aggressive as it tries to internalize those standards. As group members are made to feel inferior, they begin to disdain their own culture. Because the oppressed group won't engage in violence against the more powerful dominators, its members turn on one another, dividing and infighting, sabotaging one another.

Some scholars contend that nurses are an oppressed population because of a history of dependence and submissiveness to mostly male physicians and administrators. I believe the same could be said about teachers, another female-dominated profession overseen mostly by males. Since the 1800s, supervisors, administrators, and/or government officials—many of them lacking classroom experience, most of them men—have dictated classroom requirements. Without control over their occupation and treated by supervisors as inferior, teachers took on the characteristics of an oppressed group. Many teachers feel their autonomy has severely declined over the last 30 years. It might not be coincidental that in many schools, workplace hostilities have risen during that time.

Overpowered by superintendents, school board members, district officials, administrators, and parents, many teachers grew to accept bullying as an inevitable part of the job. Because unleashing anger toward those powerful stakeholders could jeopardize educators' employment, they might redirect their frustration or fear through lateral violence against coworkers, for which there are few repercussions.

Stress

Research has shown that "workplaces with high levels of job insecurity, low levels of autonomy, and high workloads" correlate to higher levels of workplace bullying. As discussed previously, many teachers bear heavy workloads with a significant pay gap and are expected to cater to students, parents, administrators, and district officials with a smile. With lunch and prep periods often consumed by work and meetings, teachers aren't often afforded time during the workday to take a walk or compose themselves. A whopping 93% of teachers reported high stress levels in a pre-pandemic study of midwestern elementary school teachers. When some educators are stressed, they might become hostile toward the people they most frequently encounter during the workday: other educators

Competition

In a race for statistical success, fueled by skewed, misleading magazine rankings and narrow-minded government mandates, school officials have fostered a hypercompetitive culture based on test scores. During a movement that began in the 2000s, officials created a climate of fear regulated by those scores; teachers could be fired if their students didn't perform well on standardized tests. That zeal to "factorize" teaching represented "a fundamental disrespect for the profession. That kind of hate and polarization is ready-made for bullying. It undermines teachers and it creates this [notion] that they need to be sanctioned and penalized in order to do their job. It's a poisonous atmosphere," said AFT president Randi Weingarten.

The Teachers

The use of testing data as the ultimate indicator of a school's success has been a "destructive game changer" that has deteriorated teacher collegiality, said Tia, a South Carolina school librarian. When she first taught in the 1990s, she had fewer high-level administrators and high-stakes tests. "There might have been some cliques, but mostly we treated each other kindly and felt like a cohesive, mutually supportive group. We could encourage and commiserate comfortably with each other."

When Tia moved schools, all of her new coworkers stopped by the library to warmly welcome her to the team, and teachers included everyone in the staff lounge at lunch. But that changed in the mid-2000s. As testing elevated their stress levels, Tia said, teachers' schedules became so overloaded that they ate lunch by themselves in their classrooms, catching up on work. "Today's climate has eroded the support system that used to help me through the day. It's been years since I got together with other teachers for lunch. Anything we learn about each other is usually during a quick distracted hallway encounter. Teachers are denied opportunities to spend time together during the day. There's a sense of mistrust and paranoia instead of the camaraderie that once made our difficult professions less stressful and more creative, energizing, and gratifying."

Teachers also may be pitted against one another in competition for plum assignments or resources. K–12 education has an "increased emphasis on interpersonal relationships with colleagues and superiors," Konda observed. "The evaluation of the quality of an educator's work, along with that the potential for promotion or other rewards, depends upon exerting influence in interpersonal relationships with colleagues and supervisors to improve one's own position."

At the same time, teachers report a decline in opportunities to collaborate. Even teacher workdays, which, according to *Education Week*, "were originally created to allow teachers and support staff to prepare for classroom work directly related to students and centered around curriculum," no longer necessarily feature planning with peers. These cooperative opportunities "have been replaced by district trainers administering generic professional development."

Because of the rise of competitiveness and reduction of collaboration, the teachers most likely to be bullied are "the best and brightest. It's the stars," Blase said. They are, like Penny, team players and rule followers. Teachers "have a strong prosocial, do-gooder, humanistic orientation," said Workplace Bullying Institute director Gary Namie. "They're always for the underdog and they're altruistic. So they make for a ready pool of easily exploited targets."

~☞~

What can bullied educators do? Most bullied teachers do not receive an acceptable response from administrators when they report the behavior, studies show. Often, bullied teachers don't speak up, because they're afraid for their jobs. This could explain why scant research exists on teacher bullying, and why the behavior is under reported. Unless victims are in a protected class, such as if they are whistleblowers or are experiencing racial or sexual harassment, experts said there's little a teacher can do to seek redress. "We are behind much of the rest of the world in fashioning protections against this form of workplace abuse," said David Yamada, director of the New Workplace Institute at Suffolk University Law School.

NEA literature on workplace bullying suggests, if all else fails, "Consider requesting a transfer to another school instead of risking your health." Before taking that step, former NEA president Lily Eskelsen Garcia suggested teachers report the behavior to their union representative; if they aren't represented, they can still utilize NEA and AFT resources. "The worst thing is to feel so vulnerable and afraid because you're being bullied, you take it to the person you think will help, and they ignore you or tell you to ignore the problem. When you ignore bullying, it ramps up. You have to put an end to it and you have to call the bully out so they can no longer hide behind 'I'm just kidding around,'" Garcia said.

Schools and districts must create a safe, supportive culture, with strict anti-bullying policies and enforcement plans, risk-free ways to report incidents, predetermined specific consequences for perpetrators, whether administrators or staff, and strategies to address bully-victim relationships to prevent future mistreatment. Administrators also should receive training to prevent and resolve workplace bullying.

Many bullied teachers stay the course, for some of the same reasons that make them targets in the first place. "Teachers in general are very kind. They love those kids," said Karen Horwitz, a former teacher who founded the National Association for Prevention of Teacher Abuse. "They're so traumatized by this, but they stay because they want to give these kids a chance."

That's why Meg, who strongly considered leaving her school, ultimately decided to stay. "The students believed in me," she said. "Bitches be crazy, but the kids are awesome."

Miguel Garcia   Middle School Special Ed Teacher

The days following Winter Break were tough for many kids, but special ed students especially had to be reminded of routines, and children who were food insecure could experience behavioral spikes. Miguel desperately needed an assistant, but the district still wouldn't budge. Dewayne was even more challenging than before. His gen ed teachers were now telling Miguel that Dewayne shouldn't be in their classes. Miguel timed Dewayne on several occasions: His attention span was down to three seconds.

Eli, however, was making great strides. During a book discussion, Miguel mentioned that the class would read the final chapter the next day.

"I already read it," Eli said.

"Really? What did you think?"

"The ending almost made me cry. It was really beautiful."

"Why do you think the son didn't want his father around after his sister died?"

"He was unworthy of being allowed to grieve when he was never a present father when she was alive. He abandoned them and all he did was drink. Hey, he's just like my dad, haha," Eli said.

"Unworthy. That's a really good word." Miguel tallied a point on the board next to Eli's name for using sophisticated vocabulary.

The next day, Eli came to school late, in the middle of second period. He seemed harried, but Miguel noticed he exhibited none of the "Ugh, I have to be at school" body language that accompanied his arrivals in August. Instead, Eli quickly put away his things, stacked his folder in the bin, and proudly showed Miguel his completed homework. He now did his homework every day. He hadn't once bolted from Miguel's class.

Miguel smiled at him. "You know, your IEP meeting is Thursday. I have a lot of good things to tell your mom."

Eli grinned as he quietly took his seat.

Miguel was looking forward to the meeting. Eli's mother's attitude had come a long way since her initial defensive stance. She'd written in the planner, "I've never seen him get these grades before." Formerly a D student, he was pulling straight Bs this quarter. Miguel was excited to celebrate her son's progress with her and to show her Eli's impressive collection of good work.

Miguel often told his student teachers and mentees, "When you call home, always start with a positive. Don't be the bearer of bad news." Miguel had made a practice of occasionally calling parents when he had only good things to say; he'd left a few such voicemails for Eli's mom.

Thursday morning, Eli didn't come to school. *Maybe his mom's bringing him with her for the IEP*, Miguel thought. But at the appointed time, neither Eli nor his mother showed up. Miguel and the other team members waiting around the office table looked at the assistant principal, who shrugged. "Well, I guess we should call her."

"Hello?" Her voice sounded slurred on the speakerphone.

"Hi, we're just checking in. We have Eli's IEP now. We can do a phone meeting if you'd like."

"Uh, I'm on allergy medicine. I have really bad allergies." Eli's mom sounded loopy.

The meeting proceeded over the phone. "His attendance is much better," Miguel said.

"He gives me no issues about coming to school," his mother said, sounding distracted.

"That's great! I'm really pleased to say he's working well in groups with other kids. His strength is reading. He's participating a lot. He's doing his homework. His challenges are: We want to work a little bit on fluency and comprehension skills. His main issue is writing. So his major IEP goals are for writing, punctuation, and spelling; and for math, order of operations. I'm really happy with his progress."

"Huh."

Miguel was disappointed by her apathy. As he listed additional positives, he wondered if she was depressed. After Miguel's mother had gotten sick, everyone in his family had been depressed for a time. Heck, Miguel worried that his job conditions were causing him to be depressed now. *Maybe it isn't an allergic reaction*, he thought. *She's probably really stressed. Maybe she couldn't get out of bed this morning.* Everyone struggled with something that others couldn't see.

The next morning, Eli was at school on time. "Hey, we had a meeting scheduled with your mom . . ." Miguel began.

Eli shrugged. "Yeah, she had this allergic reaction and couldn't come in."

"I told her all the good things you're doing," Miguel said.

"Okay." Eli seemed off.

"What's wrong?"

"I'm not real happy because I can't go to the park anymore."

"Why not?"

"I don't want to talk about it."

Miguel never learned what actually happened to Eli the day of the IEP.

CHAPTER 7

February

A New York 4th grade teacher: "I emailed my principal to let him know I was going to the hospital in labor. He called me about something six hours later, while I was in the labor and delivery room."

A father to a Missouri public school teacher: "I pay your salary and I can get you fired."

A science department chair to a Maryland high school teacher who was in tears because of overwork: "Stress is good for you."

Penny Davis   6th Grade Math Teacher

In Penny's class, Zach was now comfortably whispering to other kids to tell Penny tidbits about his day. From what Penny heard around school, he acted out in classes with teachers who didn't empathize with him. Blair and Wilma, who refused to communicate with Zach in alternative ways, continued to argue that he shouldn't be in their classes and that "his mother should just punish him until he talks." In classes with teachers who connected with Zach, like Penny and the art teacher, he behaved.

He did not, apparently, connect with the lunchroom monitors.

Penny was surprised to hear from the assistant principal one February afternoon that Zach had instigated a major food fight. (Penny's first reaction: "Ohh crap. It's grape day.") Although a dozen students and a lunchroom monitor saw Zach start the fight, he denied involvement.

That evening, Zach's mom emailed Penny that Zach's story had changed after school. He did start the food fight, yes, but only because students at his table had goaded him into it, teasing him that he wasn't "brave enough" to throw food. "He wanted to be cool," his mom explained. "When the other kids egged him on, he felt like he had to do it. The whole thing is really upsetting him."

Administrators gave Zach in-school suspension and lectured the students at his lunch table. As Zach's classmates turned on him in retaliation, he became more subdued.

Penny, too, was backsliding. Because there were so few substitutes, administrators kept assigning Penny and other teachers to cover colleagues' classes during their lunch and planning periods and to combine classes with their own, doubling their student numbers. Earlier in the week, administrators had pushed Penny to come to school when she had a fever because Southern couldn't find enough coverage for staff. Meanwhile, Penny had been determined to "put my personal life, my grad school life, and my school life in three separate windows that don't affect the others," but the lines kept bleeding into one another. She couldn't compartmentalize her emotions. And she dreaded seeing Blair; in any given interaction, she didn't know if Blair was going to blow up again.

After several hours at school for the student Talent Show, Penny was getting ready for bed when she got a text from Kent: "Heard you spent the whole night in Ed's classroom."

Penny dropped her phone as if it had burned her. When she recovered, she texted, "What the heck are you talking about? Ed wasn't even there!" Ed was at home, taking care of his daughter, who was sick. Penny had spent the evening in the audience, cheering for students.

"All I know is someone called me and said you were in there all night," Kent said.

Penny was unsettled. Either Kent was lying or someone at school had seen her at Talent Show and twisted the reporting on her where-abouts. Worse, with Ed on Kent's radar, her spousal support could be jeopardized if Kent claimed she was unfaithful before they were officially divorced. She texted Ed.

"Someone told Ellen the same thing," he replied.

Penny didn't know what to do.

The next day, the intercom beeped before school. "Ms. Davis, please report to my office," the principal said. Penny, who never once got in trouble as a student, still felt tremors of anxiety when as a teacher she was summoned to the principal's office. The principal asked several questions about the district office position Penny had applied for. "Do you know yet if they're going to give it to you?" the principal asked.

That's weird. If I'd heard, she knows I'd tell her, Penny thought. "You'd know better than me."

"I'm just asking because I have a teacher I want to put in your place just as soon as I know," the principal said. Every staff member the principal had handpicked for Southern was her personal friend.

Penny felt like she'd been gut-punched. Parents and students often requested her, and her classes consistently got top scores, yet the principal was eager to push her out the door.

"I'll just make a phone call and see what I can find out," the principal said.

Penny recognized now that for her mental health, she had to leave Southern if given the opportunity. She was passionate about doing as much as she could to advance the math curriculum and her own growth as a teacher, both of which she could accomplish in the district office job. The raise would be significant, too, at a time when Penny desperately needed to better supplement her teacher's salary. But she loved her students and many of the parents in her hometown. She didn't want to leave her new work best friend; although she'd known him for only six months, Ed had already had a strong, positive effect on her life and added an extra lift to her workday. Likely, she wouldn't have to make the call to leave. Hundreds of teachers had applied for the position. What were her chances?

Penny was already having a tough week. Between her divorce and the workplace bullying, she felt like shutting down. She wondered if this perhaps was not the best time for her to earn an advanced degree. *How will I support the boys on this salary? How will I pay for college in two years? Why did I think I could handle grad school on top of everything else going on right now? Maybe I should quit grad school.* She still tutored and worked extra jobs. She stayed up late most nights to do her grad school work. She took no shortcuts; she read every word of every assigned text. One assignment in particular paralyzed her: a semester-long 100-page paper for which she'd have to design extra lesson plans, create innovative class activities, and evaluate her students' responses

Penny was daunted by the breadth of the research and classwork the paper was supposed to cover. She'd have to teach the extra material required for her project and also meet district requirements for the unit's testing and pacing. Because of the timing, her research with her students would have to cover proportional reasoning, a unit students usually struggled with.

Meanwhile, Penny's physical health declined. Even after a round of antibiotics, her cough persisted. When she saw her ENT, he prescribed steroids and extra breathing treatments on top of a new course of antibiotics.

"This is unusual, though," he said, flipping through her file. "Tests from five years ago indicated that you're highly allergic to mold. Is it possible there might be mold in your home or workplace?"

"There is so much mold on my classroom wall and ceiling that when the roof leaked during a downpour, I could have showered in the mold. But the school won't do anything."

The doctor suggested that if she regularly sprayed the mold with Clorox, it might subside, as would, he suspected, her symptoms. Penny agreed to give it a try.

After a lunchtime meeting at the high school about one of their sons, Kent informed Penny that he could take some of her retirement and pension benefits from her in the divorce.

Penny was still in tears when she returned to Southern. As she hurried down the hall to her classroom, she passed Ed's room. "Hey, can you come to my room in a minute?" she asked. He took one look at her face and nodded.

Penny broke down in her room as she told Ed what had happened. "It's hard enough to be married to him, but now he wants to take everything? He's not even paying child support! What am I going to do?"

"This isn't right," Ed said, hugging her as she cried on his shoulder.

Then—footsteps. Penny and Ed looked up from their embrace to see the instructional technology specialist enter the room. They jumped apart.

"I was just trying to cheer her up," Ed said.

The guy shrugged. "I'm here to fix your Promethean board?"

"Yes, thank you," Penny said.

Less than an hour later, Savannah, Blair, and Vivian were huddled next to Savannah's doorway, whispering and sneaking sideglances at Penny.

Miguel Garcia   Middle School Special Ed Teacher

Miguel felt like he was shouldering too many responsibilities. In late February, two new students joined his second video class, although Miguel had told administrators not to add kids to that already difficult group.

Miguel had two big IEP meetings this week, which entailed a large amount of paperwork. He'd been working through lunch and prepping for classes and IEPs until he collapsed at night. He barely had time to eat, subsisted mostly on coffee, and had trouble sleeping. Meanwhile, he had to administer endless assessments and he worried about his daughter, as well as his widowed father living alone across the country. He caught himself snapping too often at his students. He loathed how his stress and, he feared, possible depression were affecting the people he loved. When he saw Jim and his daughter at home, he was often too preoccupied with work to give them his full attention.

"And for what?" he asked Jim. "So it all starts over again next year? It's like this treadmill of crisis after crisis. I don't want to live this way anymore. If I could have a job where I could disconnect when I'm done, that would be perfect." Maybe he could go into educational consulting, he thought, or ed tech.

Jim listened, supportive and loving as always.

"Dewayne alone is so draining to deal with now without the other jobs I have," Miguel continued. Miguel also had a new weekly high school intern, another variable he had to manage. "At the end of the day, I'm dealing with not just one but sixteen kids with special needs, a lot of them with behavior issues. And simultaneously dealing with additional classes, being a mentor, and planning lessons. Geez, I could be making a lot more money for doing less. The stuff that made me feel like teaching was worth it isn't there anymore."

"You're working too hard and you're making other people look good. You have to speak up because this is going to make you sick," Jim said. "When you don't speak up, everyone assumes you're fine with it and they pile on more and more."

"You're right," Miguel said.

That night, Miguel contacted a former colleague who was looking for a job. "I get these pangs sometimes where I feel sad about leaving my special ed students. I've gotten very attached to them," he told her. "You've got to apply because I'm not doing this job next year. I'll give you everything. You can just walk into my classroom and you'll have nothing to buy. I'll give you all you need to know about the kids."

She said she'd consider it.

During math the next day, as Miguel reviewed the homework, he noticed that Dewayne didn't touch his paper.

"I don't wanna do this," Dewayne complained.

The intercom clicked on: "Mr. Garcia, can you please send Gabe to pick up something in the office?" Miguel sent Gabe downstairs.

"I really don't wanna do this," Dewayne said again.

"Can you please make sure he finishes this? He hasn't done any homework in a month," Miguel asked the intern.

As Miguel returned to the lesson, the intercom buzzed again. "Mr. Garcia? Please tell Kavon his mom will pick him up, so he shouldn't get on the bus."

Dewayne took advantage of the interruption to complain about the intern: "Why is she bothering me? Why is she always shadowing me? Why is she always breathing down my neck? This isn't fair. Why—"

"ENOUGH!" Miguel bellowed, slamming his hand on a table. "Look, you know what? I'm not going to deal with this. You're going downstairs, bye. You can go to the office."

"What?" This was a first.

"You can go now."

Dewayne slowly, warily left the room.

After a while, Frank walked him back to the classroom.

"Here's your homework," Miguel said to Dewayne.

"I didn't bring my bag."

"Put it in your pocket."

"Mr. Garcia," the intercom interrupted again, "can you also remind Dewayne not to get on the bus today?"

Miguel had a pounding headache. He kept losing his train of thought. *Everything is stacked against teachers to not let you do your job properly,* he thought.

"Okay, you know what? Everyone just finish what you're doing. You can get your computers and do math games," he said, and he immediately disliked himself for being a teacher who stuck kids on the computer for convenience. *I just can't do this anymore. I can't function. I've always said when I turn into that teacher, it's time to go. It is clear I'm there now.*

When Miguel left the classroom at the end of the day, he was dismayed to spot Dewayne's homework on the floor. On his way out, he coincidentally saw Dewayne's mother talking to another teacher. He ran back to his room to retrieve the homework.

As Miguel told Dewayne's mother why he had to throw Dewayne out of class, Dewayne tried to argue with him. She saw what Miguel wanted her to see.

"Can I get your email please?" Miguel asked. "Let's communicate by email every day because he's consistently not bringing stuff home."

Latrice, a new teacher Miguel mentored, whom he'd asked to set up appointments with him rather than corral him at school, rushed over. "Hi, can I talk to you? I just can't—"

"I'm sorry," Miguel interrupted. His headache flared. "I can't talk to you right now." He felt guilty; his mentee was lovely. Miguel was unhappy with the person he'd become. Demoralized, he went to Frank's office and closed the door.

"Frank, I'm miserable. I feel like I'm depressed. I'm not getting a lot of sleep. I feel like I'm always in crisis mode. This is nothing against you, but everything from the district, parents, and students—it's like, 'This needs to be done yesterday.' I'm doing several jobs and it's just too much. I'm neglecting my dad, who's alone across the country. I'm neglecting my child on her days at home with me. Why am I doing this, missing my kid growing up?"

"I know you've had a rough year. Your mom died just before school started," Frank said.

"I don't think I've processed it yet. And I always promised myself when I stopped caring, it's time for me to go. Every teacher I know is sacrificing time with their family. People don't understand how stressful it is."

"I understand. I'm so sorry."

"Taking on that sixth class was a mistake. I bit off more than I can chew," Miguel said. "I can't do this anymore. For teachers to do their job well now, you have to not have anything or anyone else in your life. It's like that's what districts want, that's the only way to be in education. I feel like all the joy is gone, Frank. I'm snapping at people; I feel like a grouch. I think my personality's changing. I'm seriously thinking of leaving teaching."

"You're getting a teaching award," Frank responded.

"What?"

"I'm not supposed to tell you, but you won the county's Excellence in Teaching Award. It comes with a small cash prize and a local news segment. People were wondering why the school was getting painted. That's why."

"The day I decided I'm done with teaching?"

"Isn't that funny how life works."

"Wow. Okay, well, thank you. I don't feel like a very good teacher. I feel like I'm doing three jobs and none of them very well."

"Don't be hard on yourself. Your halfway-good job is equivalent to other people's full effort."

"That's very nice, thank you." Miguel felt guilty again. "Can you give my second video class a sub one day a week? Because Latrice just asked me for help and I didn't have time. I can't mentor the teachers I'm supposed to because I can't do my job. If someone covers the class, that will give me time to do observations of the teachers I mentor, the other job I promised to do."

"Absolutely."

"Classroom Contagion": The Myth of Teacher Burnout

Prisha was a special ed English teacher at a low-income Illinois high school where 25% of the students had special needs. When her co teacher had to take medical leave for two months, her school refused to provide coverage, leaving Prisha by herself to manage classes of 28 to 35 special ed students.

With a high teacher turnover rate, the school's staff was mostly first- or second-year teachers who, like Prisha, didn't know what to do when, for example, the principal screamed at special ed teachers that they were "fucking morons." She told me, "Instead of provid ing support, the administration began monitoring my grade book, sending weekly screenshots of how I didn't include enough grades or there were too many of a certain grade. I was so stressed that I started experiencing chest pains and thought I might be having a heart attack."

Teachers' occupational stress had been on the rise long before the COVID pandemic began; in Gallup polls, teachers tied with nurses for the highest rate of daily stress on the job among all occupations. Historically, teachers' rates of "job strain," a strong measure of stress referring to high demand/low control work, are higher than the average rate of all workers. In 2021, nearly 80% of teachers reported experiencing frequent job-related stress, compared to 40% of employed adults. Globally, a UK study reported that teachers are among the workers "with the highest levels of job stress and burnout on the job."

"Burnout" is a buzzword the media often uses to describe stress, depression, exhaustion, and overwork. Teacher burnout, specifically, is a popular umbrella term. In fact, both of *Merriam-Webster Dictionary*'s featured contextual examples of burnout are about teachers: "Teaching can be very stressful, and many teachers eventually suffer *burnout*" and "the *burnout* rate among teachers." Experts say that burnout is one of the top reasons teachers leave the profession early.

Social psychologists define burnout more specifically as a syndrome consisting of three dimensions: emotional exhaustion, depersonalization (disconnection from or cynicism toward the workplace and colleagues), and diminished feelings of workplace accomplishment. According to the *International Journal of Occupational Medicine and Environmental Health*, "It is confirmed that teachers have the highest burnout levels as compared to other professionals in social services."

"Teacher burnout is a huge problem. Many of us put the burden of all our students on ourselves and take full credit for every failure, but little credit for their success," said Naomi, a Virginia 3rd grade teacher. "Teachers struggle with anxiety and end up leaving the profession. Those of us who stay have coping strategies: setting boundaries, exercise, hobbies. But even when we aren't working, we carry our work with us in our hearts and minds."

Experts have identified several causes of teacher burnout, including inadequate workplace support and resources, unmanageable workload, high-stakes testing, time pressure, unsupported disruptive students, lack of cooperative time with colleagues, and a wide variety of student needs without the resources to meet those needs, most of which describe Miguel's situation. An *Educational Psychology Review* article summarized, "Teacher burnout results from the unbalance between teaching demands (e.g., problematic student behaviors, administrative demands) and teaching resources (e.g., school support personnel, the existence of instructional materials)."

Many teachers described similar conditions. A California private school math teacher explained, "My time card says I'm only allotted eight hours a day, but I spend anywhere from nine to twelve hours at school daily. This itself is exhausting, not including the emotional wear and tear from students' behaviors." A Michigan public school English teacher said, "Teachers are overworked, and it gets worse every year. Every fall we hear, 'This year we need you to do more with less,' but we're past the breaking point. What kind of business would follow this model year after year and expect to increase performance levels?"

Because teacher burnout is often associated with individuals' mental health, both Penny in February and Rebecca in October wondered whether what they called their burnout was caused by their self-perceived perfectionism and, therefore, their "fault." But a study examining links between burnout and perfectionism found that only certain aspects of perfectionism are associated with teacher burnout. Teachers who personally strive for perfection by setting high standards or who perceive pressure from coworkers to achieve excellence are not more prone to burnout. Teachers who feel pressured by students' parents to be perfect and/or who are overly worried about imperfection, however, are more likely to burn out. The researchers found a close relationship between negative reactions to imperfection and emotional exhaustion. This link, they said, "is particularly noteworthy because emotional exhaustion has been shown to be the component of burnout that predicts teachers' intention to quit the teaching profession."

That's what happened to Naomi, the Virginia teacher. She loved her students but felt she didn't have the necessary support to meet parents' and her district's surging unattainable expectations, particularly for students with severe behavioral issues. The overambitious curriculum didn't give teachers enough time to include all the lessons they were supposed to teach at the appropriate level of depth. "I felt overwhelmed by the expectations of student success. I've always taken the expectations of others very seriously. I constantly felt I wasn't good enough. I had moments where I would look at the students' scores on their latest test and just break down crying. The negative self-talk and feelings of inadequacy got worse; I lost my joy. I was emotionally and physically exhausted. I rarely get sick, but in one year I had the flu, a stomach bug, strep throat, and shingles. The stress was taking a toll on me," Naomi said. She began looking for other jobs.

Coverage of teacher stress and burnout often emphasizes the negative effects of teachers' stress on students. Various studies have associated teacher burnout with students' decreased social and academic adjustment and academic achievement. Pennsylvania State University researchers described a "burnout cascade" with "devastating effects on classroom relationships, management, and climate," in which burned-out teachers become emotionally exhausted, can't manage "troublesome student behaviors," and quit. Or, the researchers claimed, teachers cope "by maintaining a rigid classroom climate enforced by hostile and sometimes harsh measures bitterly working at a suboptimal level of performance until retirement." Authors of a 2020 study concluded that, "as hypothesized," students viewed teachers reporting higher levels of burnout as "significantly less socially and emotionally competent."

February

As I read those examples of teacher burnout literature, I was dogged by an unsettled feeling that something had been mischaracterized. While researchers seemed sympathetic to the plight of burned-out teachers, their conclusions sometimes portrayed these professionals in a way that I found vaguely disconcerting. Then I read two relatively splashy studies that crystallized what bothered me. A 2020 Belgian study warned of "burnout contagion," in which teachers can catch burnout from colleagues. The researchers concluded that because teachers in close coworker relationships exhibited similar levels of burnout, their study "indeed demonstrated that burnout is—to some extent—contagious."

In another paper, University of British Columbia researchers said that teachers experiencing higher burnout levels had students with higher morning cortisol levels. They called this transference "stress contagion." "It is possible that spending most of the school day in interaction with a stressed and burned out teacher is taxing for students and can affect their physiological stress profile," they wrote. The resulting media headlines further sensationalized the issue. A *Quartz* article, titled "Classroom Contagion: Stress in the Classroom Can Be as Contagious as the Flu," discussed "stressed teachers propagating at-risk students by 'infecting' them with elevated cortisol." *Time* magazine's coverage announced, "Stress Is Contagious in the Classroom," but didn't mention that the study authors also briefly allowed for the possibility that higher student cortisol levels might indicate a challenging working environment for teachers and "teachers of those classrooms might therefore have more troubling interactions with students, experience more occupational stress, and consequently experience higher rates of burnout." Namely, the students may have stressed out the teachers, rather than the other way around.

What the headlines ignored seemed to me to be the most plausible explanation: Burned-out teachers weren't directly causing student stress. School conditions were stressing out both teachers and students, and the teachers were being blamed.

Instead, the takeaways depicted teacher burnout as a contagion that brought down coworkers and students, with teachers as the disease vectors. Rather than address the root causes stressing out teachers in the first place—insufficient classroom resources and administrative support; not enough teaching assistants; lack of decision-making input; unpaid overtime; too much high-stakes testing; and lack of disciplinary and other policy enforcement, thereby undermining teachers' authority, all of which make a teacher's job harder and a student's experience worse—the messages scapegoated educators who are put in the impossible position of being ordered to meet shifting and expanding expectations by districts that don't give them the tools necessary to do so. Burned-out teachers aren't "significantly less socially and emotionally competent." They're handicapped by lousy school systems, ignorant officials, or out-of-touch administrators.

While reading the 2020 burnout contagion study, I kept wondering whether the teachers in those close workplace relationships could have similar levels of burnout because they dealt with the same unsupportive environmental factors causing their jobs to be more difficult. Sure enough, at the end of that paper, the authors acknowledged that "some interaction partners, who have stronger ties, have similar levels of burnout due to comparable contextual demands"—a point that could negate the paper's argument that teachers contaminate one another with burnout.

I asked the authors of the stress contagion study whether they tested the same students' cortisol levels with a control teacher who was not, as they put it, "stressed and burned out." The authors said they did not. Without studying those students in that classroom with a different teacher who was not burned out, researchers can't plausibly suggest that teachers generate a contagion. The cortisol levels could be a similar reaction to a poor work and learning environment caused by school conditions, students' group dynamics, or even one disruptive student.

⁓

What if the premise of teacher burnout is a myth, a convenient fiction that blames teachers for not being able to cope rather than faulting school systems that set both teachers and students up to fail? Instead of presenting the problem as "teachers have the highest burnout levels," we should reframe the issue: "School systems are the employers worst at providing necessary supports and resources for employees."

This line of thinking isn't meant to diminish educators' very real and thoroughly justified feelings of helplessness, stress, sadness, anxiety, frustration, and exhaustion. But let's shift blame to where blame is due.

For decades, teaching was considered a profession that was compatible with family life because teachers' working hours theoretically coincided with their children's school hours. But teaching is no longer that kind of job. Experts point to the seminal 1983 Department of Education report *A Nation at Risk* as the catalyst for that change and others. The report sparked an education "reform" movement based on an assertion (later proven wrong) that U.S. students' academic performance was sinking and that educators weren't properly trained to teach the curricula. Expectations of teachers rose dramatically in the following years, adding management of high-stakes tests, new pedagogical practices, curriculum development, and other responsibilities. However, most schools didn't incorporate these duties into the regular workday, leading teachers to work extra unpaid hours, and as teachers' work increased, their relative pay comparable to other professions dropped. By the early 2000s, researchers were reporting that the drastic expansion of teachers' responsibilities often wasn't accompanied by the structural support teachers needed to execute them. But teachers strove to meet these new obligations anyway, though their overwork led to stress and exhaustion.

Why did teachers put up with such a monumental uncompensated job shift? UC Santa Cruz education professor Lora Bartlett posited in 2004 that teachers internalized the new unrealistic professional standards. She attributed their acceptance to "1) teachers' equation of the expanded role with good teaching practice; 2) the moral imperative of teaching; and 3) the desire to live up to the expectations held by themselves and their colleagues."

Another major change in the teaching profession was the push for high-stakes state-mandated testing, which escalated in 2002, when No Child Left Behind became federal law. NCLB, which mandated rigorous standardized testing and penalized schools and teachers based on students' scores, remains "the worst federal education legislation ever passed by Congress. It was punitive, harsh, stupid, ignorant about pedagogy and motivation, and ultimately a dismal failure," as New York University research professor of education Diane Ravitch, a former assistant secretary of education and leading educational expert, has written.

Race to the Top, a federal competitive grant program that began in 2009, relied even more heavily on test scores to evaluate individual teachers. As a result, teachers' job security in many districts hinged on students' performance on specific tests on specific days, without regard for students' circumstances, such as whether they recently experienced a trauma, or were well-fed, homeless, supported by involved parents, or frequently absent. The program failed: The test scores did not rise.

By 2015, the average large city public school student was required to take 112 standardized tests, about eight per year, between prekindergarten and high school graduation. The Every Student Succeeds Act (ESSA), a new law that replaced NCLB in 2015, somewhat reduced punitive consequences of test scores, said Bob Schaeffer, executive director of FairTest, the National Center for Fair and Open Testing. But ESSA "did nothing to reduce the number of federally mandated tests." ESSA continued to require annual testing of every 3rd to 8th grade student, "a practice not found in any high-performing nation in the world," Ravitch wrote in her enlightening book *Slaying Goliath: The Passionate Resistance to Privatization and the Fight to Save America's Public Schools.*

Most states have eliminated at least high school exit exams, but students are still overtested and teachers are still criticized when their scores are subpar. "The unrelenting focus on standardized testing ignores all the other ways we can measure student progress and academic achievement and hampers the use of valuable teaching methods like project-based learning," AFT president Randi Weingarten said. "Our current system of accountability relies heavily—almost exclusively—on standardized exams, particularly in math and English language arts."

An elementary school ESOL teacher told me that the year before the pandemic, she spent 21 weeks of a 40-week school year administering state-required assessments to ESOL students, "tests whose individual sections took much longer than a child should ever have to sit for at one time, that were not necessarily aligned to curriculum, and that did not reflect what the students actually knew."

While the pandemic pause on testing should have been an opportunity for districts to rethink assessment policies, most states resumed their pre-pandemic testing practices, Schaeffer said. "The testing's had a very negative effect. It downgrades teachers professionally to, in the worst cases, leaders of test prep centers where the curriculum is defined as getting kids ready to pass the state testing requirements."

The emphasis on testing is another reason teachers can become so stressed that they leave the field. Callie, a Kentucky 5th grade teacher, worked in a socioeconomically depressed district where the superintendent humiliated teachers whose students didn't achieve the testing goal that teachers were required to set during the summer before they even met their class. The district, which Callie said frequently gave teachers professional development sessions with "passive-aggressive pushes about how to raise test scores," encouraged teachers to drill students constantly on questions similar to those on the tests.

The year after Callie's class scored one of the highest test averages in the district, she was assigned a class consisting mostly of at-risk children, who were dealing with abuse or neglect at home, demonstrated behavioral challenges, had family members with drug issues, were homeless, or whose parents had died or were absent from their lives. Her students came to school so hungry that Callie regularly bought food to stuff into their backpacks when they were on the playground. Near the end of the year, despite taking anti-anxiety medication, Callie felt so much pressure to raise their test scores that "I would shake violently, get physically sick to my stomach, sweat, cry. I'd have to get someone to watch my class because I'd go to the lounge, sometimes vomit, and try to get myself together. I couldn't sleep because I was ruminating over what I could do to get those test scores up," she said.

When her class's test results were released, her principal admonished her for the drop in scores compared to her prior year. Soon afterward, she said, "I had a nervous breakdown at school from the testing pressure," and a week later, she quit teaching. "I dearly loved the kids. Their success in life was my mission. I just caved under the pressure. It was very demoralizing," she said.

Callie's word choice—"demoralizing"—is important, and right on point. Teachers do not have characteristics that make them more prone to burnout than other workers. Penny was crushed because she was bullied by colleagues and dismissed by administrators. Rebecca was exhausted and Miguel was depressed because they weren't provided with the time, resources, or staffing to meet the diverse needs of their students. All of these factors were out of their control and not their fault.

In the end, is "burnout" actually the wrong term? After studying teacher dissatisfaction and attrition for almost 15 years, Bowdoin College education professor Doris Santoro determined that "teacher burnout" was an inaccurate diagnosis that only led school leaders to tell teachers they needed to learn how to relax. "It is the term most commonly used to refer to teachers who appear unhappy in their jobs, say they've considered quitting, or seem resistant to adopt the latest reform initiative," Santoro wrote in an excellent *Phi Delta Kappan* article. "The better and more accurate story is that teachers want to engage in good work that benefits students, communities, and the profession, and they become frustrated when they cannot do so." Good teachers leave the profession when they believe "I can't teach students as they deserve to be taught, and I won't do wrong by students."

Santoro includes this situation as part of what she calls "teacher demoralization," which is "a professional problem, not a personal one. It arises due to the context and conditions of the work, rather than with deficiencies in the individual teacher."

Granted, teachers' exhaustion can't always be attributed solely to external factors. A New York high school art teacher encourages students to work in her room during their lunch and free periods. "My door is always open to my students. When I was in high school, I felt like an outcast and hated the cafeteria, so I'm sensitive to students who feel the same. I like to give them a safe space to hang out. Because of this, from seven a.m. until the end of the day, I feel like I'm running just to keep up. I love most of my students and would do just about anything for them, but most days, I can't even fit in a bathroom break. I'm on the go for seven or eight hours a day. Fortunately, about the time you think you can't go on at that pace, there's a school vacation or a holiday built into the calendar, which is usually enough to recharge me."

The responsibility for resolving teacher demoralization, or what the public calls burnout, should lie with districts and administrators. Telling teachers to relax doesn't cut it. A meta-analysis of 20 years of intervention studies on teacher burnout, including strategies such as therapy, mindfulness, and relaxation, concluded that "intervention effectiveness is generally small." Instead of halfheartedly attempting to mitigate the effects on teachers, school leaders should fix the underlying causes—their school climate, staffing numbers, and resources—not just to prevent employee demoralization, but because that's how a proper workplace should operate.

Until that happens, some teachers told me about strategies that helped them cope. A Washington, DC, history teacher said she reached "full-scale burnout" when "I was being pushed to do things that weren't good for learning or there was adult dysfunction from leadership." She realized she felt better when she had "the space to bring my full energy to this job, when I can see that I'm being impactful, and when things outside my classroom don't make it worse." She instituted a no-work-on-Saturdays rule and allowed herself to fall slightly behind in grading when she needed extra time. A Texas high school language teacher changed schools until he found one with a fabulous leadership team that valued teachers. Prisha, too, switched Illinois schools.

Many studies highlight the importance of social support from coworkers, whether through friendships or peer collaboration groups, whose empathy and experiences in the same workplace can help teachers view their situation more positively. Conversely, a Missouri middle school teacher said that her "best support is a friend who doesn't teach. Venting to someone who doesn't have her own classroom helps my perspective better than 'Oh I *know*, let me tell you what he did in *my* class,' one-upping each other and spiraling downward."

Opening up to both coworkers and an outsider helped Naomi deal with her demoralization. "I talked with my teammates and my therapist. I looked at the scores of kids in other classes and the progress my kids made since the beginning of the year, when many of them came in well below grade level. I looked at their progress that wasn't measured on tests. I reread thank-you notes and recalled positive feedback from students and parents. I set personal goals that had nothing to do with test scores," she said. "I'm allowing myself to make mistakes and not be a perfect teacher, to struggle and try again. I am giving myself the benefit of the doubt. I am trying to take to heart the success of my students as much as I do their failures. I am trying to let neither define my self-worth. I feel much more positive and optimistic. It is getting better."

Rebecca Abrams	Elementary School Teacher

Rebecca was about to teach a new math lesson on the rug, but JJ was still sitting in his chair. "Hey, JJ," she said. "Can y—"

He looked up. "Is this a 'humor the teacher' moment?" he asked.

Rebecca cackled. "Yes, yes, it is. Please come to the floor." He gamely complied.

JJ was a fascinating student to teach. He referenced various historical facts that made classmates blink in confusion, created his own unusual but valid strategies for mathematical operations, and made impressive connections between subject areas. He now often asked questions confirming what Rebecca had taught him so he'd remember the steps later on. Rebecca tried to find spare moments to teach him things that interested him, like American Revolution trivia or how to make tables in Google Docs.

As she was doing at home, Rebecca was working on injecting more fun into her school life. One day, she handed each of her students a xeroxed photo of Evangeline and announced, "Prank War!" She told them to draw a costume on their music teacher. Students dressed their paper Evangelines in Elmo, snow cone, pirate, chicken, banana, and other funny getups. They plastered their creations all over the school.

By now, Rebecca had gone on two dates with Pete. Although they had a lot in common, she wasn't feeling sparks for him. "I'm not giving up on him yet, maybe it'll change. But I'm really not good at boys," Rebecca told me. Aiko, by contrast, was happily dating one man exclusively.

Rebecca went out dancing every week or two, visited her family often, and exuberantly threw herself into her musical rehearsals. All of these activities made her world feel richer (if her sleep scarcer), for the moment. She was a teacher, first and foremost, but she was also a singer, dancer, animal lover, daughter, sister, aunt, and friend. She hadn't focused on some of those aspects of her identity in years. "I finally feel like I'm 'lifeing,'" she said.

Rebecca was so busy that she barely had time to check the dating site. She was about to cancel her profile when she got one last alert. A 30-year-old named Nathaniel had written a funny message. She checked his profile. *We have compatible geekiness and he's really cute. Okay, I'll get back to him*, she decided.

The next day, Rebecca was surprised to hear from Nacho the dog's rescue organization. Though last year she had desperately wanted to keep Nacho, a toothless, middle-aged weirdo with anxiety issues, she didn't have as much time to take care of him as the couple who adopted him. But one of Nacho's many anxiety triggers, the rescue staffer told Rebecca, turned out to be babies—and the couple just had one. The staffer asked if Rebecca could dog-sit Nacho temporarily as the couple settled in. *This is a sign from God*, Rebecca thought. She welcomed Nacho with open arms.

In ELA, Rebecca led a brainstorming session about poetry. She conducted a "popcorn": Students called out answers, taking turns quickly without raising their hands.

Rebecca stood at the Smart Board, marker in hand. "What are things we can write a poem about?"

"Friends!" someone shouted. Rebecca wrote it on the board.

"Family!"

"Death!" The shouting ceased for a moment as students digested that idea.

"That's right, we sometimes help ourselves feel better about sad things by writing poems about them," Rebecca said.

"Sickness!"

"Springtime!"

"Cookies!"

"Okay," said Rebecca, adding to the list. As usual, when one student broke the silly ice, others followed.

"Cake!"

"Ice cream!"

"Cheez Its!"

"That's random, but okay," Rebecca said, as she wrote "Cheez-Its" on the board.

Around the room, Rebecca could hear students muttering, "Cheez-Its? Why would anyone write a poem about Cheez-Its?"

"Hey, no judging," Rebecca said. "If we can write poems about cookies, cake, and ice cream, why not Cheez-Its?"

"Miss Aabraamms?"

"Yes, Mia."

"That was me!"

"Okay. I'd love to read a poem about Cheez-Its."

"I didn't say Cheez-Its! I said Jesus!"

From then on, whenever Mia mumbled, Rebecca said, "You're talking about Cheez-Its again."

Mia was still grappling with her testing self-esteem. Rebecca scheduled a lunch bunch with her to discuss how to feel better about taking tests. She went over a list of study strategies. "Number one is to reread old notes and mark them up in a new way to monitor what's important and what still confuses you," Rebecca said. "Remember when we did a reading activity about tigers and used an exclamation point for 'I didn't know that!' a question mark for what we didn't understand, and a star for 'That's important'?"

"Yeah!"

"That's something you can do with your notes! And then if you have question marks, ask me about them, and I'll help clarify those ideas."

Rebecca reviewed the rest of the list, giving Mia specific examples of class activities that demonstrated each strategy. "Which of these examples have you found most helpful in the past?" Rebecca asked. They settled on choosing two strategies Mia wanted to try. Mia left lunch bunch with a skip in her step.

⁂

On their third date, Pete leaned in from his spot on Rebecca's couch. "Do you mind if I kiss you?"

"Sure?" Rebecca replied because she thought she should.

I'm not feeling it, she thought as she kissed him. *This isn't sparking anything. Ugh, how do I get out of thi—*

Nacho jumped onto the couch between them. *Saved by the dog!* Rebecca rejoiced. "I'm sorry, I can't do this with a straight face," she said.

After a while, Pete asked, "So where do you see us?"

"Look, I'm going to be honest with you. I don't know if I see an 'us,'" Rebecca said, as kindly as she could. "I'm not really feeling rainbows and butterflies. I would like to be that person for you, but I'm not sure if I'm going to."

Pete eventually concluded that he didn't want to be someone whom Rebecca had to persuade herself to like.

Later, Rebecca admitted to Aiko, "I'm not actually looking for rainbows and butterflies."

She choked on her soda when her friend replied, "Would you be open to unicorns and daffodils?"

The next night, Rebecca had a rehearsal for her synagogue's musical. The male lead, Sam, was a gracious, mild-mannered man who chatted amiably with Rebecca during breaks. He was cute, Jewish, and, Rebecca was surprised to learn, 50; he could have passed for 10 years younger.

After rehearsal, Rebecca ran into her neighbor, who told her that Nacho had barked for a long time while she was out. Rebecca was puzzled: When she was home, Nacho was usually quiet and mostly just napped and cuddled. She apologized and said she'd take steps to resolve the situation.

As she approached her first date with Nathaniel, Rebecca felt schvitzy walking from the pouring rain into the fancier-than-she'd-expected candlelit restaurant. She'd wanted so badly for her hair to look nice, but it was frizzed out wide because of the humidity and she was wearing jeans and muddy sneakers because she'd walked Nacho in the rain, carrying him over mud puddles so she wouldn't have to bathe him. She was the most casually dressed person in the room.

Rebecca and Nathaniel both reached for a hug. They'd talked on the phone every day for a week. "Hi, it's good to meet you," Rebecca said. "Wow, I am so underdressed for this place."

"You're not underdressed."

"Yeah, I am, but I've been carrying a dog around in muddy clothes."

"Why?"

Rebecca explained the saga of Nacho and they didn't stop talking for the rest of the meal. When the conversation veered to their favorite jokes, Nathaniel charmed Rebecca with his: "A pirate walks into a bar. The bartender notices something weird about his pants. He says, 'Uh, do you have a steering wheel in your pants?' The pirate says, 'Arr, yes I do.' The bartender says, 'That doesn't seem very comfortable.' And the pirate says, 'Arr, no,'"—here, Rebecca joined in for the punchline—"it's driving me nuts."

Once the restaurant closed, Rebecca didn't want the night to end. They walked to a nearby coffee shop for a long discussion about semantics and wordplay. They said good night with a warm hug.

"That," Rebecca told me, "was the best date of my life."

The date went so well that Rebecca lost interest in other guys— even Sam, who made overtures at every rehearsal. He sat near her, flattered her, rushed to her side during breaks, and hovered after rehearsals until she left so he could walk her to the parking lot. Rebecca was careful to be friendly without being flirty.

She was excited to get to know Nathaniel.

Miguel Garcia   Middle School Special Ed Teacher

Finally, finally, Miguel got an assistant. André had been assigned to support a Western feeder elementary school student who had just left the district. Miguel happened to be friends with that school's assistant principal, who called him as soon as she got the news: "We have an aide floating around who I can send you," she said. "I can't promise you anything because they'll probably take him away." She shared Miguel's skepticism of district officials. "But you might get Mr. Dixon on Monday."

On Monday, André, a friendly, easygoing thirtysomething with dreadlocks, arrived with a smile. "Hey, I hear that I'm here," he said. Miguel was excited for his Black students to have a role model who looked like them.

The difference in Miguel's classroom was immediate. Having an experienced, talented teaching assistant in the room, let alone one who the students thought was cool, modified the kids' behavior and allowed Miguel to teach the way he should have been able to teach all along. André was proactive, made helpful contributions to class discussions, and gently redirected students who acted up. Miguel didn't have to give André more than a quick shorthand of what he needed and André understood and tackled it right away.

Over the next weeks, Miguel was able to work with students in small groups. He could teach units more quickly and his students gained ground. Another aide told Miguel that André "really likes your class. He says it's really interesting and fun."

Miguel felt renewed.

At the end of February, Chad Tucker finally held a meeting at Western about the takeover. The crowd included a surprising number of parents for a weekday morning, considering that most Western families couldn't afford not to work.

The information the Citywest librarian had reported spurred parents and educators to action. Western, Central, and Citywest parents, many of whom spoke through translators, angrily challenged Tucker with pointed questions and accused him of promoting a segregationist, discriminatory plan. When he gave excuses, they did not back down. Hope blossomed.

CHAPTER 8

March

An irate father to an Illinois high school counselor: "When is graduation? Do I get tickets? Did you let my ex-wife steal them, too?"

Text from a parent to a Maryland middle school English teacher about a book the class was reading: "Why are you having my daughter read porn?" The book was Anne Frank's *The Diary of a Young Girl.*

Rebecca Abrams   Elementary School Teacher

On their second date, Rebecca worried about whether she'd feel the same hesitation with Nathaniel that she'd had with Pete. After their evening together, Rebecca and Nathaniel were at her door when Nathaniel leaned in to kiss her. *Oh god,* she thought, *I hope there's as much chemistry in this kiss as there is in just being together . . . Oh good! There is.* Rebecca was simultaneously comfortable and giddy.

For the next couple of weeks, their relationship progressed. They had a lot in common—their family lives, taste in books, and Rebecca's favorite, "our nerdiness!"—but they weren't so "in lockstep that it would be boring," she told me, thrilled. "We really are very compatible. So I keep waiting for the other shoe to drop, for Nathaniel to decide he's tired of dealing with this crazy person. I keep feeling like this is too good to be true."

It was the most promising start to a relationship that Rebecca had ever had. And then . . .

Santiago, a student in Rebecca's homeroom, came back to school after he'd been out sick for two days with a stomach bug. As she walked the class to recess, Rebecca reminded Santiago to take it easy and not run around too much. Outside, he grew pale and shaky. "Miss Abrams, I think I'm going to BLARGHH!" Santiago puked practically on Rebecca's shoes. Relieved it had happened outside, Rebecca patted his back during round two and walked him to the nurse's office.

Whenever a kid was sick in Rebecca's vicinity, she got sick, too; she'd never acquired the legendary teacher immunity. This time was no different. She had to stay apart from Nathaniel for a week, he had work travel the next, and she had a quick trip scheduled to visit her parents the following weekend. They talked on the phone and Face-Timed when they could.

But it was hard to make time for Nathaniel when she had so much else going on. After school, she had show rehearsals and work for her continuing ed course. She'd rush home to be with Nacho, but she couldn't give him enough attention because she had to grade and prep for her students. "I'd signed up for these shows thinking, 'I love theater, I want to reclaim my life,' and then came Nacho," Rebecca told me. "This is what I wanted! I wanted a life! Well, now I have a boy, a dog, and two shows. Everything is happening at once and I don't know how I get through all this. Lesson learned: Be careful what you wish for. You just might get it!"

Rebecca still had to write interims and change her hallway bulletin board; it could take a while to gather student projects, design a board, and arrange it to her satisfaction. She was behind on grading from February, but taking a day off to grade would require the extra work of writing sub plans and there were no days off in March this year. She felt stretched to her limit at school as she continued to try to meet all her students' needs without the class time to differentiate instruction, and she blamed herself for not successfully connecting with the student or students stealing from her classroom. After rehearsals, which ended at 10 p.m., she graded and prepped until 1 a.m. She woke up at six to walk Nacho and make her lunch before leaving for school. She hadn't gone dancing or been out with friends in ages. FaceTimes with Nathaniel dwindled to texts only. She didn't have time for pranks. "I still can't work enough with my truly advanced kids because the small group of kids who are struggling need so much more of my time. Eastern parents advocated for gifted classes in the first place so their kids would get the attention they deserve. It's all still extremely frustrating. I feel like I'm veering toward a nervous breakdown." When Nathaniel finally came over, she was barely awake enough to keep up a conversation.

Worse, Rebecca felt like she was letting her coworkers down. She hadn't even chatted with Trixie this month. She turned in materials at the last minute, didn't have time to track down resources she wanted to offer her teammates, and didn't volunteer to do as much for the team as she normally did. "The guilt is overwhelming," she told me. "I feel terrible that I'm not helping as much as I should or could be."

At the same time, Oliver, who still hadn't been tested, seemed to have suffered a setback. At recess, when he lost games or got tagged, he banged his head against the wall or wrapped his arm around a playground pole to try to break his wrist. He stopped only when adults told him to and talked him through his feelings. Rebecca called in his mother for another conference. After a long conversation, she generally agreed that testing could be beneficial, but insisted that her son wasn't at a point where he needed it.

March

In the middle of rehearsal for the synagogue show, Rebecca's phone dinged several times. After Rebecca's next song, she sat in the back of the room to check her messages. They were all from her neighbor: "You're not home, are you?" "How long will you be gone?" and then "Rebecca, I'm sorry, but I can't take it anymore. I like being your neighbor, but your dog is insane. He barked nonstop all day, like every day this week. You need to do something about him!"

Rebecca was taken aback by both content and tone, because she had always gotten along well with her neighbor. When they'd previously spoken about Nacho, the situation hadn't seemed urgent. With her neighbor now added to the list, she felt she was disappointing too many people—and Nacho—and so she fell apart. She covered her mouth with her hand but couldn't hide the sobs. The director stopped the song in progress. "Rebecca? Are you okay?"

The director called for a five-minute break and Rebecca sputtered out what had happened. An older, motherly castmate hugged her, murmuring comforting things about how Rebecca couldn't have known what was going on. Sam left the room, returned with a cup of water, and hovered anxiously behind Rebecca with it until she took a drink.

Later that week, the rescue organization informed Rebecca that Nacho's owners didn't want him back. They asked Rebecca to adopt him. Rebecca was torn. She badly wanted to keep him. If she didn't, he would go to a kennel until the rescue staff could find him another foster home. "But I have an insane month, including a full week where I won't be home because of tech week," the last week of rehearsals before opening night. "If I back out of stage crew, I'm an asshole because I'm reneging on a commitment," she told me. "But I can't go to work all day leaving him alone in my house, be home for ninety minutes, and then go to rehearsal every night and abandon him *again* every single night for a week."

Rebecca recognized she couldn't manage everything she'd taken on. She decided the only obligation she could drop without affecting others was the continuing ed class she was taking to earn her certificate to teach gifted students. She had never withdrawn from any kind of class in her life. When she apologized profusely to her professor, he assured her, "It's an academic class. Don't worry about it. It's really okay."

Rebecca also tried everything she could think of to solve the Nacho problem: a crate, ThunderShirt, music, plug-in pheromone infuser, CBD oil pills, a pair of Rebecca's old socks that smelled like her (she assumed), a peanut-butter-filled Kong, leaving him in the house for just a few minutes at a time to desensitize him. But her neighbor said nothing changed. On rehearsal nights, Rebecca begged friends to come over after work to keep Nacho company. During the community show's tech week, Sam saw her Facebook pleas and Nacho-sat several times.

At a 4th grade team meeting, Trixie called out all three of her teammates; Grace and the 4th grade special ed teacher had been AWOL this month, too. "Look, I want to talk about where we are as a team," Trixie said. "I feel like we're struggling right now, and we don't normally. Where do you see us as a team right now?"

The teachers looked at one another for a long moment. They were used to Rebecca being their workhorse. Grace was stiff and silent as she tried not to cry.

"I think as a team we generally work very well together," Rebecca said, sniffling. "I have personally been crazed and I haven't been able to hold up my end. I haven't met all my responsibilities and I'm sorry for it."

"Yeah, that's true," Trixie said. "Apology accepted, let's move on."

Rebecca was grateful that her friend and colleague didn't dwell, try to "fix" her, or scold her. "Any of those would have made me feel even worse than I already do. Trixie knows the things I hate *the* absolute most in the entire world are not fulfilling my responsibilities and disappointing other people," Rebecca told me. "So just forcing me to acknowledge it was enough. I'd do better and she knew it, and that gave the others a chance to own up to *their* issues. Which they did. It was a pretty crappy, but necessary, meeting."

In one of the last rehearsals for the synagogue show, when Rebecca and Sam were preparing to sing their big duet, the director said, "So, the ballad . . . I didn't want to ask before, but we need a kiss. It really calls for a kiss. Would you be willing to do that?"

"OKAY!" said Sam.

Shoot me now, Rebecca thought, slumping. *This is so awkward.*

The director and Sam were looking at Rebecca hopefully. "Okay, sure, let's do the kiss," she said. After the song, Sam leaned in and kissed her.

"Aww," chorused the rest of the cast, and the "So, when's the wedding" jokes commenced.

Sam was caring, supportive, and the only friend of Rebecca's to attend her community musical. "Sam saw me with no makeup, hair a fuzzy, nasty mess, shapeless clothes, huge eyebags, in a meltdown in the middle of a rehearsal, and Nathaniel saw me close to that bad," Rebecca told me. "Life is stupid. When I tried to be impressive and pretty and clever and all, no dice. But when I was an absolute disaster, I somehow found *two* keepers. Why didn't they both run as far and as fast as they could? Save themselves while they still can!"

At the end of the month, Eastern had an assembly with a visiting author who gave a presentation about storytelling. "What are examples of things you can write a story about?" the author asked.

Among the kids wildly waving their hands, Luci, her arm practically halfway out of its socket, hooted, "Oo oo! I know one!"

The author called on Luci. "There was this one time! In writing! We were brainstorming ideas for poetry!"

Rebecca knew where this was going and started to laugh. The rest of the gym was so quiet that it was impossible not to hear her snorting.

"And Mia said we could write a poem about Jesus! But Miss Abrams thought she said Cheez-Its! And everyone was saying, 'Why would you write a poem about Cheez-Its?' And it was so funny!"

Rebecca's students turned around to smirk at Rebecca as Luci told the entire school about her mistake. Teachers looked at Rebecca in amusement. "Did that really happen?" one asked Rebecca.

"Yes. Yes, it did."

Miguel Garcia   Middle School Special Ed Teacher

Miguel liked to jazz up roll call with daily icebreakers to build a community in which students learned about one another. "The attendance question of the day is 'Who would you want to be friends with, fake or real?'" he asked his first period video class one morning in mid-March.

As he called roll, most students named celebrities.

"Jon?" Jon looked bewildered.

"Come on now, listen to the question." Quiesha quietly prodded him like an older sister. "It's who would you want to be friends with, anyone fake or real."

Jon named a video game character, Quiesha a singer.

"Who is that? Is that appropriate for a ten-year-old?" Miguel asked. He occasionally talked to his classes about his daughter.

"Nah, she's too young. Don't share that with her yet," Quiesha said.

Quiesha was now Miguel's best student. There was an elegance to her reserve that Miguel admired, and she extended patience and empathy to Jon when most kids did not. She had a toughness that

Miguel knew she was going to need if she pursued a career in the film industry.

Later that period, a student fiddled with what looked like a small toy camera.

"Mr. Garcia, look at this," Quiesha said.

Miguel recognized her attempt to connect with him. Knowing what would happen, he picked up the prank camera, pressed a button, and immediately got zapped. "WAAHH!" he shrieked, treasuring Quiesha's laughter.

Spring was when classes tended to reach their sweet spot: Teachers and students had a rhythm, chemistry, and inside jokes that made them like a little family. Miguel's special ed class was no exception. His students were hitting their stride, their behavior was largely under control, and André was a godsend. "This is the time of year when teachers really get to see the fruits of their labor," Miguel told me.

Miguel's special ed kids were able to work independently enough that Miguel started them on Prodigy Math, a Pokémon-style educational video game. Immediately, the kids were obsessed. Even Dewayne sat still at his computer to play Prodigy; he didn't want to stop for lunch. Miguel hoped Prodigy would help him catch up.

One morning, Dewayne trudged into Miguel's first period video class. Since Winter Break, teachers had kicked him out of class often, but usually not this early in the day.

"What are you doing here?" Miguel asked.

"Oh, I got in trouble. They said I wasn't listenin', but I was listenin'," Dewayne said, finding something interesting to look at on the wall.

Miguel asked André to escort Dewayne to his elective, a computer class, to see what was going on. After 20 minutes, André returned with a report: Dewayne was distracting other kids, getting out of his seat and walking around, playing video games instead of working, and closing his computer or switching tabs when someone walked by.

Miguel slipped into Dewayne's classroom. "I understand you're having a hard time focusing," he told Dewayne.

Dewayne was surprised to see Miguel there. "Naw, I'm good."

"From now on, when you're having a hard time focusing, I'm going to have to leave my class of thirty other kids and come help you." Dewayne's eyes widened.

"Have him sit over here, right next to you," Miguel told the computer teacher. "Use a [cardboard] separator. Don't make it punitive. Make it about helping him focus."

Miguel assigned André to sit next to Dewayne permanently in first period. In Miguel's room, Miguel stayed within three feet of Dewayne during lessons. Between Miguel and André, Dewayne slowly improved. When he started to get work done, Miguel gave him extra points for motivation. "I feel bad for him because it's not his fault," Miguel told me. "I'm worried he's going to get to the point where it's so hard for him to try that not trying is going to be easier. What happens a lot in middle school is kids fall behind and develop certain behaviors to mask that they're struggling. By the time they get to high school, they either drop out or become labeled as 'the bad kid' because it's easier and then that'll be their personality. In seventh grade, kids start getting that edge. Like, 'Well, if this isn't working for me, I'm just going to be the badass.'"

Before Dewayne's IEP meeting, Miguel told Dewayne's gen ed teachers he planned to suggest moving Dewayne to special ed for all academics. "I think that would be for the best," the science teacher said.

"Oh, thank goodness! Oh, yay, thank you!" Harriet rejoiced.

Miguel shot her a look. She had never stopped complaining about Dewayne's behavior, but she hadn't seated Dewayne close to her. She left him in the back of the room. "Kids can tell when you don't like them," Miguel said and walked away.

Dewayne's mother was a nice woman who worked at a nearby

nursing home. Miguel outlined the period of time that Dewayne's behavior temporarily improved, but he wasn't certain that she made the connection to medication.

"I love Dewayne. When he's focused, he does such a great job," said LaShonda. "He's got a really good heart. Sometimes he gets out of his seat and it's really hard to keep him focused."

"Yeah, I know," Dewayne's mom said. "So what's this about an assistant going to class with him? He doesn't like it."

"That's not what I'm advocating for, a one-to-one," Miguel said. "He needs to learn how to develop executive function skills on his own. I wanted someone to take data and the data matches the data in my room. The fact that that teacher has thirty-four other kids means he spins out of control."

"I could see that. It happens at home."

"He's not doing this out of malice. He just can't control himself, so I have to keep him next to me. I've been tracking his behavior: He has a three-second attention span."

"I know he has a lot of problems with one teacher and tunes her out after a while," she said. Harriet had requested to come to the IEP meeting, but Miguel convinced her to write a statement instead so she wouldn't spout off at Dewayne's mom. Her statement relayed that Dewayne didn't listen, he distracted other kids, and other students asked not to sit near him.

"Yeah, I understand," Miguel said. "You know, we're all nice here and we know what Dewayne's like, but it's not always going to be like that."

He didn't think he had to spell out for Dewayne's mother the root of his concern: Western was a small enough school that the administrators and most of the teachers knew Dewayne was a good kid. But Miguel lost sleep worrying about what would happen to Dewayne in high school if "no one gives him the benefit of the doubt that we give him and they just see him as a problem. When he's in a big high school and gets some teacher who just sees a big Black kid she can't control, there'll be police on campus. If he starts arguing with them, it's going to be a problem. It's time he understands that," Miguel told me later. "Eli, too: Especially as he gets into high school, people might think, 'Oh, he's this angry Black guy.' At a school level, that's concerning, but even more so on a societal level, it's terrifying to me because he's such a sweet kid deep down."

Dewayne's mom nodded, comprehending what Miguel left unsaid.

"I honestly think he's better served being in my class all day except for electives," Miguel said.

"Some of the stuff in your class seems too easy."

"I agree my class is too easy for him. However, if he can't get through assignments because of attention, that's a problem as well. Cognitively, if I'm able to sit with him constantly he can get everything done, but that's not feasible." Miguel didn't mention the district's plans to cut special education; as of now those plans were neither public nor concrete.

"I understand he needs extra support. Okay, let's try it," Dewayne's mom said.

"If he does better, we can do an amendment to put him in one gen ed class next year. Mainstreaming him in two classes plus electives is too much."

"He's going to be upset, but I'll explain it to him," she said.

"I will, too."

The next day, Dewayne's behavior was noticeably better. *His mom must have had a talk with him*, Miguel thought. *When parents and teachers communicate, things get done.*

The next day, Miguel told Dewayne, "The reason this is changing is because I want you to be successful. It's not a punishment. I know you think my class is too easy and I agree with you. The issue is you're behind because you're not doing the work. I'm going to help you with that."

Dewayne nodded. "Okay."

Miguel told me later that he was disappointed Dewayne's mom hadn't raised the topic of medication. "At some point he'll reach an age where he'll be tired of being in special ed and ask for the meds himself."

Penny Davis	6th Grade Math Teacher

In the middle of lunch, Penny's phone dinged a moment after Ed's did. "I know you're with Ed right now," Kent texted. "You need to stop lying about your relationship with him."

Penny slid her phone across Ed's desk so he could read the text. He showed his phone to her—a text from Ellen: "Why do you eat lunch with Penny all the time?"

Penny was rattled. It was no secret that Penny and Ed ate lunch together. They were friends. They left the door open. But who had reason to report their daily whereabouts to their exes? Because they didn't know who was keeping tabs on their private life, they couldn't trust their colleagues, the people whom they saw more than anyone outside family.

That afternoon, in a parent conference with Robert's mom about Robert's lack of motivation, Penny provided examples of some of the best work Robert had done in spite of challenges related to his autism. "He can do this. He just needs you to help me encourage him to do it," Penny said.

"I see him helping his younger brothers and sisters."

"This is what's been going on," Penny said, and described how Robert was giving up instead of maintaining the stamina to work through problems.

Robert's mom told Penny that a church had reached out to them to ask how members could help their family with clothing donations, for example, and childcare help. Penny was hopeful that, with more adult supervision and support at home, Robert could pull up his math grade. "You can see the good underneath that whirling dervish!" she told me. "He has a good heart under there."

For her grad school paper, Penny had to conduct group activities to help students learn how to demonstrate proportional reasoning. She had decided to move forward with the paper and her master's after her professor offered a generous deadline extension.

Penny explained to her students that the project both covered curriculum and, if it was successful, would be helpful for her grad school work. For a week, Penny assigned tasks to teach them proportional reasoning. Students would work toward delivering a group presentation about two situations: one proportional and one nonproportional.

The first two days of the project were rocky. Penny wasn't sure how to make proportional reasoning more accessible to 6th graders. On day three, she decided to put the kids into groups and ask them to come up with sample situations. "Remember, a proportional relationship is 'If x happens, then y happens,' and the relationship stays proportional," Penny explained.

As Penny circulated among the groups, she saw Zach whisper to the student next to him. The student announced to their group, "Zach says that if you buy ten shirts from Amazon and you're not Prime and have to pay seven dollars extra shipping, that's not proportional because if you're Prime you don't pay shipping." Penny was floored. She'd never seen a child make that accurate and creative a connection in this unit for as long as she'd been teaching.

"Holy cow!" Penny said, clapping. For a student—and Zach, no less—to apply this particular math concept to real life was a major success. "That's exactly right, Zach! That was amazing!"

As the group huddled closer, Zach took the lead, whispering to them. Penny still didn't know what Zach's voice sounded like, which was odd because she could identify any student's voice blindfolded, having heard "Mrs. Davis! Mrs. Davis!" a hundred times a day.

By coming up with a relatable example, Zach had not only proven to Penny that she could teach this unit, but also given her the breakthrough she needed to finish her paper. "All students, regardless of ability, can connect to math in some way. This taught me to not give up on any child because they may not be able to express it, like Zach, but they can *apply* it. Sometime it's going to click and maybe they'll say, 'Oh, that's why Mrs. Davis taught us that math!'" Penny told me. "Today's class reminds me to keep going no matter what. I've already done the hard stuff by leaving Kent, and I've proven I can do difficult and messy things."

At the end of class, Zach handed Penny a note: "I was really proud to help with your grad school because I know how much it means to you."

Penny held in her tears. "I had been feeling so defeated. I care so deeply about my students," she told me. "That note meant so much to me. A student recognized I was working toward a major goal in my life and how much I wanted to succeed. He had no idea that I was going after something I'd been told I could not do, but somehow he saw inside me and realized how important education is for myself, not just my students."

Soon afterward, Zach's mom emailed to thank Penny for her patience with Zach and to tell her he was loving math. "He wants to talk to you so bad," she wrote. "He communicates with you more than any other teacher. If he's going to talk to one teacher, it's going to be you."

A few weeks after Penny began spraying her walls with Clorox, her respiratory symptoms disappeared. As she felt better, her confidence grew. At one of Blair's parent-teacher conferences, Penny announced, "I just want to say that I have zero problems with this child." The parent smiled. Blair shot her a dirty look, but Celia agreed with Penny. *I had the guts to say something, so now Celia did, too,* Penny thought, feeling validated.

Teacher Confessions: Behind-the-Scenes Dish

Ever wonder what teachers really think of your emails, your child, or your parent-teacher conference? Here, teachers share secrets about what it's like on the other side of the desk.

Don't call us in Fucktober

The longest-seeming months of the year for many teachers are January, March, and October (also known to some educators as "Fucktober" because "the shine has worn off but there's so much more to go," said a Maine high school history teacher). In Fucktober, there's no break in sight and students, over the initial honeymoon period of being back at school, are more likely to act up. January is like a groggy school restart with a Winter Break hangover, and March (which some teachers call "Death March") is a wintery slog with standardized testing in some states and no holidays except in the years when Spring Break clips the end of the month.

During these tedious months, parents could refrain from making non-urgent requests and take care to read the emails or notices sent home so they don't ask repetitive questions. PTAs or administrators could schedule a teacher appreciation lunch or Pi Day (March 14) staff celebration. Parents could also offer to help out. "I've had parents help me sort field trip forms, cut out math materials, and put together packets," a New York 4th grade teacher said.

A California math teacher at a high-achieving high school said that parents should also understand that "the same exhaustion and malaise that hits teachers is also hitting students. I'm an adult professional. I can handle March the way I handle Friday traffic: From experience, I know it will pass, even though it sucks. So parents can help kids with a month that moves so slowly. They can check in with their kids in a way that has nothing to do with grades. Go for a walk, cook a special meal, anything that helps remind the child that they are seen and they are more than a school machine."

Parents could also lobby their school district to schedule early release days or a three-day weekend in March by adding a day elsewhere during the year, a Pennsylvania AP English teacher suggested.

We might not want you to friend-request us on social media

Teachers often avoid visiting hot spots in the town where they teach, thanks to stories of former students spotting their teacher at a club or current students waiting on their teacher's restaurant table. Awkward! Similar boundaries apply to many (not all) teachers' social media presence. "Don't send me friend requests on social media," said a Missouri middle school teacher. "This is so tricky for me, and I don't want you to take it personally, but I cannot mix my professional life with my personal life."

Teachers also don't want to witness or be targeted by social media drama. "Social media can be a really bad thing. Parents go there to air dirty laundry before speaking to a teacher or administrator first and it's really damaging," said Licia, the Tennessee library media specialist.

Even if they aren't friends with parents on social media, teachers might still be wary about their exposure. "You're always conscious of your teacher life. I always have to be aware of myself as a public figure in behavior and presentation, always have to watch my tone and wonder if an errant comment will get me fired, especially on social media. Sometimes I'll say something off the cuff in class and then worry for weeks whether it's going to come back to bite me in the ass if a student tells a parent and a parent complains," said a Pennsylvania high school English teacher. Similarly, a Nebraska high school teacher admitted, "I'm sometimes scared to teach because one misunderstanding happens and you're on the news defending yourself, your profession, and your job. It's very nerve-wracking."

We have secret codes

Just as parents might converse in another language or via gestures to evade little ears, educators, too, use codes. Some examples:

- **"The principal wants to see you":** To rescue coworkers from unending student or parent situations.
- **Staff development:** Happy hour.
- **Put in the Z-file:** Toss an assignment in the trash.
- **Ninth period:** Also happy hour.
- **The lounge:** The closest bar.
- **Hallway prowler:** District administrator or principal popping into classrooms.
- **Frequent fliers:** Students who often visit the health room or administrators' offices.
- **Book club:** Again, happy hour. Though sometimes it actually means book club.
- **Opportunities for growth:** Problems with a student's learning or behavior.
- **Titanic/Chernobyl:** Impending student meltdown.
- **Milk and cookies:** Happy hour!
- **Gone to the dark side:** Moved from a classroom teacher position to a district administration position.
- **Choir practice:** Yep, happy hour.

- **I need to see the principal:** I'm going to the bathroom; please keep an ear out for my class.
- **Going bowling:** Going bowl—nope. Usually happy hour.
- **Parking lot drill or pest control is coming:** Admin is letting teachers leave early on a teacher workday or right after dismissal the day before a holiday.
- **"I'm appreciative that Johnny is always on time":** "If a teacher starts out a parent-teacher conference with this kind of positive comment, rather than about a student's personality or academics, your kid is probably giving the teacher hell in class," said an Indiana science teacher.

We know your secrets . . . even if we wish we didn't

Teachers get a lot of insight into families' lives; what happens at home does not stay at home. "We do everything for the kids when they're in our buildings. We are their friend, their parent, their nurse, we care about them as if they were our own kids. We're often the only people they will confide some things to. Because of this, when you come to parent-teacher conferences, we know a lot about what goes on in your homes. We just don't tell anyone," said a Nebraska 5th grade teacher.

"Teachers are social scientists. We see what goes on in people's homes, parenting styles, abuse and neglect, we know who's on drugs and who has been to jail. We have a lot of privileged information and much of the time we don't want it. We actually would love to come in and just teach," said a Kentucky middle school English teacher.

What we really think about communicating with parents

Teachers have mixed feelings about calling parents—some are happy to do it and some are apprehensive because the call won't be well received. "I hate calling parents. Hate it. I always feel like when I contact them, it's a bother," a Texas high school English teacher said. "I'm tired of hearing, 'You're the only person to say that about my kid.'"

Other teachers feel that parents have unrealistic expectations. "Be patient with response time. My plan time is 7:40 to 8:30 a.m. and I have a twenty-minute lunch at 10:30 in the morning. I might not get back to your email until tomorrow morning if it isn't pressing or it requires some thought. Give me the grace you would want at your job," said the Missouri middle school teacher.

Parents can get better responses to emails if they are kind and polite (which sounds like a Captain Obvious thing to say, but many parents aren't). "Everything is in the presentation. You can ask me the same thing in two different ways and I guarantee you'll get a much more favorable answer if you're respectful. I had a parent who asked many questions this year—constant emails—and ended every email, 'Thank you for your time.' It makes a difference," said the New York 4th grade teacher.

The "schedule send" email option is handy for communicating with teachers. Parents can write a note when they think of it, but schedule it to arrive during school hours. The timing is considerate to teachers and the grace period could give upset parents the opportunity to cool down, rethink their wording, and cancel the email.

Even better, students in middle or high school can speak to their teachers directly. "Teach your child to talk with their teachers themselves. High school teachers have around one hundred sixty to one hundred eighty students. We can't keep in touch with parents as easily as an elementary school teacher," said a Texas high school Spanish teacher.

What we really think about parent-teacher conferences

Parent-teacher conferences aren't any easier for teachers than they are for parents. "We have feelings also, and when we need to have hard conversations, it's difficult for us to see how upset parents get," said a Maryland private school kindergarten teacher.

Another challenge is how to offer constructive feedback that doesn't raise parents' hackles. "It's tricky to pretend you 'like and enjoy' their kid when you don't. It's like acting. I've always been told to start with a positive about the child and dig really deep if it's difficult. Then you dive into the negatives, but you always have to tread lightly and pepper the conversation with 'We are here to help,' 'I know she can be successful,' 'I know he is smart and capable.' It's hard not to wonder what kind of parents are these people that they have a kid who acts like this, even though I've met many good, genuine parents who are also at their wit's end with their child's behavior. Sometimes I've asked other teachers or administrators to sit in on meetings to help redirect the conversation if I start to get too negative. I can name about five students in my career, which isn't many based on the thousands that I've had, who I could not find one good thing to say about because they were just that awful," said a New Jersey middle school English teacher.

"Parent-teacher conferences can be an ego boost or a battle; you have to mentally prepare yourself for each meeting. Some parents just come in to say how much their kids love your class, but you'll always get a couple who aren't so pleasant. Sometimes divorced parents treat it like a counseling session, parents yell at their kids in front of you, or parents try to argue with you about the student's behavior or grades. I wish more parents wouldn't come in on the defensive and would realize we're on the same team," said an Illinois high school English teacher.

Another tip: Bring the teacher a snack! "A parent once brought me Levain cookies at her conference. I will remember her and love her forever," said a New York elementary school teacher.

What simple expressions of gratitude really mean to us

Those thank-you notes your children write their teachers mean more than you know. "In my workbag I keep every single kind note I've ever received from a student," said a Georgia private school teacher. "I discovered that most of my colleagues do something similar. If I'm having a bad day, I reach for those notes." A New Jersey high school teacher said thank-you cards are her favorite part of teaching. "Having tangible proof that I matter to people is something I didn't realize would mean so much to me. I didn't realize how many days go by without gratitude," she said. "This year, I actually cried at one card, which is unusual for me. I also occasionally get emails from past students who share how much they gleaned from my class. Whenever I'm feeling particularly low, I either reread these letters or I serendipitously run into a former student who reminds me why I stay in this amazing profession."

The Texas high school English teacher said that students' expressions of gratitude validate her career choice and teaching style. One student gave her a card that said "how happy she was to have me as a teacher and that I was the only teacher who bothered to keep it real with kids and tell them about issues happening in the world. She said I had made her a stronger critical thinker and more 'woke' as a young lady of color. I did cry at that card because what she said is what drives me to get out of bed every single morning, what makes me keep pushing."

What we really think about our administrators

School administrators can make or break a teacher. Supportive admins give teachers the headspace to shine in the classroom. But toxic admins, whether they overtly bully employees or punish teachers they dislike by assigning them undesirable classes or duties, can drive superlative teachers out of the profession. Here's what some teachers from around the country told me about the administrators they work with:

- "Some have our backs. I was called into an IEP meeting and the special ed teacher began by asking what everyone's goals were. The parent leaned across the table, pointed at me, and said, 'Our goal is to get her fired!' My administrator looked at the parent and said, 'Well, she has tenure, so I think you're going to have to think of a different goal for the day.'"—Delaware high school teacher
- "I once had a principal who positioned her chair at a higher level than the other chairs in her office to assert her authority over others."—Florida 3rd grade teacher
- "A former administrator had candy in her office. Students got in trouble on purpose so they would be sent down there, get candy, and get to play on the iPad."—Nebraska school librarian
- "Our principal publicly tweeted offensively about transgender students and didn't get reprimanded. I was disappointed in him as a human. It was sad to see someone who was allegedly so supportive of student achievement and goals hating a growing segment of the student body."—West Virginia teacher
- "My subject level administrator is a fantastic former English teacher, and she really gets it. She supports us on curriculum choices, outside-the-box methodologies, and interventions with difficult students and parents. The support she's given me both

directly and indirectly has been priceless."—Pennsylvania English teacher

- "Administrators take parents' or students' sides with frustrating frequency. School policy is teachers are supposed to give a student detention at three lates, and a student had five or six before I finally told him he had to serve. He went straight to administration and said it was unfair. The vice principal told me I couldn't keep him after school and had to hold him in my classroom during lunch. I wasn't allowed to leave the room or attend my collaborative meeting. Instead I had to sit and essentially stare at this student who got his way. After that, knowing I wouldn't get support from administration, I've stopped giving detentions for lates."—Virginia middle school teacher

- "The public doesn't know that administrators play favorites, move around money, exchange favors, and punish the squeaky-wheel teachers."—New York middle school teacher

- "There's no money, but we're getting a new football field. I haven't gotten new books since 2002. Our district administrators give the illusion of asking for and collecting input from students, teachers, and the community, but then they do exactly what they set out to do before the survey was issued. I love teaching and I love my students, but administration is making our jobs harder and harder. They changed the hours of the school day, but athletics still start at the old times. Kids who play baseball are missing an hour of class three times a week for games."—Pennsylvania AP English teacher

- "I worked in a school that chose not to have bells. When I offhandedly stated that I didn't want to set alarms on my phone because as a woman, I often don't have pockets and my phone would be across the room, one admin seriously suggested I purchase Apple Watches because 'then the bells can be on your wrist!' It was the epitome of transferring responsibility to teachers."—Washington, DC, charter school teacher

Yes, some teachers hook up

Whether because of the school setting, long work hours, the shared mission of taking care of children, or the feeling that only fellow teachers "get" what it's like to be a teacher, many educators report that hookups with coworkers are common. "Walk into any school here and I guarantee you can find at least ten teachers who either dated or fucked. It's an incestuous little pool," said the Texas high school English teacher. "I can't tell you how many guys I nearly swiped right for on Tinder, until I looked more closely and saw they were a teacher on my campus or in my district."

A Pennsylvania social studies teacher said at her school, hookups happen often among the younger single teachers. "Many of the teachers who've been there for ten or fifteen years were all hooking up when they first started out. There have been a few teachers who met at school and are now married." At an Iowa school, the science teacher and the social studies teacher hooked up and eventually got married. After they moved away, the science and social studies teachers who replaced them also hooked up and got married.

When a Massachusetts middle school teacher began teaching at her alma mater, her first coworker hookup was one of her former teachers. "It felt extra naughty even though we were colleagues by then, and weird because it was in the parking lot of our school. But it was a fun one time thing."

Anecdotally, staff hookups seem to be more common in secondary schools, where there are more coworkers to meet and more spaces to rendezvous. "At a large suburban high school, I witnessed more than a couple affairs among teachers," a New Jersey school librarian said. "One teacher got caught in the faculty room with a maintenance worker."

An Illinois high school has so many interfaculty relationships that "the secretaries love to meddle in teachers' personal lives, and they often try to set people up. Sometimes it works," a foreign language teacher said. "Students also like to meddle. My students often pick a male teacher they think I'm dating or should be dating and make up little stories to try to rattle or distract me."

What our daily lives are really like

"People don't realize that unlike most 'professional-level' jobs where you can take a moment for yourself when you need to—a walk around the block or just taking thirty seconds to stare into space in a quiet environment at your desk—teaching is like being onstage for six to seven hours per day, performing for an audience. This is why my duty-free lunch isn't something I'll ever budge on unless there's an emergency. I need that recharge time," said a Nebraska elementary school teacher.

What really happens during class placement

A New York City private school holds at least five several-hours-long meetings to place students, said a 2nd grade teacher who has since switched schools. "We have five classes per grade. We give each student a card with their race, ethnicity, gender, whether they have 'problem parents,' a single-parent household, gay parents, any kind of parent request of students or teachers to place them or not place them with, and ranking them in three categories (math, reading, writing) as high, medium, or low. We're allowed to give our top five at-risk students first preference for each class. Each teacher takes a turn placing a student in a class for next year, and there are many rounds of trading and switching. The goal is to make sure each class has an even amount of diversity and student ability."

Many public elementary schools similarly assign students cards listing their academic, social, and behavioral information; some schools also include strengths and weaknesses. Grade-level teams create classes that aim to balance students' academics, gender, race, behavior, and other considerations. Teams may try to ensure that each student has a friend in class and is apart from children they've had issues with. "Parents don't appreciate what a nuanced, difficult thing this is and how moving one child has a domino effect on an entire class," said a New York 4th grade public school teacher.

Private schools don't necessarily have better working conditions

"I typically worked twelve hour days every day, came in on some weekends, and still felt like I wasn't working enough," said the 2nd grade teacher. "At private schools there's an enormous pressure to make the classroom look 'perfect' for the parents and prospective parents, since they pay so much tuition. I felt like I lived in a fishbowl. At my last school, tour groups came in several times a day to watch us. I often felt like I was working more to show off for the parents than toward the students' progress. Also, private schools often defer to families who fund the schools' endowments. I taught a kid who was essentially illiterate and should have been in a special education school, but his parents refused to get an evaluation. Because they gave the school so much money, we couldn't do much. It was a shame because the school was ill-equipped to handle his needs. Manhattan parents are crazy about getting their kids into the top-tier private schools and don't listen to red flags that the school isn't the best place for the child."

What we really think about recommendation letters

Families aren't aware of just how many recommendation letters teachers are asked to write on their own time. One year, a Michigan AP English teacher wrote 137 college recommendations. She asks students wanting letters to request them after the AP Exam in May. "I couldn't have written that many if I didn't write them over the summer. I finished 121 before we returned to school in August," she said. "I develop close relationships with my students as we work together to conquer the AP English exams, and I think of them as my kids. I will do anything I can to support them."

That number is rare. Many teachers won't automatically write a letter for every student who requests one. "Recommendation letters can be a harsh wake-up call to students. If a student has been cruel or abusive in class, like talking badly about a peer, or even another teacher, I will not write them a letter. I never hesitate to explain why," said a Rhode Island high school teacher. "If I see backstabbing, ruthlessness, or lack of empathy, I'm very clear I don't want my name to be associated with them. It's interesting how students respond to that feedback; some cry and are disappointed, but some aren't surprised at all. It's like they've waited their whole life for someone to point this out about them."

A Pennsylvania AP English teacher asks requestors to complete an extensive form before she writes a recommendation, which helps winnow down the numbers. She declines students with whom she doesn't have a rapport. "I just had that happen with a girl who never talked to me in class or one-on-one, never asked a question or offered an opinion. I told her, 'I'm sorry but I don't feel like I know you well enough to write a recommendation letter.' But when I get the opportunity to write a letter for kids who were super-engaged in the class? Boy, do I love writing those letters! I make myself cry talking about what amazing students they are and how any learning community would be lucky to have them."

Some of us find various outlets to deal with our stress

The stress on teachers doesn't automatically lift when the afternoon bell rings; it often escorts teachers home and lingers during off-hours, leading educators to seek relief in a variety of ways. At a Nevada elementary school, some staff members go running together or work out at night with a teacher who shows exercise videos in her classroom; others meditate, bike, or do yoga. A group of their coworkers utilizes a different set of outlets: drinking, smoking weed, or consuming edibles at night or on weekends. "Not everyone understands how much effort it takes sometimes to stay positive throughout the school day," said a kindergarten teacher. "Some teachers drink hard in our free time. For staff like myself who drink harder sometimes, I think it comes from the need to relieve built-up stress. Others are more occasional or recreational smokers; I consume the occasional edible. This work is so all-consuming that sometimes it takes chemicals to get your mind off it. No one I know consumes marijuana in any way before or during the school day. A lot of us also take pills for anxiety or depression. I've been taking Paxil for anxiety for a few years. Some of the strongest connections I've made with coworkers are around this. Many of us are pretty open about anxiety and depression and how we medicate it. We share some general anxieties: student loan debt, potential health-care bankruptcy, Social Security, climate crisis, school shootings. Add to that how emotional this work is, and the number of things we're juggling and accountable for in and outside of the classroom, and yeah, it takes a toll. Just about every teacher I know has *some* release."

A South Carolina school librarian said that stress drinking is a common outlet among teachers she knows. "Stress drinking is a real thing for many teachers, especially in high-risk, tough schools. I'm nowhere near prepared for the heart-wrenching needs of the neglected and abused children at my school. At the end of the school day, I have no emotional or physical energy to pursue any of the 'normal life' activities that most workers enjoy regularly," she said. "A lot of my drinking is coping and recovering from the day, and occasional weekend binges."

What we really think about the first day of school

"I love the first day of school!" said the Illinois high school English teacher. "I love meeting new students, reconnecting with returning ones, catching up with colleagues, and the overall energy on campus. It's also nice to get back into a routine."

Even the most seasoned veterans get first-day-of-school jitters. "Teachers who've been teaching for twenty-five-plus years tell me they still get nervous on the first day. It's exciting, too. You're anxious to meet your students and see who's going to be reliable, who's going to give you headaches," said a Connecticut middle school teacher.

The first day of school can also be bittersweet when teachers miss the students who left in June. "A classroom is a microcosm and each class has its own chemistry. It's the main reason teaching is never boring, even when you've taught the same material many times," said a Maryland middle school English teacher. "I remember vividly individual classes. One had a fat bird we named Cheese who sat on the bush outside our window. One class wouldn't stop asking me to sing 'Forest Friends,' a little ditty I'd made up once while passing out animal cards to sort students into groups. In one class, I almost broke down in tears as I addressed an embarrassingly personal piece of writing of mine that students had discovered online. I remember the class I told I had miscarried—a student's mother was my ob-gyn and would be operating on me the next day. I remember the class that threw me a surprise birthday party. Many classes have secret jokes, strange rituals. In all of them, students read aloud in funny voices. They took risks by reading their most personal stories and intimate thoughts aloud. They learned, formed relationships, felt like they mattered. When you dwell in a microcosm like that for fifty minutes a day, one hundred eighty days a year, you get attached to it. I'm always sad on the last day of school. Many years I cry because I know those unique little worlds will never exist again. And on the first day of school the following fall, as excited as I am to get to know new students, I feel a little pang of nostalgia for last year's kids. For a moment, I look out at the new faces and think, "Who the fuck are you people? This is all wrong!"

CHAPTER 9

April

A father to a North Carolina middle school history teacher as he stared at her and mimed punching her: "My daughter is not to be crossed. I taught her how to punch."

An administrator told a Texas art teacher she'd be teaching world history—an extra class for no extra pay. When she said, "I've never taught or taken world history," he replied, "You taught AP Art History. That's just like world history with pictures."

Rebecca Abrams   **Elementary School Teacher**

Rebecca sat beside Sam in the middle of their show, her head on his shoulder. In front of them, actors sang and danced. Sam leaned over. "I saw on Facebook you said something about how you have a little bit of a love life," he whispered.

Rebecca froze. A large audience, including her family, watched the stage. "This is not the time to talk about this!"

Sam didn't hear her. He leaned in closer, put his arms around her, and repeated himself.

"We are in the middle of a performance!" she hissed. "We are not having this conversation right now!"

April

That night, Rebecca sent Sam a friendly email explaining that she liked him, but she also liked someone else, that she was sorry if it seemed she was leading him on, she wasn't ready to be more than friends, and she enjoyed spending time with him. Sam wrote a considerate reply about how he cherished their friendship and that was enough.

Actually, Nathaniel hadn't responded to Rebecca's texts in more than a week. Wondering if he'd lost interest, Rebecca cycled through sadness and anger. Had she misjudged him?

She didn't have time to continue reaching out to him; she had nearly 40 kids to engage. Near the end of math, when a student suggested that to solve a problem with a numeral, "we have to move it," Rebecca sang the entire chorus of "I Like to Move It," complete with booty shaking and a dramatic hip-shot/hands-out freeze finale.

"OMG would you just stop!" Santiago said, laughing.

In April, Rebecca finally got a dog cam so she could see for herself what Nacho was like when he was alone. When she left the house, Nacho barked and howled, running in circles for nearly two hours. When he stopped barking, he lay down on the floor mat and stared despondently at the door. "As desperately as I want to, I can't keep him. This is one of the most heartbreaking decisions I've ever made (let alone had to make *twice*)," she told me. "It's also killing me that my neighbors have to put up with the barking, I can't have family over because Nacho can't handle children, and every time I leave my house, I worry about Nacho instead of being fully present doing whatever I'm doing. I can't do this anymore, for any of our sakes. But especially Nacho's."

She contacted the rescue organization to tell them she believed Nacho was unhappy, and she put out a call to friends for help finding him a home.

～

Rebecca and Grace finally had a chance to catch up after months of working through their lunch period. Grace shared her latest class drama, which Illyse's clique had instigated at arrival that morning.

"I don't see much drama from her in my room, but I cut her a little slack," Rebecca said. "She wrote a personal essay back in the fall about what a tough time she was having with the divorce."

"What divorce?" Grace asked.

"Uh, her parents'?"

Grace cocked her head. "Illyse's parents aren't divorced."

Rebecca lowered her eyes as if she were peering over glasses. "I beg your pardon?"

Grace said that Illyse had lied about various matters all year. Once she claimed to have siblings who didn't exist. She wrote an essay about her nanny, but she didn't have one. "And remember when she said Rory was cutting herself? Eventually it came out that Rory was totally fine, she was just frustrated about something. Illyse told her to cut herself to fix it. Illyse is kind of Jekyll and Hyde."

If the teachers hadn't been rushed during team meetings, if they'd had time to eat together instead of working through lunch, perhaps Rebecca would have learned this helpful information earlier in the year.

Mia stopped Rebecca while she was checking on students' reading activity groups around the classroom. "Miss Abrams, I have a question."

"Okay, shoot."

"What's a 'tit'?" she mumbled.

"Wait, what? You're talking about Cheez-Its again."

"What's a 'tit'?"

Rebecca struggled to keep a poker face. "Where did you see or hear that word?"

"Santiago. He said it was on a book."

"You saw it in a book?"

"No, *he* said it was *on* a book."

Now Rebecca was confused. "Wait, did you see that word, or did Santiago? And it was on the cover of a book?" *Was he harassing her?* Rebecca thought. *Are they passing around inappropriate books?*

"No, he saw it."

"The word 'tit'?" Rebecca asked.

"No, it was on the floor."

"*What* was on the floor?"

"The tit!" Mia said, befuddled by Rebecca's cluelessness.

Another girl broke into the conversation. "Mia, he thinks he saw a TICK."

Rebecca, relieved: "OOOOHHHH."

"Oh, okay," Mia said. "So, Miss Abrams, what's a 'tick'?"

Later that week, the class took a major science test. When Mia saw her 14 out of 15, she gasped and covered her face to hide her tears of pride.

Rebecca wanted to stand and cheer for her, but she didn't broadcast students' test performances. She subtly patted Mia, smiled, and whispered, "Congratulations." She saved her jumping and cheering for dismissal, when the other kids were leaving or too distracted by the chaos to pay attention. After they hugged and high-fived, Rebecca asked, "What did you do that helped you succeed?"

Mia said she reviewed her notes for a full week, read the study guide every day as her reading log activity, and rewrote what she'd learned in a "mind map" with color-coded themes and patterns.

Rebecca pointed to the growth mindset bulletin board. "Earlier in the year, when you were so worried about tests, did you think you could accomplish something like this?"

Mia beamed. "Nope! But now I know I can!"

Penny Davis   6th Grade Math Teacher

When Kent asked Penny to meet him at McDonald's to discuss the divorce, Penny agreed because he asked nicely. She hoped to soften his latest settlement proposal, which had shocked his own attorney and would leave her in debt. At first, he was courteous enough that Penny thought the conversation would be civil. But as he shifted into the topic he really wanted to discuss, he grew increasingly heated. "I know you and Ed have a relationship, and you need to stop lying about it," he said.

The couple sitting at the next table were their old neighbors. Penny didn't want them to hear him getting angry.

"That's not true," she said.

"I know it's true."

"How? Where are you getting this?"

"I have my sources."

The more Penny thought about how he was trying to trick her into admitting a romantic relationship that didn't exist, the stronger she felt. She vowed she would not cry until she was in her car. *I am not going to let him win.*

"Who?" she asked.

"Everybody!" Kent shouted. "People see you all the time, so you need to just stop lying about it."

She remained calm. Their neighbors were staring at Kent losing his temper, but she didn't care anymore. "I don't know what you're talking about and it's really none of your business," Penny said. "If you're so interested in my life, you might as well tell me who's talking about me."

He blinked. Penny had never stood up to him before. She had always let him have the final say, or she repeated "I'm sorry" until he stopped yelling at her. "Everybody's talking about you all the time!" he said. "You're only hurting the twins by not settling. Your sons will be the ones who are damaged and it will all be because of you."

"Settling" on his terms would mean he would take more money from her than he would pay in child support, even though his salary was nearly four times hers.

"We're done here," Penny said. She walked away, head held high.

The call came during Penny's lunch period while she was grading tests alone in her classroom. "You've been on our radar for years. We hear frequently from parents who adore you," the district official said. She told Penny that hundreds of math teachers from across the county had applied for the position, which would oversee the district's mathematics program. "We are just so proud of your accomplishments," she said and told Penny the district chose her.

When she hung up, Penny burst into tears. Later, she reflected that she was emotional for several reasons. "It's bittersweet that I'm leaving my students and a couple friends at school, but I'm finally being recognized for all the work I've put into my career," she told me. "Also, I'm a creature of comfort and even though I'm in a toxic soup now at Southern, I'm scared because I don't like to let people down. I'm wondering if I'm going to be able to successfully transition from working with students to working more with teachers and administrators. Will I be able to teach adults how to teach and think about math?"

To celebrate, Penny invited Ed for dinner on a night the boys were with Kent. They chatted over a bottle of wine as she finished cooking. "I can't stay at Southern for you. But you'll be in my life. You're my best friend," she said.

"I don't want you to stay for me."

As she plated dinner, Penny realized she'd forgotten to clean a spill off the corner of the table. "Oh my gosh!" she exclaimed, alarmed. As Ed jumped up to help with whatever the emergency was, she flew to the table with a towel.

"What? What's wrong?" Ed asked.

"I'm sorry, I'm so, so sorry! Oh golly, I'm so sorry." As Penny cleaned up the mess, she continued to apologize.

"Penny, it's just a spill," Ed said.

She had told Ed before about how a mess in the kitchen, however insignificant, would send Kent into a rage. He'd scream at her about how inconsiderate she was, about how if she didn't have the kitchen gleaming at all times, "you're not thinking about my feelings."

When Ed made the connection, he put his hand on hers, stopping her from scrubbing the table, which was already clean. "Penny, I am not Kent," he said. "Things are imperfect. You're imperfect. I'm imperfect. It's okay."

From their dinner conversation through the moment when Ed gave her a warm hug goodbye, Penny kept thinking, *What did I do to deserve a best friend like Ed?*

Miguel Garcia   Middle School Special Ed Teacher

André's classroom presence continued to invigorate Miguel. It was a shame the district hadn't provided the support earlier this year, or, for that matter, the year before. Last year, Miguel's students constantly attacked him. Every few months he had to get HIV and hepatitis tests because of student bites. He had frequent doctor appointments to address his multiple injuries. The district kept putting Miguel in dangerous situations by sending Western violent, severely disabled children without assistants.

Midyear, the district had sent a new student who didn't have bathroom skills and smeared poop on the walls. The district did not supply a behavioral specialist. Miguel was expected to drop everything to integrate him into the class. There was nothing Frank could do.

When Miguel demanded support—an assistant or more training because he didn't know how to toilet one child while simultaneously teaching the others—a district official told him during classroom observations, "You're making great gains! You don't need assistance."

"Don't patronize me," Miguel said. "You've got to do something!"

"We're trying."

"Try harder. This is a safety issue."

Miguel went up the chain. He told the district that a large student constantly body-slammed him. The district did nothing. He told the district that another student kept grabbing women's breasts in school. The district did nothing. "The district doesn't care," Miguel told me later. "If parents complain, they don't want to get sued, so they respond right away. If a teacher complains, they do nothing."

When the district administrator in charge of hiring assistants finally visited his classroom, Miguel described his constant injuries. She responded, "That's part of the job."

"Madam, that is not part of the job and I resent that," Miguel said. "You're implying that teachers aren't supposed to feel safe on the job and that's completely uncalled-for."

That spring, Miguel attended a special ed conference. When he took off his jacket, the older teacher next to him saw his arms and gasped. "My god, what happened to you?"

Miguel looked down at the lines of purple bite marks. "Some of my students attack me."

"You need to see a doctor! You need to document this!" the woman said.

That night, Miguel relayed the conversation to a friend who was also a teacher. "You've gotta sue," she said.

"I'm not going to sue."

"I'm calling you every day until you get a lawyer," she said. She hounded him every day for a week.

The lawyer told him he had a case. An independent doctor found that, because of his students' attacks, Miguel had permanent disabilities in his back and the tendons in his arms. "This is crazy! This is terrible!" the doctor told him. "They're tormenting you and you're too nice of a person! You've got to get out of this. You're not a young man anymore and this is going to cause you more permanent damage." His doctor's insistence was the reason that Miguel had switched to teaching mildly to moderately disabled students.

Ultimately, Miguel sued the district and won lifetime medical care for the injuries he sustained.

One afternoon when Eli wasn't at school, the counselor came into Miguel's room and pulled him aside. "Did you hear about Eli?" she asked.

"What?"

"He was hit by a car."

"*What!*" Miguel straightened, alarmed.

"No, don't worry. I was just in the hospital with him. He's fine."

"What happened?"

Every morning, Eli took a public bus to Western's neighborhood and scootered from the bus stop to school. Today in front of school, a car sped by, dinged him, and knocked him off his scooter. When someone informed the school, Frank and the counselor ran outside to Eli.

"I'm fine," Eli insisted. "I'm fine."

"We have to call an ambulance to make sure you're okay," Frank told him.

The counselor rode with Eli to the hospital for observation.

She told Miguel, "I said to Eli, 'We had to call your mother,' and he looked worried. He said, 'Uh-oh, she's going to have to leave work.' I told him, 'But as a mom I'm sure she's really worried.'"

Eli shook his head.

"What does your mother do?" she asked Eli.

"She says she's a stockbroker."

"Really? A stockbroker? What does that mean?"

"Well . . . she stocks cards at Walmart."

When Eli's mother arrived at the hospital, the counselor told Miguel, "She was pissed" and barely looked at Eli.

"The doctor checked him out and he's completely fine," the counselor told her, saddened that Eli's mother's first reaction was anger rather than relief.

"I could have told you that," Eli's mother said. "You made me miss a day of work for this. Great. Where's his stuff?"

"Oh no, I hope he didn't get in trouble for this," Miguel said to the counselor.

"Yeah, that's what I'm wondering."

Eli was absent for two days.

When Eli returned to school, Miguel couldn't contain his enthusiasm. "Eli! I'm so glad you're back! Are you okay?"

"I'm fine," Eli said, his head down. Miguel changed subjects, knowing Eli didn't want to discuss it. But his heart broke at the idea that a child was in the hospital and thought his parent didn't care.

"Just Part of the Job": How Violence and Short-Staffing Create a Hazardous Profession

It is outrageous that Miguel was told that being assaulted at work is "part of the job." But violence against teachers is common. A nation-wide survey conducted by an American Psychological Association (APA) task force found that 80% of K–12 teachers had been a target of violence or abuse within the past year, 94% of those attacks by students. Almost three-quarters had been harassed, more than half had damage to their car or property, and about half were physically assaulted.

Educators say that violence in the classroom is increasing in both frequency and intensity and many teachers feel unsafe. But there has not been a great deal of research on violence against teachers. "It's a tough thing to study," University of Florida professor Dorothy Espelage, who led the task force, told *Education Week*. "No one wants to talk about that teaching is a hazardous profession, that teachers are at risk when they're in the classroom."

Ali, the Kansas special ed teacher, was bitten, kicked, punched, and twice sustained two black eyes and a broken nose—and that was all from just one of her students. "I love him dearly; he has a communication disorder, intellectual and physical disabilities, and obsessive-compulsive behavior," she said. "It isn't his fault. It's the fault of an administration that doesn't value teachers or accountability. We've needed two more special ed teachers and eight more para-professionals, none of which has been okayed by our district."

The task force found that high school teachers were more likely to be threatened than elementary school teachers, but elementary school teachers were more often physically abused or assaulted. A 2020 study published by some members of the task force reported a range of 38% to 62% of teachers experiencing verbal aggression and 8% to 12% physical assaults in a given year. The most recent *Report on Indicators of School Crime and Safety,* released by agencies of the U.S. Departments of Education and Justice, listed lower percentages of attacks, but the task force believed the government numbers are underreported "because teachers may fear that reporting these incidents could jeopardize their jobs."

For this reason, the Oregon School Employees Association helped to pass legislation requiring school districts to develop a process for reporting injuries relating to assault. School staff, the OSEA said, were "discouraged from filing incident reports documenting physical or verbal attacks, being told that it was just 'part of the job.'"

An Oregon statewide survey titled "Work Shouldn't Hurt" found that more than half of surveyed special ed paraprofessionals and other support staff were physically assaulted by students and about 40% targeted with threats, verbal abuse, bullying, or sexual harassment in the past year. Increased risk of these offenses was significantly associated with inadequate staffing, security, assault investigation procedures, training to deal with assaults, and discouragement of reporting injuries.

As Ali suggested, while many students' attacks are intentional, other students' aggression can be attributed to mental challenges. "The discontinuation of counselors, paraeducators, social workers, and services for special education and other needy students has only exacerbated the issue," an *NEA Today* article observed. "Whatever the circumstances, more and more educators are ending up in the emergency room. While some are forced to use their medical leave, others choose instead to resign."

When these students don't have the appropriate support, the entire class can be affected. Disrupted learning environments occur "when student behavior significantly interferes with instruction and/or school staff members' ability to maintain a stable classroom or ensure student safety," the NEA said. "At times, students can become dangerous to themselves or the classroom as a whole."

These concerns are particularly pressing given that the 240 gun incidents* in schools in 2021 were a record high, more than double the number in 2019 or 2018, the second and third worst years in history. Meanwhile, society's only nationwide substantive change between the 2012 Sandy Hook Elementary School massacre and the 2022 Robb Elementary School massacre was to train teachers to hide their students and barricade the door. Once again, the burden fell on educators to bear responsibility for larger societal failures. (For thorough examinations of school shootings and related issues, consider reading *Sandy Hook: An American Tragedy and the Battle for Truth* by Elizabeth Williamson and *Columbine* by Dave Cullen.)

In an extensive 2019 investigation, the *South Florida Sun Sentinel* "found that a sweeping push for 'inclusion' enables unstable children to attend regular classes even though school districts severely lack the support staff to manage them. State and federal laws guarantee those students a spot in regular classrooms until they seriously harm or maim others. Even threatening to shoot classmates is not a lawful reason to expel the child." The newspaper reported that "violent students have injured thousands of teachers, bus drivers and staff in Broward County alone and undoubtedly thousands more across Florida." Broward's 2019 School Safety and Discipline Survey found that half of surveyed educators said they had feared for their safety in the past year and 57% said violence "disrupts the school day multiple times a day."

---

* These incidents include "every instance a gun is brandished, is fired, or a bullet hits school property for any reason, regardless of the number of victims, time of day, or day of week," according to the Center for Homeland Defense and Security at the Naval Postgraduate School.

April

Florida law treats students with severe behavioral disorders the same as harmless students with special needs: They must be educated in regular classrooms unless it's impossible, and parents or a judge must agree before they are transferred to a special needs school. This is not at all to say that inclusion with appropriate staffing numbers is poor policy. As a 2020 analysis of violence against teachers cautioned, "Inclusion positively impacts both students with disabilities and their peers, but many schools do not effectively implement inclusive best practices due to a lack of resources, supports, and training."

The Florida law leaves dangerous students in ill-equipped schools, where teachers shoulder the burdens of both managing behavior and documenting complaints. Florida teachers compiled a mountain of evidence that public school was not the place for one particular student who had numerous mental health issues, was obsessed with guns, and was suspended 18 times in one school year. But it took five months to get him transferred to a special middle school—and when he was determined to attend public high school, Florida's disability law allowed him to. The student was Nikolas Cruz, the school Marjory Stoneman Douglas. In 2018, Cruz massacred 14 students and three staff members in one of the deadliest school shootings in history.

꧁꧂

Teaching should not be a hazardous occupation, but teacher victimization costs run more than $2 billion a year. Yet there's no uniform data collection of students' or parents' assaults on educators. Another concern is the number of administrators who brush off violent incidents. When a 6th grader hit Michelle, a New Jersey teacher, in the face so hard she sustained permanent nerve damage in her neck, administrators suspended the student for one week and then sent him right back into Michelle's classroom. In response to

Michelle's request to move the student to another class, her principal told her to "put on your big girl panties and deal with it." A Florida high school teacher attacked by a student couldn't get him removed from her class until she filed a restraining order.

The *Sun Sentinel* reported that when educators complained about violence, sometimes their bosses blamed them for not controlling the student. A Washington, DC, charter school teacher notified administrators several times about a student who attacked a classmate with a pair of scissors while saying he was going to kill him. Her principal said to her, "This incident really stuck in your craw, huh?" and suggested she seek professional development to allow her to "increase your tolerance for chaos." Instead, the teacher left the school.

When I asked teachers what else they've been expected to tolerate as part of the job, many of them mentioned administrators passing the buck. They told me about having to let student misbehavior slide so as not to anger parents or, as at Penny's school, to whitewash the school's reputation. At a publicly funded California school for special ed students, a teacher said staffers are discouraged from giving consequences for misbehavior. "If a student decides not to attend school, then we aren't funded for average daily attendance. Therefore, we're at the mercy of the students and their parents. Sometimes we have to just accept that students can get away with inappropriate behaviors or parents can complain while the staff have to take our lumps and try to appease them."

At some schools, administrators refuse to discipline students unless a teacher first contacts the parents and submits an official referral. A California high school English teacher says it's "absurd" that her school's discipline administrators require the teachers to do those administrative jobs, "but they don't give us enough time to even prepare for classes, grade and enter work, or offer students individualized help, let alone call every parent of a disruptive student to conference."

Parents' phone numbers can be outdated or parents might not call back until evening, "so all the extras happen on our own time."

At a New York high school with a similar policy, an art teacher who has 180 students said, "If we can't contact parents, we aren't allowed to submit referrals for students cutting classes and we're blamed for the cuts. The referral can be about anything: lateness, fighting, cursing, carrying a weapon, stealing, cheating, having sex in the stairwells, which actually happens, and anything else that could happen in the course of the school day. Administrators won't take any actions—in other words, won't do their jobs—without that paperwork."

A Texas high school language teacher described "ambush meetings" set up by the principal to conference with angry parents and students. (Administrators also have ordered him to tutor students online almost every Thanksgiving break for the past several years.) "Sometimes I'm given a chance to explain the grade, but much of the time the parent makes an hour-long plea for me to be fired and then I'm dismissed at the end of the meeting for my next class. These are the town Karens who think their child could only be failing due to the teacher being substandard. Teachers aren't told about these meetings until the last moment, so we don't have time to gather the student's file and work examples. When I've complained about this dynamic, administrators explain they don't take the parents seriously, but they just 'need to vent.'"

It is even more problematic when administrators don't take the teachers seriously. At too many schools, administrators have told teachers, like Penny, to substitute unpaid for other classes during their planning or lunch periods. Some schools combine classes, doubling the student load, or split the subless class, scattering, for example, a class of 25 4th graders in groups of three or four throughout the school "so if you teach music or first grade, you also have to entertain three fourth graders you've potentially never met and who are justifiably annoyed by what their day has become," a Missouri teacher said. While this practice existed before COVID, during the pandemic it became widespread. As usual, school districts put the onus on teachers to make up for the districts' failures—in this case, their shortsightedness in not hiring more substitutes or making substitute teaching a more attractive job.

A former superintendent in a Utah district liked to use the phrase "pack 'em deep and teach 'em cheap," a high school English teacher there told me. "This seems to be the motto for the state." One recent year she taught seven periods of English, some with 40 to 45 students in a class. In total that year, she had 263 students.

This type of short-staffing can be dangerous to teachers and students. Students attacked Miguel more often when he didn't have enough support staff. At a mid-Atlantic school, a 5th grade inclusion class had several special needs students. When the school pulled the inclusion aide to sub for another class, the teacher was left alone to manage 30 kids in her portable classroom. A student who often fled the room had an outburst and bolted out the door. The teacher, who wasn't permitted to leave her students unattended, repeatedly called the office staff, who didn't pick up the phone. Eventually the boy was found on a busy road, blocks away. "Despite always being short-staffed and never having adequate support for the child, I was asked to continue with this protocol and had less and less support as the year continued," the teacher said.

At a midwestern middle school, more than a sixth of teachers quit midyear and couldn't be replaced with new hires. "The buildings with the highest amounts of teacher stress and the neediest students usually have the fewest substitutes. So you know before you call in sick that you'd add to your colleagues' stress that day. Many teachers teach sick and it's not just out of dedication to their students or due to lack of sick time (most teachers I know retire with one-hundred-plus sick days unused) but because you'd hurt the people you depend on most," said a special ed teacher. "Our administration has ceased to address behavior concerns. This year so far, I've had furniture and objects thrown at me, three different students put their hands on me in anger, and I've broken up countless fights. The school keeps saying we are 'trauma informed' but this seems to equate to holding no one responsible for their actions."

When unpaid or unsafe duties mount, when supervisors don't look out for their employees, when "work hurts," it shouldn't be surprising if good teachers quit.

During a photo shoot the day special education teacher Brett Bigham was named Oregon Teacher of the Year, he was hunched over and his shirt lay strangely. This was because a few days earlier, a student had beaten him to the ground, whipped him with a TV cord, and bit him so hard he had to go to the hospital. He couldn't sit up straight during his acceptance ceremony because his abdomen was wrapped with bandages and gauze. He told me, "The bandages were weeping and I was afraid I was going to bleed through my shirt. I almost took my shirt off at that press conference. I wanted people to talk about this. I thought, *If I take my shirt off right now, the conversation will finally happen. But I was too chicken.*"

Student assaults had sent Bigham to the hospital four times. Students often slapped him, spit in his eye, or bit him. One bite gave him hepatitis; because there was no working bathroom on his floor, he poured alcohol-based hand sanitizer in the wound. "It's a nasty secret that not many districts talk about," he said. "Teachers, counselors, behavior management specialists, and paraeducators are getting beaten regularly as part of their job."

Over the years, Bigham's students hit him in the head with a chair, sticks, books, a stapler, tape dispenser, rocks, shoes, scissors, lunches, a broom, and a rusty mole trap. He had to replace his glasses four times after students hit him in the face. Students kicked him in the stomach, face, and groin so badly he had to seek medical attention. So many students had threatened his life that he stopped counting past 20. His district did nothing to help him.

After a student snuck up behind Bigham and hit him over the back and head with a chair, his doctor told him he needed to take medical leave to recover. His district's refusal to allow it convinced him to quit teaching for a time. He was tired of "everybody saying, 'It's part of your job.'"

But he eventually came back to teaching, and he keeps coming back, even though when we spoke in 2022, he had recently been hit so hard by a student that he got a concussion. When I asked him why he returned to the profession, he told me a story. While teaching a transition program for 18- to 21-year-old public school students, Bigham realized that unlike general ed kids, his students didn't get a prom. "Several girls, nonverbal and in wheelchairs, could hardly move; no one's asking them to prom. So we threw one." Nonprofit organization Abby's Closet scheduled a special appointment time to give his students free prom dresses. The following year, other special ed programs asked if their students could come, and more asked the year after that. Eventually, 350 students with special needs from as far as 40 miles away attended the prom Bigham organized.

That year, while his students tried on dresses with nurses and Abby's Closet employees in the fitting rooms, Bigham was in the waiting area when the front doors opened. "The first thing I see is a white cane with a red tip and in comes a group of girls from the Vancouver School for the Blind. I had just spoken there two weeks before; some girls I knew by name. Then in comes another group doing sign language. And another group in wheelchairs. The woman who runs Abby's Closet told me the names of the groups coming in—the School for the Deaf from Salem, the kidney transplant branch from the hospital . . ." Bigham choked up as he recounted the event. He explained that he's unable to share this story without crying.

The woman told him that because of his efforts to make special ed students feel included, "you showed us that we could be doing better." She pointed to all the girls now examining the racks of dresses. "They're here because of you."

He told me, "I saw these blind girls walking through, feeling all the fabrics until they found the one that felt beautiful to them. It was such an amazing experience. And that's why I stayed in teaching. Because I can do things like that for kids who don't get anything sometimes. Making joy happen is a driving force unlike any other I have ever experienced."

Bigham works at a different school now, one that is "doing it right," he said, with a coach system set up for de-escalation; every teacher and para has support a walkie-talkie away. He never blamed his former students for their violence. Instead, he emphasized that they and their educators needed more support from their districts and in the classroom. "If I have a student who's about to blow up, the best thing I can do is have him go on a walk with a paraprofessional so he can calm down." But many school systems don't provide enough staffing for that kind of supervision.

"People often look at special education and the violence and say we're saints for putting up with that. And that's not the case," Bigham said. "We don't want people to tell us we are heroes. We want them to change the system so we are safer."

CHAPTER 10

May

A mother at a Virginia school door when it was closed to parents during the pandemic: "I DEMAND to be let in. I know workbook pickup is tomorrow, but I want it today and I pay tuition for my son to go here." (The school was public.)

A North Carolina private middle school mother in response to an English teacher who said her son was dropping the F-bomb in class: "What the fuck do you want me to do about it? It's your job to teach him manners."

Penny Davis   6th Grade Math Teacher

"We talk a lot in this class about setting goals and how anyone can achieve anything regardless of who they are," Penny told her students. "And I want to remind you that not everyone's meant for college. Some people do trades, some will be hairdressers. You don't need to go to college to be successful. And you don't need to have money. My dream was to go to grad school. I didn't have the money to pay for it, but I applied for a grant and made it happen. Now, I know you hear a lot about standardized tests at Southern. You are more than a number to me. That test score doesn't show your creativity, your kindness, your friends, your fun. No test can ever tell you what type of person you are on the inside. This test is only a snapshot of that particular moment of time. That snapshot may show you were having a bad day, or not feeling your best. It may show you were doing great. But no test will ever define you and I'm going to be proud of you no matter what score you get as long as you give it one hundred percent."

May was testing season, and Southern students were stressed. Some overachievers, upon confirming that they weren't graded on standardized tests, would tear through the computerized assessments—click, click, click—just to get the test over with. As long as they met expectations and kept up their grades, they would still be allowed to take advanced classes the following year. Their anxiety instead surfaced during class tests that affected their grades. Penny occasionally had to ask Birdie to pull distressed overachievers out of class and proctor them in an empty classroom where kids who finished early wouldn't distract them. Some of those students had gone to psychiatric hospitals and/or threatened suicide because of test pressure.

Southern teachers felt the pressure, too. "Teachers are held to extremely high standards as to how students perform on tests. We're penalized for things that are out of our control," Penny told me. Each year, some kids had meltdowns and parents flooded teachers' email inboxes with test related concerns and demands. The week before, Zach was hospitalized for a panic attack triggered by standardized test season.

The students who most feared the state and county tests were the ones at risk of failing, though they wouldn't have to repeat the grade. Robert was one of those students, having never once passed a standardized test in all his years of schooling. He had been learning much better in Penny's class since she'd conferenced with his mother. Penny also believed Robert was becoming more confident as his family's church took them under its wing and gave Robert extra attention. Now he was regularly doing his homework.

A few days before the tests, Penny was eating lunch in Ed's classroom when Nel walked by, did a double take, and stuck her head through the doorway. "How's Ellen doing?" she asked. "Haven't seen her at spin class lately."

Penny quirked a brow.

"She's fine, thank you," Ed replied.

"That sweet, sweet wife of yours, I just love her." Nel glanced at Penny and strode off.

Penny and Ed looked at each other, understanding. "It's been Nel all along," Penny said.

"She must have been reporting to Ellen, who was somehow reporting to Kent," Ed said.

"You know what, I don't care anymore. Kent doesn't know anything and he can think whatever he wants," Penny said. Penny had told him if he didn't accept her counteroffer, she would file suit, and that she was done with his mental abuse.

That afternoon, Penny attended a meeting with a few teachers and administrators about whether Zach could qualify for an IEP. His mom was concerned about him going into 7th grade without stipulated accommodations.

"The reason I requested this meeting is because there have been issues with two of Zach's teachers," Zach's mom said. Neither of those teachers, Blair and Wilma, was invited to the meeting.

The counselor said that because Zach's condition wasn't medical, he couldn't have an IEP, "but the administration could agree on accommodations and Zach's teachers would have to provide them."

"Well, okay, if Southern guarantees they will be done," Zach's mom said.

"I will absolutely make sure the teachers know what Zach needs," the special education teacher said.

As Zach's mom visibly relaxed, the conversation turned to Zach's panic attack. "Is there anything in Zach's past that caused all this?" the special education teacher asked.

And that was when Zach's mom, after nine months, explained that Zach had been touched sexually by a student in elementary school. Even though he and his teacher, a witness, reported the incident, the school did nothing, the district did nothing, and "Zach shut down." When the perpetrator tried to do it again, Zach shut down further. In the five years since, he hadn't spoken to an adult outside the family.

"You could have picked me up off the floor, I was so shocked," Penny told me later. "This whole year I've had this poor child and I was wondering why some of his behaviors were occurring, and the whole time it was the result of a traumatic situation he had endured at school. And he's still surrounded by those same kids!"

Penny, having learned from Ed that bluntness was not necessarily offensive, spoke up now. "Well, golly, why didn't you tell us this? This information could have really helped me and now I feel bad," Penny said.

"Don't feel bad," Zach's mom said. "It's just not something I thought was important to the story."

Penny continued her streak of nearly 100% of her students meeting or exceeding expectations on the state test, dipping only slightly because the test was new and Penny had chosen to teach all the inclusion kids. A handful of students failed, including Brentley, the egotistical jock whose mom had doctored a fake IEP for his twin (who passed just fine on her own).

Diamond failed her standardized tests in every subject, as well as all her classes. Penny had to bump up the scores of 21 of Diamond's class tests to a 60. Occasionally, Penny had a breakthrough moment with Diamond: She'd give her a little pep talk about doing her work and Diamond would say, "I can do better!" She would, for a few days, but then she'd regress. Or Penny would encourage her to ask someone at home to keep her on task with her homework. Diamond would take the initiative and get help for a few days, but the assistance would stop. At Penny's parent-teacher conference, Diamond's mom was full of excuses.

Nevertheless, the principal told Penny, "You need to just move Shanaynay on to seventh grade."

"First, that's racist, and second, Diamond did nothing all year," Penny said.

"Look at her size," the principal said, referring to Diamond's chest. "She looks like she belongs in tenth or eleventh grade. She's very . . . mature . . . in her knowledge compared to other students and it just isn't going to do her any good to spend another year in sixth grade looking like that."

"But how does moving her on help her learn?"

"Because she wouldn't do the work next year either," the principal said, and signaled the conversation was over.

The teachers were supposed to tell their students if they passed or failed the state test. Penny called them up one by one to her desk, where she wordlessly showed them the score she had written on an index card and a document with the pass/fail rates. Afterward, she took the kids outside to the basketball court to relieve their stress. Jake, a teddy bear of a kid, approached her in tears. "I did my best, but I let you down," he said. He'd been absent from school often because of his overbearing mother. Once she'd supposedly kept him home because of a hangnail.

Penny hugged him. "You did not let me down. You did your best. A test does not measure anything about you. It doesn't measure your heart."

As soon as Penny got home, her phone dinged with emails and texts from parents. Jake's mom was the first email in: Jake's aunt had been recently diagnosed with cancer, his brother had broken his leg, and she had forgotten to give Jake his ADHD medicine that morning, she claimed, apparently throwing everything at the wall to see what stuck. *You're telling me I've been through a whole year with this child and I didn't know he had ADHD?* Penny thought. *Had I known, the days he wasn't focused, I could have worked with that better. Had I known he forgot his medication on testing day, I wouldn't have let him test that morning.* Because his score was below the retake range, Penny had to file a waiver with the superintendent's office.

A girl who hadn't done her work all year in any classes besides art also didn't pass—and told another student she was going to kill herself if failing the test meant she'd fail 6th grade (it didn't). Penny reported the conversation to the school counselor. The girl's parents took her for a psychiatric evaluation that determined she was suicidal. She was out of school for weeks.

When Penny saw Robert's math score, she was optimistic. He didn't pass, but for the first time on any state test, his score fell in the range that permitted him a retake. "I know you can do this. We're going to review day and night, we're going to push through, and we're going to do this. Do not be discouraged," Penny told him.

"Okay, I can do this," Robert repeated.

For the next week, Penny spent extra time working with Robert individually and in small groups. When he needed breaks, Penny gave him breaks. When he was engaged, Penny worked him hard.

"Look, you can pass this test. You know how to do this math. You just sometimes choose not to," Penny said. "You think nobody believes in you"—other adults had written him off—"but I do. Just because something is hard doesn't mean you can't do it." She knew his mom worked multiple jobs, his father was still in prison, and Robert spent a lot of time looking out for his younger siblings. "When things are hard, you can ask me, Birdie, or someone else for help."

Robert nodded.

One evening after school when both Penny and Ed were working late in his classroom—it wasn't unusual for Penny to grade and prep until six or seven at night—Ed asked if he could see the headshots Penny had gotten for her new job. "I don't know," she said. "I don't even know if I like them."

"Please?"

It seemed show-offy to hand him pictures of herself while she watched. "Okay, look, if I accidentally leave my phone unlocked and on your desk, there's nothing stopping you from going through my phone. Oh gee, I gotta go to the office and pick something up," she said.

When she returned 10 minutes later, joking about having left her phone in his room, Ed looked at her seriously. "I'm just going to flat-out tell you that I think you're beautiful and these pictures really capture who you are."

Ed rolled his chair around from behind his desk. "I think you're incredible. You're intelligent. You're warm, open, and loving. You are the complete package. I've never met anybody like you. I didn't think girls like you existed."

He really just said that! Penny thought. No man had ever spoken like this to her before.

"You're what I've always wanted, but I always settled," Ed said, standing up next to her. He leaned in and looked at her questioningly. She leaned in, too.

May

As they kissed, her thoughts swirled. *I've heard about people saying they fell for their best friend, but I never understood,* Penny thought. *This is what they mean.*

On the day of the test retake, Penny met with Robert before class. "If y'all need a break, ask. You can have as many breaks as you want and you can take all day on the test. Just take your time. You can do this," she said, her heart cracking a little because he so badly wanted to please people by passing a ridiculous state test that wasn't created with him in mind.

"I can do this!" he said.

Later that afternoon, Robert's special education teacher texted Penny Robert's name and a number. Robert had passed his first standardized test. Penny rushed down the hall and asked Robert's teacher if she could speak to him. Robert stood up, saw Penny smiling through her tears, and asked, "Did I pass?"

"YES!" Penny shouted. The entire class gave Robert a genuine, caring standing ovation.

After school, Robert visited Penny's room again. "Mrs. Davis, I got an A in math and it's because of you!" he said, jumping up and down with excitement. Penny jumped with him and he laughed.

"Robert, I am so proud of you!" she told him. "You just keep working hard. You can do this!"

"I know I can! I like math! I know I can do it and I got a good teacher this year!" he said, reaching for a hug.

She embraced him tightly. "Have a great day, love you!" she said as he bounded happily out the door.

Just a few hours later, Penny learned that on the way home from school, Robert was hit by a car. He was killed instantly. Penny was the last person to give the child a hug.

Rebecca Abrams   Elementary School Teacher

After Rebecca sprayed Trixie's hair blue and yellow for School Spirit Day, Trixie returned the favor. The pair were known at Eastern for going all out on School Spirit Days.

"Did you see my text?" Trixie asked.

"Noooo . . . What text? When did you send it?"

"Two days ago? And the other one last weekend?"

They figured out that Rebecca hadn't received most texts sent to her, and her outgoing texts hadn't been delivered for weeks; something was wrong with her phone. *Nathaniel!* Rebecca thought. He'd been silent for ages, and Rebecca reluctantly had accepted that the relationship was over. Immediately she emailed Nathaniel screenshots of texts she'd sent him to prove she hadn't been ignoring him. He emailed back screenshots from his phone to convey his confusion when he didn't receive responses.

Their date that weekend seemed more like a platonic get-together. They were relieved they hadn't ghosted each other but also strangely tentative after their long absence. There was no urgency to their reunion. So when Nathaniel emailed Rebecca an amicable note to say that while he truly enjoyed her company, his feelings hadn't developed romantically in recent weeks, she wasn't surprised, only resigned. She'd already cycled through her sadness and anger back when she'd thought he was ghosting her anyway. She commiserated with Aiko, who had discovered that the man she was seeing seriously was also dating another woman.

Rebecca decided, for now, not to resume dating. *Maybe over the summer,* she thought. *And certainly not while I have Nacho.*

Coincidentally, the next day the rescue organization notified Rebecca they had a family for Nacho: a middle-aged woman and her parents, who were mostly homebound. "Man, in February, I had a thirty-six-hour span where I met Nathaniel, found out I'd be getting Nacho again, had a ton of rehearsals, and was totally crazed because of work," Rebecca told me. "Now, I'm having a thirty-six-hour stretch where I have no shows, Nathaniel ended things, and I'm *losing* Nacho. What the hell is up with this all-or-nothing timing, Life?"

When Luci told Rebecca during social studies that her Pop-It had disappeared from her backpack, Rebecca had a class meeting. She reminded the students yet again, "We are a classroom community, really trying to be more like a family. The community and I need your help and your honesty. Does anyone know anything about the missing Pop-It, either because you saw someone take it, or overheard someone talking about taking it? I'm calling on you to be upstanders for your classmates whose property has gone missing and, frankly, for yourselves, so this will *stop* happening and won't happen to *you* in the future."

This time, several students' hands shot into the air. "Illyse has one of those!" "She was showing everybody at recess!" Illyse was currently in Grace's social studies class.

Rebecca asked Luci to describe her Pop-It. "There's a mark on it! From where Mia accidentally got marker on it!"

"I'm sorry again!" Mia said.

"It's okay!"

"There was a mark on Illyse's, too!" someone shouted.

During ELA, Rebecca took Illyse into the hallway to ask her about the Pop-It. Illyse looked right at her. "I didn't steal it."

"Okay, then where did you get it?" Rebecca asked.

Illyse's eyes flitted around the hallway. Her mouth hung open.

"Where did you get it?" Rebecca repeated.

After a few beats, Illyse said, "Well, I didn't take it, but still, if—"

"No. There are no 'buts' or 'stills' or 'ifs' in stealing. If you take somebody else's property, it's stealing, period. So, for the last time: Where. Did. You. Get it? If you did take it, this is the time to be honest about it."

Illyse shrugged and said nothing.

After school, Rebecca conferenced with the principal. The next day, the principal and assistant principal called Illyse to the office. With Illyse in the room, they called her mother and asked her to look for the Pop-It. She found it within minutes.

As a consequence, the principal wrote up a discipline report and told Illyse she couldn't bring a backpack to school through the end of the year; everything she brought to and from school she had to carry in her hands. Rebecca had mixed feelings about this consequence. "Part of me is glad to move on, but part of me wanted something strong enough to happen that she might actually regret it, because we spent months trying to solve this," she told me. "She kinda got away with it."

Miguel Garcia — Middle School Special Ed Teacher

As the end of the year loomed, and with it possibly the students' last special ed class experience, Miguel focused on giving his students strategies to succeed. While the district was fixated on data and curriculum, Miguel estimated that 60% to 75% of his special ed work was teaching executive functions, social skills, behavior modification, and behavioral support. He continued to try new strategies with Dewayne, who evidently had not resumed taking his medication.

"Dewayne, you didn't finish writing the sentence. Will you please finish writing the sentence?" Miguel asked him.

Dewayne was busy poking the boy across from him. Peripherally, Dewayne knew Miguel was talking to him, but he couldn't seem to stop his own feedback loop. Miguel wondered if he could make the act of not listening so irritating to Dewayne that he would choose to listen.

"Dewayne, I asked you to write the sentence. Dewayne, I asked you to write the sentence. Dewayne, I asked you to write the sentence," Miguel repeated.

Other kids stopped and stared.

"Dewayne, I asked you to write the sentence. Dewayne, I asked you to write the sentence." Miguel kept going.

The boy Dewayne was poking stopped paying attention to Dewayne. Eli cracked up.

Finally, Dewayne looked around. *"What!"*

"Dewayne, I asked you to write the sentence. You didn't respond to me, so I figured I'd just keep asking until you did. I had to ask you nine times," Miguel said.

The next time Miguel repeated an instruction to Dewayne, after only a few seconds, Dewayne said, "Okay, *okay,* I got it."

Meanwhile, Prodigy Math had been a game changer. Miguel had noticed that Dewayne was able to focus on Prodigy because it offered nonstop action. Miguel could set assignments on the game and monitor the results to assess students' skill mastery. He could frame lessons as ways "to help you on Prodigy." While the kids were engaged online, Miguel could work with students individually or in twos on specific skills.

As a result, Dewayne's math skills were improving; technology was an antidote to his ADHD. Because Miguel and André couldn't be with him all the time, at least Dewayne could learn on the computer while Miguel worked with other students and intermittently checked on Dewayne's progress. Miguel now had hope that by the end of the year, Dewayne would jump to a mid-5th-grade level, which would put him only two and a half grade levels behind.

By building Eli up as the good student he knew the boy could be, Miguel had set in motion a self-fulfilling prophecy. Eli now came to school nearly every day, and on time. When Miguel asked for feedback during class discussions, Eli gave advanced answers that Miguel continued to reward with casual compliments and points on the board. Since Spring Break, Eli consistently garnered the most daily class points, which earned him a granola bar every afternoon.

Eli continued to mention his anger management issues occasionally, but he was learning to handle them. André was also skilled at deflecting. One morning when Eli was getting precariously close to his boiling point, Miguel watched him try to cope. Eli took a deep breath, then started to catastrophize: "This is not good. I'm really upset. This is a really BAD DAY . . ." André leaned over and whispered something to him. Eli listened, took another deep breath, and put his head down on his desk. After about 15 seconds, he was fine.

Then, in late May, Eli got an 8 out of 10 on a spelling quiz. The next morning, Miguel saw a planner note from Eli's mom, asking to see the test. Eli showed him the note with a shy smile. Sensing that Eli didn't get much praise at home, Miguel wrote, "I'm really proud of him. He did a really good job."

Just before the holiday weekend, the school board quietly mentioned that they would postpone further discussion of the academy. Miguel's movement had succeeded. Because the district had made no progress on its quest to eliminate special ed classes, Miguel hoped that plan, too, would not come to fruition.

"Do No Harm but Take No Crap": Bribery, Workarounds, Happy Hours, and Other Pro Tips for Educators

Every teacher has their own MOs for interactions with students, parents, and coworkers. There is no one "right" strategy, and what works in one situation might not work in another. With that said, teachers here share tips and tricks they believe could help fellow educators.

How to Interact with Students

Connect before you correct

In her book *The Good News About Bad Behavior*, author Katherine Reynolds Lewis advises, "Connect before you correct," a phrase I've never forgotten, and one I've adhered to often as a sub and soccer coach. Veteran teachers do this instinctively. "These kids need you to be there for them emotionally," said a PE teacher at a high-poverty Texas school. "I've noticed kids coming in my gym misbehaving. I don't yell at them. After a couple times I'll tell them to sit down, but my first reaction is not to yell. I pull them outside because you never know what reaction you're going to get and I don't want to have an audience. Most times it's something deeper."

When they're alone, this teacher tells students, "You're not in trouble. This is just me and you. What's going on? Because you don't act like this." He said, "Sometimes they break down and tell me. Sometimes they just start crying. Sometimes they just be like, 'Nothing's wrong,' and I'm like, 'No, I know you. Something's wrong. If you need someone to talk to, I'm here. If you don't feel comfortable talking to me, we have a counselor.'" He suggests the student stay outside with the door open for a few minutes to get fresh air. "A lot of times you don't know what's really going on at home. You never know if the parents got arrested last night or what. Sometimes kids just have a bad day. I've had kids want to give me a hug. I'm like, 'Man, why you hugging me?' But sometimes they just need somebody to listen and to know that somebody cares."

In like a lion . . .

Many teachers begin the year no-nonsense and gradually soften the tough love once students adapt to their new routines. A Pennsylvania 7th grade teacher lays down the law from day one. She has her students practice entering and exiting her room by lining up along the wall, waiting for the prior class to exit, asking permission to come in, and going straight to their seats to do their daily warm-up activity. "They cannot use the bathroom when I'm teaching unless it's an absolute emergency. I have so many rules, and some people may think this is drill-sergeant behavior, but it works at my school," she said. "When you don't follow the rules, there are consequences. Because of this, I have very few behavioral issues. A lot of kids try to test you in the beginning and see what they can get away with. You can't back down. Stick to it."

Get real

A Georgia private school English teacher said he strives to always "be genuine" with his students. "I don't mean you should be their buddy or overshare. I mean be a real, honest human being with them. Teenagers can smell insincerity a mile away. Don't BS or condescend to them. If you make a mistake—enter the wrong grade, call a student by the wrong name, say something incorrect—just acknowledge it, apologize if necessary, and move on. Treat them with respect and hold them consistently to appropriately high standards and they will go to the ends of the earth for you."

This strategy can boost disciplinary efforts, too. "Always take the time to get to know students and talk to them about common interests. Let them see you as a human," said a Pennsylvania high school history teacher. "When you have a problem student, take them away from the rest of the class to talk and let them know how their actions affect you personally so they can see how they can affect others and will think more deeply about their actions in the future."

But don't beat yourself up if you can't get through to a student, teachers advised. "You cannot save them all, as much as you'd love to. You can't get emotionally destroyed when you fail to turn a troubled student around. Keep trying, because you'll save many, but not all," said a California high school English teacher. "Be their teacher, not their friend. They have loads of friends and only a handful of good teachers. Be fair. Be consistent. Make them laugh. Love them so strongly that you convince them to love themselves. Do no harm but take no crap."

Fake it till you make it

"I use my minor in theater every day," said a midwestern science teacher. "I never make up things or lie to the students, but I can change my demeanor to project like all is good and I have everything under control."

Raise the bar

When a Louisiana science teacher attended a training for a new curriculum, a presenter said she didn't give multiple choice questions and her students wrote every day. "I said to her, 'Wow, I don't know if I could ever get that from my students.' But this year I did. My students said it was the first time they've ever had a class like this. It really changed their mindset about critical thinking and writing," he said. "The kids who tended to be behaviorally 'high-fliers' not only bought into this type of teaching, they excelled at it: always asking the deeper question, putting out hypotheses, trying to piece together a conclusion from the tidbits of evidence. I asked one of the more challenging students why and he said, 'Because we always mess up, so we have no fear of being wrong.' Which explains why my honors students struggled at first. They were so afraid of being incorrect, they'd hold back from answering any questions."

Home in on "that kid"

"Find the kid the other teachers complain about in the lounge, the kid who repulses other teachers, the one whom teachers seem to take too personally. Be the best teacher that kid has ever had," the Missouri teacher said. "It will make your job easier and potentially change the trajectory of that child's whole life. And if it doesn't, you can at least go to bed with a clear conscience that you tried."

Share that you're learning, too

A California special ed teacher said when he was a student, he connected most with teachers who "didn't act like they knew more than students." "For me, being open with students helps them not feel intimidated in the classroom setting. I try to point out new information I'm learning along with them while staying enthused about the topic, which helps them stay interested as well. We're all lifelong learners, so why not continue the process with them?"

When in doubt, interpretive dance?

Two teachers brought up stories that mentioned interpretive dance. An Iowa science teacher said, "I once had a dream that I made my biology class do an interpretive dance demonstrating the steps of mitosis. So I actually had my classes do it in real life. It was hysterical to watch."

At a North Carolina magnet school, an 8th grade history teacher was covering industrialization with a "jigsaw," a technique that assigns small student groups a topic to teach the others. One group repeatedly asked how they should present their material, even after the teacher told them to come up with their own method. After the fourth time they asked, the teacher said, exasperated, "Whatever kind of presentation you want! Do an interpretive dance for all I care."

Well, they did. "The joke was on me," the teacher said. "Three of the girls were in the dance track and the other was in the creative writing track. They composed a spoken word poem with a solid beat that the three danced out. It was amazing. They climbed on each other to create skyscrapers; baseball players became opera stars to show urban entertainment, who then barfed and keeled over, illustrating the spread of disease. The other students dutifully took notes because they had been trained in how to read art as text. I maybe learned a more valuable lesson than any of my students that day."

Dance can be an effective learning strategy. Science writer Annie Murphy Paul, author of *The Extended Mind*, reported that whole-body movements can help someone "commit knowledge more firmly to memory; the 'enactment effect' shows that we remember what we *do* much better than what we read or hear."

How to Interact with Parents

Give them a hamburger

In conferences and meetings, many teachers offer parents a "hamburger," also known as a "compliment sandwich" or "two glows and a grow." A Texas art teacher explained, "Parents love to hear good things about their kids and are willing to hear an area for growth if you offer two good things." An Illinois high school English teacher offered an example: "Your child has such a positive attitude! Unfortunately they failed a test, but I know they're trying so hard and we'll be able to get their grade back up."

To help develop the parent-teacher relationship before those situations arise, the Illinois teacher periodically sends complimentary emails to parents, sharing that their child aced the vocab quiz, helped another classmate, or asked a great question. She explained, "It helps create a positive relationship with parents, so if you have to have a harder conversation (say, about poor grades or cheating), you've already established that you see the good in their kid."

Also, when raising a negative, the Texas teacher suggested, "Never lead with 'Your child.' I say something like, 'I find it challenging to teach my class when a student persists in standing up and loudly acting like a fool.' Invariably, the parent's head snaps around and they say to their child, 'Do you do that?' If you lead with 'Your child,' the parent becomes defensive and won't listen."

Validate them

Parent emails used to "spook" a Pennsylvania middle school teacher, she said. Now she avoids checking her school email after work hours or on weekends. "I'd be up all night worrying about it, especially if it was negative. But I've learned that most of the time, the parent is aggravated at the situation or their child, not at me. So I usually wait a day to respond if it's not urgent, because by then I've calmed down and so have they. I try to validate what they're feeling ('I can't imagine how difficult this must be for you'), which goes a long way in turning the email from negative to positive. Parents want to be given the benefit of the doubt, so I try to provide that while still addressing the issue."

A Missouri middle school teacher said that validating parents' concerns is particularly important in low-income schools like hers. "Listen. Let parents talk. They'll eventually run out of steam and then it can be your turn. If you're having a difficult meeting, lean forward and say something like 'Your child is really important to me and I want to leave this meeting with everyone on the same page,'" she said. "Parents walk into schools with all the feelings they had when they were students, and many of them didn't have good experiences. You have the chance to be the first educational professional who *sees* them, who talks like they talk, who wants to be on their side instead of telling them what they or their child are doing wrong. A parent who trusts you conveys this to the child you see every day, who will be more willing to also trust you."

Find the humor

Two New York elementary school teachers often commiserated about the outlandish parent emails they received each week. After one ran a class spelling bee, she got an email from a parent whose child came in second. "The parent accused her of not being able to spell, because clearly her son would not have spelled a word wrong and gotten out, since he knew how to spell everything," the other teacher said. "After that day, she and I created a 'spelling bee jar' where we added money to the jar every time we received a parent complaint and we used the proceeds to go to a well-deserved happy hour."

How to Stay Sane

Protect yourself

"Document everything, and I mean everything. Also, when asked to do something you think is questionable ethically, illegal, or a grade shakedown [pressure to bump up a grade], ask for the request in writing. This makes many unethical requests evaporate," the Texas high school language teacher said.

Try to find times to compartmentalize

A Kansas high school teacher uses her commute to transition into and out of work mode so she doesn't dwell (as much) at home. "On the way there, I think about what went well and wrong yesterday and what I want to change today. I record on my phone when I have a goal. On the way home, I review my day and brainstorm. Then I try to leave it as I rejoin my family until the next day (or until two in the morning, when I'm still trying to create a plan). When you deal with students with behaviors, somehow plan times always get sucked out within the chaos of the day."

A few days a week, the Pennsylvania 7th grade teacher selects a time she'll stop working for the day. "Teachers could work 24/7 if you really wanted to because the work is always there, but that's just it, the work is *always* there. If I have a day where I just want to get home or I have plans in the evening, I set a limit: 'Okay, I'm leaving at three thirty.' Other days, I want to get stuff done, so I'll stay later. But don't overdo it if you're feeling exhausted. Your family deserves the best of you when you get home. I am extremely dedicated to my job, but a few years ago, that almost ended me. My anxiety was spiraling out of control and I was depressed. I was too involved in work. You cannot be an effective teacher, spouse, or parent if you aren't in the right frame of mind. Set limits."

Don't take on everything yourself

"Don't re-create the wheel if you don't have to," said the Pennsylvania history teacher. "Borrow as many lesson plans and resources from other teachers or online as you can." The Iowa science teacher agreed: "Other people have already created great lessons and will share them. I then just have to tweak them to fit my equipment and students' interests." One of teachers' favorite resources is Teachers Pay Teachers, an online platform in which teachers can "exchange instructional materials and access easy-to-use digital tools."

Pro tip for observations

Educators can cajole students into behaving during a classroom observation, said a Minnesota middle school science teacher. "I've one hundred percent bribed kids for observations and I'm sure any teacher will say the same," she said. She offers candy, fun activities, or a movie day and explains the observation's purpose. "For the most part, they get it."

Consider workarounds

A Maryland high school math teacher who retired after 50 years was not on board with her district's policy that any student who turned in work automatically received at least a 50% score. "Teachers do not agree with that and feel it undermines their ability to do what they believe constitutes teaching. I figured out my own way to get around this in a stated class grading policy that no one questioned," she said.

How to Interact with Colleagues

Choose your own mentor

"You might be assigned a mentor, but you can also informally pick a teacher you admire, get to know her, and take her advice," said a Texas high school language teacher. "My 'mentor' was a teacher who taught for many years prior to my joining the field. She taught me invaluable lessons."

A Georgia English teacher often tries to observe his coworkers and discuss best practices. "Seek out colleagues who are good teachers and learn from them," he said. "Good teachers need to be able to collaborate and learn from one another, just as we ask students to do. Also, think of the bad teachers you had, and the things those teachers did that made them bad teachers. Then don't do those things. It's harder than it sounds."

Check your—and your colleagues'—implicit biases

When a Texas high school English teacher was a student, athletes and cheerleaders sat at one cafeteria table, band kids at another, and "all of the Black kids (there weren't a lot of us at my high school) sat together." At the school where she now teaches, "the kids blend together so beautifully. However, that doesn't always translate to us adults. Some of my peers continue the culture of low expectations. Here are some comments I've heard: 'These kids are the reason I drink.' 'Nobody's going to take these kids seriously.' 'It doesn't matter, she's not going to go anywhere.' 'They're not going to college anyway, so do they really need . . .'"

She continued. "These comments are defeatist and kids pick up on it. I want to ask my colleagues, 'If we were in a majority Caucasian school, would y'all still say these things?' It gets annoying hearing 'Our kids won't do that.' My response to this statement has been, 'Kids rise to any challenge set before them. You're going to have a few that don't. Just like adults.' Overall, I get infuriated by the culture of low expectations because it not only puts all students at a disadvantage heading into the next level, it cripples children of color, the group of students who have historically had academic disadvantages. The majority of my peers don't understand and their privilege—that they claim they don't have—allows them to not understand."

She hopes fellow educators can learn to check their implicit biases and remain aware. "I've seen white teachers tense up or get extremely defensive and combative whenever we've had workshops on how to teach children of another color or on implicit biases. And for the record, I've taught in schools where I was the only Black teacher. You better believe I had to check some of my biases before I walked in the door. Once you're aware of your biases, you can work to overcome them."

Christopher Emdin makes a similar point in his book *For White Folks Who Teach in the Hood . . . and the Rest of Y'all Too*: "The work for white folks who teach in urban schools . . . is to unpack their privileges and excavate the institutional, societal, and personal histories they bring with them when they come to the hood."

Fraternize in the workplace . . .

Some teachers rely on coworkers to help boost them throughout the day. "Support systems of other teachers are essential," said a Tennessee library media specialist. "Some of my best friends are teachers. A group of us meets every week for margaritas and laughter even through the summer." A Colorado kindergarten teacher agreed:

"Having at least a few strong staff relationships is key, because other friends and family members, even those working in the field of education, can't really understand the toll this work can take on us."

The Georgia English teacher explained the allure. "When teachers get together socially, we always end up talking shop. Our spouses with jobs usually want to leave work at work; the last thing they want to do is talk about work when they're socializing. Teachers may try to avoid it, but like Coleridge's Ancient Mariner, we are eventually compelled to talk about it. 'Why would you want to hang out with your coworkers after work?' our spouses ask. 'Don't you spend all day with them?' No, that's the thing. We spend all day with our students. We see our colleagues at lunch when we aren't running a club, conferencing with a student, or returning a parent phone call."

. . . Or not

A Delaware English teacher cautions new teachers not to go to happy hour because of a gaffe her student teacher made. "People let down their guard at happy hours and you might be tempted, too. Until you know the connections among your peers, you don't want to be anywhere where you might gossip to the wrong person about the wrong thing," she said. At a happy hour with other student teachers, hers complained about her department chair. Another attendee told her co-teacher, who told the chair. "When I finally got wind of it, I had to have a really difficult conversation with her about gossip as a professional," the teacher said. "This seemingly small slipup ultimately cost my student teacher a future job, which was a shame, because she was promising."

Other teachers said that depending on the school culture, it's possible to find a middle ground between coworkers and friends. "Dealing with colleagues is *hard*. I've had some great ones and ones I never want to see again. People told me, 'Don't confide in people at work.' How can you not? You spend more time with those people than you do with your own family sometimes," said a New York English teacher. "But you have to find the ones you can trust. And you will. Follow your gut. Those you can't trust? Be polite, watercooler chatter, but don't complain to them or tell them anything personal."

How to navigate the staff lounge

Teachers also have mixed feelings about the staff lounge. It can forge friendships, but it can also be a lion's den. A California middle school math teacher eats lunch in her room with students. "I don't really talk to the other teachers at my school much. That can be hard, but I don't share interests with them and sometimes I don't like the way teachers vent and the feeling that I have to go along with it. I'd rather eat and hang out with the kiddos than be around negativity, so I mostly stay in my room to keep my sanity. I'm happy to work with the kids, though. One year two eighth graders ate with me nearly every day."

The Missouri middle school teacher suggested that new teachers start off in the lounge to understand staff politics, but then proceed with caution. "Eat in the lounge for a while, if that's what's done at your school, until you figure out who's on your side. Then casually invite them to eat in your room," she said. "Talk about benign things from your personal life, your own kids' soccer games, your yard, the cute thing your toddler did. Do *not* complain about parents or students. Find a partner you can go to for real problems, and complain about your job to people who aren't teachers. Don't mix it up in the lounge because it will come back to bite you every time."

Teachers who want to hang out in the staff lounge at least should "stay away from complainers," the Pennsylvania English teacher suggested. "You won't change them, and they'll always bring you down. Surround yourself with people who are kind and willing to collaborate. They will be your heroes, in terms of both your emotional support and helping you support your students. I always say that my kids are as successful as they are because of the hidden team I have that works with me behind the scenes."

CHAPTER 11

June

A principal to a Massachusetts high school teacher: "You smile too much."

A mother, as she handed a California AP English teacher a Starbucks gift card: "I know you teachers don't make much, and [my daughter] has never gotten less than an A in any of her other classes, so what can we do to resolve this? Because I know you don't want to ruin her future."

The teacher said she couldn't change the grade.

Mother: "You haven't heard the last from me, bitch."

An upset mother to a Maryland elementary general music teacher about the school musical: "I don't understand why [another student] has fifty-six words and my son only has forty-three!"

Penny Davis	6th Grade Math Teacher

Eleven years ago, at another school, Penny taught a 1st grader with a learning disability and other special needs. During her first parent-teacher meeting with Penny, Ben's mom was a wreck, sobbing about her son. Penny sat her down, took both her hands, and said, "It's going to be okay. Maybe not today or tomorrow, but it will be okay. Ben has limitless potential, two parents who have tirelessly worked to ensure he has the support he needs, and me—and I believe in him."

Ben grew by leaps and bounds that year, and until she left his school, Penny tutored him so that he remained at grade level. She heard from his mom over the years that Ben continued to thrive.

In June, Penny learned that Ben was one of a small number of graduating high school seniors who would receive an Outstanding Senior Achievement Award, recognizing students who had met certain academic and extracurricular requirements and completed an exceptional number of community service hours. For the awards ceremony, honorees were allowed to choose one teacher who had been influential in their success. Ben had named Penny.

Penny glowed with pride when the young man walked across the stage to receive his award. He planned to double-major in business and computer science at a state university. During dinner afterward, Ben's mom told the table about how Penny "believed in him but also in me. She constantly supported me by finding things to help not only at school but at home. She researched different strategies and programs she thought would help support him. She nurtured his academics and also his social well-being and self-esteem by believing he could be successful. I was worried about him, but Penny was always one hundred percent positive. It takes a village!"

Zach's mom, too, expressed her appreciation. She said Penny had an enormous impact on Zach. She had been terrified to send Zach to middle school, she said, and was overwhelmed with gratitude that he'd made so much progress, particularly in Penny's class. In math, Zach had gone from a low B to a high A, and he'd aced the standardized test. "He hated math until he met you. He loves you very much. You made math fun and now he loves it because of you."

Zach approached Penny after class on the last day of school. He looked straight at her, his eyes crinkling as he smiled. Then he gave his teacher a warm, tight, extended hug. Penny understood. "There was a lot behind that hug," Penny said later. "He was communicating with me. That hug said, 'Thank you for taking care of me.'"

On a hot summer day in mid-June, Penny and Ed drove a few hours out of town to go hiking together. Their divorce attorneys had told them they were allowed to date, but advised them not to go out close to home. Both private people, Penny and Ed were fine with that. They didn't tell anyone they were now more than friends. They hadn't even told their children.

When they reached the section of a trail that started up a mountain, Penny hesitated. The trail had several difficult stretches of rock climbing and uneven terrain. "I don't know, this one looks harder than any other I've done," Penny said. "I don't think I can make it up this one."

"I know you can make it. If you can nail a huge thesis paper about math, you can certainly climb this mountain," Ed replied.

As the school year wound down, Penny had stopped taking anti-anxiety medication and turned to hiking to clear her mind. Southern's toxic work culture, rife with cliques and distrust, had been her trigger, and she was leaving that behind. The administrators were so indifferent to staff morale that they didn't host the annual End-of-the-Year Staff Farewell Lunch. The teachers didn't know where the money budgeted for that tradition had gone.

Three hours later, their arms and legs aching, drenched in sweat and streaked with dirt, Penny and Ed reached the peak. As Penny gazed at the sweeping view, the metaphor wasn't lost on her. "I never would've thought I'd be able to get up this mountain. My soul needed this. A year ago, I just went along with the status quo. I never questioned. I did what I was told, what was expected of me. By the school system. By the town. By my husband," she told me later. "I always doubted myself. I had to find an inner drive, a backbone. I did the hard part by leaving. I realize I let everybody walk all over me at times. You know how you envision what your life is going to be like, and you think you'll be able to do great things? I just saw myself giving up on myself. But I had to realize"—now she spoke through tears—"that I needed to be more independent. I got married right out of college, which is fine for some people, but I think I wanted to maybe go experience life. I needed to climb a mountain. These are happy tears. These are tears of 'Good lord, you were so hard on yourself.'"

It was quiet here where the world was still. Penny couldn't hear "the noises in my head," the voices of expectations and judgments. She sat on a boulder near the precipice, feeling the warmth of the sun on her face, breathing in the clean, fresh air, reveling in the calm. *Golly, you made it up this mountain. Think of how many other hard things you've done this year*, she thought, and smiled. She had left her husband, found her financial footing, gotten a new job, met a best friend, begun a relationship with someone who truly supported her, and finished her first semester of grad school—the goal she'd dreamed of for 20 years. And, as always, she'd successfully guided some challenging students through 6th grade math. While she would dearly miss teaching children, she would always be an educator. *If you can go up the hardest mountain you've ever hiked and go through a divorce, and deal with people who are horrible to you, you really can do anything*, she thought.

When she stood up, she saw Ed waiting for her patiently, hanging back to let her be alone with her thoughts. They had grown closer in recent weeks. They routinely shared home-cooked dinners when the kids were out for the night. Sometimes they just sat out on Ed's back porch and had cerebral discussions. And sometimes he reminded her that *Dirty Dancing* passion was possible after all.

"Penny, I didn't believe there was such a thing as soulmates, but clearly there is," Ed said. "I've never experienced a connection to another human being as much as I have with you."

"Thank you for believing in me when I really wasn't believing in myself."

"Sometimes it takes somebody to see it in you and encourage it," he replied.

"I'm not the same person I was a year ago," she said. She felt independent now, confident, resilient. She'd been through hell this year and yet here she was on top of the mountain, her world righted, her heart full.

Rebecca Abrams   Elementary School Teacher

Rebecca gave the class a spelling pretest. "Ship. I would like to own a ship someday. Ship."

"But you DO own a ship already!" Santiago said.

Rebecca raised her eyebrows. "Oh?"

"In your IMAGINATION!"

Rebecca laughed. That was a Miss Abrams thing for a student to say. "Okay, good point. *Everyone* has a ship already in their imaginations!"

"Yaayy!" The kids at the table cheered.

The second week of June, Rebecca and Grace convinced Oliver's parents to attend a child study meeting, the first step of a local screening process. Oliver had come a long way since August. He continued to exhibit the same issues, but he was happier and more frequently able to roll with the punches. He had even made a second friend.

By the end of the meeting, the assistant principal, counselor, and teachers had persuaded Oliver's mother to let his father initiate evaluations and testing. "We will work with you next year to see what to do about it," Rebecca told them, certain Oliver would have an IEP that would get him the support he needed. "If you want, he could have a set number of hours working with a counselor on social skills.

And he'd have a writing goal; the special ed teacher would be required to spend some time helping him with his writing. He'd still be in the gifted classes, but where he needs support, he'd get it."

Afterward, Rebecca told me, "This past year it was me doing what I could with him because we built a rapport quickly. But I'm not a special ed teacher, and I was making up stuff as I went along. We're all so relieved they're finally going through testing. Hopefully, next year he'll learn so much easier."

Illyse, too, was getting help. Grace told Rebecca that after she'd suggested for months that Illyse should get counseling services, her parents had finally found her a therapist.

On the last day of school, JJ handed Rebecca an envelope at dismissal. Rebecca read the letter at red lights on her drive home. Every time she got through another few sentences, she cried harder. She received lovey notes from students fairly often and short thank-you cards from parents every June. But she'd never gotten a note like this, long and detailed, full of specifics about her teaching methods.

JJ's mom told Rebecca that she was the most influential teacher her son had ever had, that she had sparked in him a love of true learning and an eagerness to understand the reasoning behind everything from math problems to historical events. She thanked Rebecca for developing JJ's growth mindset and pushing him to reach his full learning potential. She listed examples of social studies and ELA units she'd overheard JJ discussing with friends, and funny stories he shared at dinner, like "killing birds" and "Cheez-Its." Rebecca had changed his life, she wrote, and he was so enthusiastic about Rebecca's class that when he realized it was the last day of school and Rebecca would no longer be his teacher, he put his head on his mom's shoulder and cried.

June

When Rebecca finished reading, she pulled into a supermarket parking lot because she couldn't wait to share the letter. She read it out loud to her mother. "Mom," Rebecca said, "this is the best validation I've received in my entire teaching career."

The note also validated a perspective that had crystallized for Rebecca over the last several weeks. "Getting a dog and having a love life were meant to help improve my work/life balance, but I've realized that in reality, as fun as they were at times, overall they were counterproductive. While I'd hoped they would decrease my stress, they ended up being additional time commitments that made me put myself last even more than before," Rebecca told me. She decided not to resume dating. She might have been interested to see what could happen with Sam, but she knew he'd want a commitment she wasn't sure she could give. "I think I'm done with boys for now. I don't need to date to be happy and fulfilled with my life."

Rebecca would spend the summer taking a new gifted learners course to make up for the one she'd dropped, prepping for classes, doing a musical, and reconnecting with friends and family. Most of her summer would revolve around teaching, which was what she wanted. "I'm going to reclaim my own life," she told me, but this time she meant doing what she already loved, rather than adding new things into the mix. Rebecca had come to the realization that the life she truly wanted—the one that was most personally meaningful to her—was one in which being a teacher came first. And for Rebecca, for now, that was enough.

Miguel Garcia   Middle School Special Ed Teacher

When Frank asked Miguel to help him with an administrative duty, the counselor covered his class for 20 minutes. Afterward, the counselor effused in front of the class, "Your kids are so great. They're so well behaved. They were listening and they were participating. They were just a joy." Miguel realized then that he had gotten his students behaviorally to where they needed to be.

Eli's behavior had been top-notch lately. He constantly asked Miguel if he could help—pass things out, pick things up—and his hand shot into the air whenever Miguel asked for a volunteer. He was unfailingly polite, thanking Miguel for things other students would never have thought to. He routinely requested extra homework so that he could earn more points.

One afternoon, Eli joked around with a classmate who took the teasing too far. Miguel silently watched from a distance. Instead of coiling into his usual rage, Eli immediately asked Miguel, "I'm upset. Can I get up and go out?"

"Yeah, sure. Go."

When Eli returned just a few minutes later, he said, "Thank you. I really needed to go out."

Miguel was heartened. He didn't need to worry about Eli anymore. Eli was going to be okay.

In Miguel's video class, Quiesha was now confidently leading a group of students making a short film. At the end of the school year, Miguel would present her with the school's Cinematographer Award. The counselor told Miguel that while Quiesha had difficulty in her other classes because of reading and writing, thanks to her success in Miguel's class, she was passionate about pursuing a career in cinematic arts. Quiesha, Miguel knew, would be okay, too.

Miguel had finished his 7th and 8th grade history units and had rotated back to 6th to teach about ancient Egypt. The students were fascinated in particular by how the Egyptians removed liquefied brains out the nose. Using a stuffed anatomical model, Miguel demonstrated how the Egyptians extracted organs and stored them in jars. They did a class project to mimic drying out a body, liquefying the brain, and rewrapping the model (in toilet paper) to make a mummy.

Naturally, the brain-out-the-nose topic led students to disrupt the lesson with booger jokes. "All right, you want to talk about boogers instead? Let's talk about boogers. What kind is better: brown, yellow, or green?" Miguel asked. The kids laughed. "No, seriously, do you like dry boogers, wet boogers, the really disgusting ones?" Now their laughter was more uncertain. "I want you to go home and tell your parents you wanted to talk about boogers because that's what you're interested in."

The novelty wore off. "No, we want to talk about King Tut," said Eli.

"I think we should delve into boogers, since you guys keep talking about that," Miguel said.

"No, we don't want to anymore," said Gabe.

Miguel resumed his lesson, pleased to have regained their attention in less than a minute.

When the class finished preserving the mummy, Miguel had them create a replica of King Tut's tomb, which he suggested they decorate with gold paint and fake jewels. On the second day of this project, Dewayne approached Miguel at the beginning of class. Usually, Dewayne was particularly challenging in the afternoons.

"Where are the King Tut materials?" Dewayne asked.

"Over there," Miguel pointed. He watched Dewayne collect the items, sit down quietly next to Isabel, and get to work.

Hm, interesting, Miguel thought.

For the rest of the afternoon, Dewayne's behavior was stellar. He concentrated on creating intricate detailed work, collaborating with Isabel to glue beautiful patterns of fake jewels onto the sarcophagus.

Miguel watched, amazed. *Oh, he needs something tactile. I have to always have him do something with his hands because as long as his hands are busy, he's laser focused.* Had Dewayne been in his science class since the start of the year, Miguel would have made this discovery a semester ago. Right away, Miguel began brainstorming how he could differentiate instruction so that Dewayne would be constantly engaged. For an upcoming poetry assignment, for example, rather than write in a notebook, Miguel could have him paint his poem onto a box.

The next afternoon, a TV reporter was scheduled to film Miguel's class for the segment on his teaching award. Miguel had warned Frank that his class would be chaotic because of the King Tut project, but Frank was unfazed. The reporter showed up near the end of the day, when some of the kids were already cleaning up. This was a time when Dewayne was usually bouncing off the walls. Miguel watched the reporter circle the classroom and settle on her shot: Dewayne and Isabel, oblivious to the pandemonium, working diligently on their design. *Wow,* Miguel thought. *He's the model student.*

After Miguel stored some video equipment for the summer in the school's most secure closet, a treasure trove of random educational paraphernalia, he poked around, curious. He came across a bunch of unopened boxes. *What are these?* he wondered as he turned them over. *Microscopes!* There were a dozen new, untouched microscopes, nearly enough for every student in his special ed class. *Cooool. If no one's using them, I will.*

For the next Fun Friday Science Experiment, he taught the kids how to use the microscopes. They looked at the slides that came with the equipment. He told them to pluck a hair from their head, inspect it under the microscope, and trade places.

"Whooaa," the students said, fascinated.

The previous week, they had dyed crystals with food coloring. Today, Miguel had them insert a tiny slice of their crystal under the microscope. The kids moved around the room to examine different colors. The effects were beautiful. The class was awed.

"Mr. Garcia," Gabe announced, "you're my favorite teacher ever." When Gabe realized he'd blurted that out in front of the class, he startled, then resumed gazing through his microscope.

Miguel blinked, initially unable to respond. The remark, from a 7th grade boy, took his breath away. He thought praise from adults was often accompanied by an agenda. Spontaneous praise from students was pure. Children meant what they said from their hearts. "I don't think I could have gotten such a gratifying, human, and life-affirming moment in many other professions. While teaching is stressful, hard, and often overwhelming, you also get nuggets that signal you're making an impact," he told me. "What's wonderful about being a teacher is knowing that even after I'm gone, my life will have meant something. It sounds corny, but it's true. I have friends who make gobs of money in finance and corporate law, but it's really sterile. I love honest and raw human interaction, even when it's messy, as it can be with kids."

～❧～

On a late June morning, when Miguel would otherwise be sleeping in, he opened the Zoom room. *Ding. Ding. Ding.* One student after another joined the video call—more students than he'd expected to show up to learn. It was the first day of special ed online summer school for 6th, 7th, and 8th graders, and Miguel was ready to teach.

Months ago, if you'd told Miguel he'd be teaching summer school, he would have laughed in disbelief. But the program was short-staffed and Miguel was glad to get more practice with the latest educational technologies. He had learned in 2020 that some mildly to moderately disabled special ed students could concentrate more easily during remote learning, without the challenging social situations, distractions of their peers in the classroom, or temptations to misbehave for attention. Some of his academic-year kids had signed up for this summer school class, too.

These weren't the driving reasons behind Miguel's decision to teach, however. Maybe he was here because on the last day of school, when the period ended, he'd said to one of his video classes, "Okay guys, have a great summer," and no one moved. An 8th grader cleared her throat, said, "I just want to say thank you. I really loved your class," and teared up. Before the students filed out, there was a chorus of thank-yous and, to Miguel's surprise, more sniffles.

Miguel was not an emotional person, but he had to pause to compose himself. *I thought this elective was just something for them to pass the time, but the class and the connections were really important to them*, he realized.

Or maybe he'd chosen this path because, he told me, "I really, really loved my kids this year, all of them." He recognized that his frustrations with teaching involved testing, unnecessary paperwork, and obstructive bureaucracy, none of which played a role in summer school. But the kids? They made his soul happy.

A week after the academic year had ended, Miguel had chatted with the guidance counselor before a meeting to interview a potential addition to the counseling office.

"You know the times I'd go to you to vent? Thank you for that," Miguel told her. "It wasn't that I hated all this. I just needed to vent and I felt better afterward."

"I know. When I went into your class and saw what you were doing, I always knew you loved the teaching part. It was just everything else," she said. "You didn't know I watched your class from the hall sometimes. You were always really involved and the kids really responded to you."

The job candidate told the interview committee that he'd initially become a teacher to help disadvantaged Black children whose background paralleled his own. After several years of teaching, when he saw the holistic impact counselors could have on students, he changed course. Now a few years into retirement, he felt the pull to return to counseling students because he realized "it's very important for me and for my life to continue doing this sort of work."

Something clicked for Miguel at that moment. *I'm looking at my future*, he thought. He wanted to keep working with communities like the one he grew up in, "where kids aren't getting support and not doing that well academically, but want to get out." He wanted to help those students share their stories, which they could accomplish through film. Because the district still hadn't figured out how to realistically mainstream special ed students, Western's special ed program would remain intact for now.

"So many of the kids in my special ed class were known for being 'problem kids'; people would say, 'You better watch out for that one.' It was meaningful to me to try to figure out why they were so guarded, angry, or disappointed and to try to right that," Miguel told me. "And so many of my students are young African American boys. Some of my kids could easily be shot by the cops in a bad situation. They might listen to me more than they might listen to someone else. So there's a sense of urgency. Of vocation. My vocation is to mentor. I'm almost at the age when my mom had her brain hemorrhage. I'm writing my DNR. If I don't have a lot of time left, I don't want to waste it. What I'm doing is good and my daughter will see that. We all want a life's purpose. Isn't that what we all want?"

Miguel's life purpose, he was sure now, was to return to Western, to protect his school community, and to teach his students in the fall.

Epilogue: December 2021

Alexandra Robbins   3rd Grade Teacher (Long-Term Sub)

"My" classroom has emptied for the last time, the tail end of my students' dismissal line having trickled outside to the buses, towing with it a wistful piece of my heart. When the kids return from Winter Break, they will no longer be mine. Now that elementary students are finally getting vaccinated and recent college grads have joined the hiring pool, our public school has found a permanent certified teacher for the position.

But I will always think of this class as mine. They are the only class I have taught for more than a few weeks at a time, the only class that thought of me as their teacher, not a sub. Teaching is a hard job, but it is harder to step away.

Initially I'd considered it sheer coincidence that I became a teacher at the same time as I happened to be writing a book about teachers. When I began short-term subbing in 2019, I viewed the work as an act of service; after volunteering unpaid in schools for years, I spent my substitute paychecks on classroom supplies, day brighteners, and, later, PPE for the teachers whose classes I covered and #ClearTheList items for others. It didn't ever occur to me, even at the start of the pandemic, that I would take on a long-term role.

When I did, just as people incredulously asked Miguel why he left a more lucrative job for teaching, some acquaintances had difficulty comprehending why I slowed my writing career to sub. They questioned why I gave up sleep, family time, weekends, and better-paid work. They were perplexed by why I allowed prepping, grading, and pondering ways to motivate and entertain students to consume my life outside of school. They couldn't fathom why I dragged myself to school while sick (not COVID, not contagious), even though I explained that there were no substitutes available. On one day that week, 18 staff members at my school were out, most without subs. If I stayed home, a coworker would have to cover my class in addition to their own responsibilities.

It was when I defended my reasoning, which echoed that of teachers I'd interviewed, that I realized that while the urgent pandemic teaching vacancy was happenstance, perhaps my agreeing to fill it was not wholly coincidental. By then I had interviewed teachers nationwide for six years, first because they wanted to share their thoughts with me after reading my book about nurses, a similarly underappreciated helping profession, then sporadically as I wrote another book, then in depth as I began reporting this one. When I explained to friends why I would show up to work unless I was contagious, it hit me that I had been so inspired by the teachers I'd met, interviewed, and worked with that their mission had become mine. I joined their ranks because a school asked for help, but I also knew when I accepted that, for me, the joys of full-time teaching would outweigh the sacrifices.

And they did. I saw students aha moments in real time when a math strategy clicked, they made a text connection, or their science experiment worked. It was exhilarating to watch their eyes brighten as they came up with original, creative story plotlines during our one-on-one writers' workshops. It was validating that they often begged for our rap/dance-offs to the silly rhymes I made up for them to remember math or reading comprehension strategies, similar to Miguel's glee when his students didn't recognize that their games were lessons in disguise. Students laughing so hard they fell out of their chairs became a regular occurrence in my classroom; I would do anything for those 8- and 9-year-old baby-giggle belly laughs. Delighting the kids delighted me. Teaching those students felt like the most consistently meaningful work I had ever done.

It was also helpful to experience firsthand the aspects of the job that teachers discussed with me during interviews. I gave Back to School Night presentations, conducted parent-teacher conferences, navigated the grading and report card system—which was more complicated than I'd realized—weathered a COVID-caused quarantine of half the class, taught hybrid. I ran our class's mandatory active shooter lockdown drill. I survived Fucktober.

At the same time, I understood how one can love teaching but dislike the profession. I loved the students and staff, adored my team, and was lucky that my class had helpful, supportive parents. The school day itself was a happy time for me. But like many school systems, ours had out-of-touch district officials, countywide bureaucratic delays and inefficiencies, overtesting, some counterproductive school board members, and a central office that demanded too much while providing too little—which partly explained why the district's number of vacant school staff positions eventually soared past 1,000.

In my now jarringly quiet classroom, I'm not thinking about any of those obstacles. I hear only the echoes of the kids' sweet voices, the familiar refrains of our inside jokes, and their genuine cheers for classmates who nailed an answer, earned a special seat, or were rewarded for kindness. I'm already awash in nostalgia for the camaraderie and rapport of, as Miguel put it, our little family.

I'm also thinking about the compassionate village of educators who warmly and enthusiastically supported my students and me, including Miguel, Penny, and Rebecca, who cheerfully dispensed advice whenever I reached out. At my school, I remember the librarians who helped stock my classroom library and taught me to use the online platforms; the secretaries who made generous extra efforts to save me time; the building services worker who adopted my classroom, coming in frequently during recess to chat with me and to check if the room needed maintenance; the super gradewide paraeducator who helped our class a few hours a week. I'm overcome with gratitude for the outstanding and hilarious 3rd grade team leader, the absolute best mentor one could dream of; my fun, considerate, rock-star teacher teammates; and the many caring coworkers who went out of their way to help an uncertified noob build a classroom and learn to teach.

Several teachers, understanding the mixed emotions, asked me if leaving feels bittersweet, because they know that while I'll reduce my workload from two full-time jobs to one and reclaim my evenings and weekends, I became deeply attached to my class, as teachers do every year. But while it was difficult to endure the kids' tears when the principal told them our time had to end, my buckets are full. And this isn't really goodbye. I know that I'll sub as my class's PE or music teacher sometime soon. I know that within days after the New Year, there will be a 6 a.m. substitute call, whether for "my" class or another class of students whom I already love or will once I meet them, and that no matter how tired or busy I am, I will take the job. Because teachers step up when students or coworkers need help, and it's the least the rest of us can do to step up, too.

Teachers Deserve Better: How You Can Help

Teachers deserve better. They deserve more trust and respect and less standardized testing, smaller class sizes, and, yes, larger paychecks. "Oh my god, pay us what we're worth!" a Texas high school English teacher said. "I can't think of another industry where you can have two degrees and a master's and still make less than 50K a year." A 2022 study found that students' math and English test scores are "significantly higher in districts that offer a higher base salary to teachers."

Teachers deserve a safe working environment in which violence is not tolerated from students, parents, or staff, and educators can report it and other transgressions without fear of retaliation. Many teachers in this book said they don't advocate for themselves because they are afraid that speaking up will endanger their job (which is why I've omitted or changed their names). They deserve fair, effective protections and mitigations contractually in place for school shootings and contagions. They deserve mold-free, rat-free workspaces with functioning HVAC systems and water fountains. They deserve a positive school climate, which SUNY Downstate public health professor Paul Landsbergis defines as including "physical and social-emotional security, support for teaching and learning, social support from peers and adults, and respect for diversity, . . . school connectedness and engagement [and] staff relationships."

Teachers deserve more staffing: paraeducators, counselors, aides, and a nurse in every school—and those staff members deserve more respect, protections, and compensation, too. They deserve an administrative assistant to handle educators' paperwork, documentation, and clerical tasks, so that teachers can focus on teaching. When teachers are told to "do more with less," a phrase they are all too familiar with, the imbalance doesn't just overwork teachers, it endangers students. "The social, emotional, and academic pressures students face today are exponentially worse than when I was in high school and get worse each year. I have more students struggling with depression than ever before," said a Michigan high school English teacher. "Our counselors are overwhelmed by the number of crisis situations they face on a daily basis. At the same time, we cut a counselor and reduced support services like social work due to budget cuts. Students often come to me for support, but I have limited training in social-emotional support techniques, and the school simply does not have the support services in place to help these students. This is not an isolated problem. It is a national crisis."

Teachers deserve to helm every committee determining school operations rather than policymakers who proclaim what should happen in the classroom despite never having taught in one. "So often, the government or administration tells teachers what we need to be doing. But we're the ones in the classroom, we're the ones spending hours a day with our students, hearing firsthand what they're struggling with, seeing with our own eyes what changes really need to happen," said a Colorado high school science teacher. "A lot of teachers leave the profession because we all know there are jobs out there that pay significantly more while demanding so much less of our time and emotional energy."

Teachers deserve student loan forgiveness, tax credits for every penny they spend on school supplies, paid parental leave, free or heavily subsidized childcare, administrators who receive more relevant teacher-supportive trainings, time to observe other classes, and to be treated as skilled professionals. "Society gives respect to doctors, lawyers, firefighters, and military personnel. We, too, are professionals with training, advanced degrees, and state licenses. But teaching doesn't get the same degree of respect as those other professions," said a New Jersey high school foreign language teacher.

Teachers deserve a well-defined, realistic job description and enough protected school-day planning time to fulfill that job within their paid contracted hours. They deserve unwavering administrative commitment to full time positions for music, art, drama, library classes, PE, and other specialties. They deserve staffing for behavioral support and/or administrators who assist with behavioral challenges, communicate with parents, and enforce consequences. Districts are wasting money on programs and curriculum initiatives that add to teachers' workloads without helping students, said a Maryland kindergarten teacher. "I've had two real moments of despair and demoralization this month alone, both of which are related to money spent on resources being pushed down teachers' throats, without asking what we really need—which is always, always *people*, because you can't buy time."

It can be hard for teachers to extricate themselves from the teacher part of their identity, especially if they're passionate about the work or consider it a calling. When districts or administrators expand a teacher's role without providing the necessary supports, they knowingly take advantage of people who will do practically anything for their students, even as the unreasonable expectations steadily chip away at educators' mental health and personal lives. But the pandemic mistreatment of teachers was the final straw that convinced many to leave their jobs. They saw that public schools, and therefore educators, were the underfunded, unequipped safety net for societal failures. Schools cannot shoulder that responsibility and teachers should not bear that blame.

Now American education is caught in a catch-22: To fix the school system, we need more educators, but to attract more educators, the system must change. The job also must become more appealing to recruit a more diverse workforce. A Louisiana science teacher told me that at a state teacher leader conference, out of more than 1,000 teachers and administrators, he was the only Asian man. Just 7% of public school teachers are Black and 9% of public school teachers are Hispanic—and even these low numbers are in danger of dropping. A 2022 NEA survey found that 62% of Black educators and 59% of Hispanic/Latino educators were considering leaving the profession earlier than planned.

Students of all races, ethnicities, cultures, and identities should be able to learn from an equally diverse teaching staff. A Johns Hopkins study found that Black students who have one Black teacher by 3rd grade are 13% more likely to enroll in college; the likelihood jumps to 32% for students who have two Black teachers. Black students who have one Black teacher "early on" are up to 39% less likely to drop out of school, according to the Center for Black Educator Development.

More universities could follow the lead of schools such as Arizona State University's Mary Lou Fulton Teachers College, which offers state-funded full-tuition scholarships to students who commit to teaching in the state for the number of years of their scholarship. Enrollment in the school's teacher prep programs has risen every year since 2017. Recruiting for teacher preparation programs that don't make similar offers can be a "formidable task," a Florida teacher education professor said. Why? Partly because for many people, the allure of teaching is the meaningfulness of the work, the opportunity for trained professionals to inspire students with creative instruction and the time and space to connect their lessons to students' interests, questions, and tangents. Education "reforms" have stripped some of those opportunities away. "As public schooling has become increasingly focused on standardization, testing, and compliance, it has become a less compelling career choice for people who are motivated by contributing to their communities, engaging meaningfully with young people, or sharing the beauty of their subject matter," Bowdoin College education professor Doris Santoro has said.

Teachers are often the only adults who spend as much direct time with children as their parents do—or more. Why does this country entrust teachers with our most precious demographics but refuse to provide the tools necessary to best educate them? Improving teachers' working conditions will improve the student experience, too, with more teacher feedback, attention, and differentiation. But that can't happen unless we truly listen to teachers and heed their calls. Teachers' requests are informed and commonsense, but too often their voices are derided or dismissed. We can help. As an educator ally, you can lobby for the abovementioned changes.

You can also ask teachers what supplies they use and purchase them, fundraise for them, or enlist friends and neighbors to collect them. Search #ClearTheList on social media or visit www.gety ourteachon.com/clearthelist, where you can help teachers acquire their classroom wish lists for books, project materials, and supplies (I also tweet #ClearTheList threads at @AlexndraRobbins). Help fund a classroom project through DonorsChoose, a fabulous teacher-founded online charity. Additionally, make a habit of keeping social media posts about educators supportive.

Most of all, "trust teachers. They're some of the most educated people in our workforce," said Badass Teachers Association assistant executive director Denisha Jones, an education professor at Sarah Lawrence College. "We expect them to know so much about so many different areas—child development, social-emotional development, curriculum development and assessment—and they do learn all that. And then we put them in places where they aren't trusted to do any of it. We know what children need to make sense of the world. It's really hard to get them there when so many people are questioning whether we know what we're doing. If you want to be allies to teachers, say you trust them. Say that you know they're putting your child's best interests at heart."

At home, parents can model this trust for their children. "Children need to hear parents say, 'I trust your teacher. I understand that lesson made you feel uncomfortable, but there is a reason for it,'" Jones said. "Parents who are against their teachers, those kids know. Every teacher can tell you which child has a parent at home that mocks teachers. Those parents are a vocal minority, but they are vocal. The majority do not stand up to say something. That's the hardest part. We don't have enough of those voices. We need allies to push back in all sorts of spaces when they hear people saying something derogatory about teachers. Being open and explicit about support for teachers and schools is really important."

To do so, consider forming community support groups that amplify educators' voices, writing op-eds, taking out ads in media outlets, or writing emails or publicly testifying in support of teachers to school boards and district officials. Parents and other educator allies can write open letters, petitions, or sign-on statements in favor of policies that help teachers. The more visible, the better.

It is imperative and urgent that we get teachers what they need, both tangibly and at a broader policy level. Teachers are heroes, but they shouldn't have to be. Christopher Reeve aptly defined a hero as "an ordinary individual who finds the strength to persevere and endure in spite of overwhelming obstacles." We must fight to remove those obstacles so that educators' jobs focus solely on the rewarding, meaningful work of teaching children. Teachers—exceptionally devoted, critical contributors to society—are the most influential professionals during the formative years of future generations, and they are the key to fixing a broken, needlessly politicized education system. It's time we treat them right.

"Why I Love Teaching"

This book describes educators' challenging work conditions in an effort to make the public aware of the realities of teaching, more inclined to appreciate teachers, and motivated to lobby to get teachers the supports they need. With that said, it is common for educators to love teaching even if they don't love the profession in its current state. The best parts of being a teacher can persist even in difficult environments. Here is a short selection of the many testimonials to teaching that arose during my interviews.

- "I love: When a kid finally does super well on something they have struggled with. Hearing about their success when they leave my classroom. The daily interactions and knowing you have a part in watching them become amazing people. Being able to learn something every day."—California private school math teacher
- "There are so many great things: students being kind and compassionate, thoughtful and insightful, being silly and reminding me how to love life; students leading me to new connections about history I never considered. This job allows me to continue

learning fascinating things and to spend time with adults and young adults who care about the state of the world and making it a better place to be."—Washington, DC, history teacher

- "I'm lucky to work with a terrific staff of well-educated and informed individuals. People from other departments often seek me out to talk about ways to teach writing in their own classes or get book recommendations. I really do love my coworkers."—Pennsylvania high school English teacher

- "I get to see the immediate impact of my work. For me, there is nothing more rewarding than being a part of that light-bulb moment when a student finally gets it. Every student leaves my class a better writer than when he or she arrived. I smile as I see my students create more compelling arguments with each essay. I am so proud of their progress and growth."—Michigan high school English teacher

- "A person can't go through life without knowing some content from history classes. In order to have a conversation, to understand literature, to go forward and try to improve the world, students need to have an understanding of what happened in the past. I love that the subject is so easy to relate to and I can connect things from the past to things that are happening today to make students understand better."—Pennsylvania high school social studies teacher

- "I love my mentor. We just click. I meet with her on Fridays at three o'clock, and it is just decompression. I ask her all my questions and she's super-supportive and complimentary of what I'm doing, which is the affirmation I need. She also sends little postcards in the mail, which is such a nice surprise. My principal is also one of the greatest people and just knows when I need extra support. Her feedback is so valuable, direct, and specific, and she knows the kids incredibly well. She has great perspective and I am so proud to work with her."—Ohio elementary school music teacher

- "Every day is different and I love learning. Some days we dissect owl pellets, then read stories, then do math or go on a field trip. It's never boring. I feel like I'm always learning and growing in my job. I love seeing kids get excited about learning and developing new skills. I like feeling like I make a difference in the lives of my students and can help them become lifelong learners. I love the people I work with."—Hawaii 4th grade teacher
- "I love my colleagues. Many adults view their high school years through a blend of nostalgia, embarrassment, and occasional revulsion. Teachers are adults who have gone back to school. We're weird that way. All teachers are very slightly weird, but you won't find a more brilliant and entertaining group of people. And if there's a trivia night at your local bar, we'll absolutely crush it."—Georgia high school English teacher
- "As an introvert with sometimes debilitating anxiety, I tend to disengage from other people and hide myself away. Teaching has kept me plugged into the rest of humanity. It doesn't matter how bad I feel; I have to be present every day for my students.

  "We teachers have kids we don't like (and kids who don't like us, of course). But it's our duty to love all of them unconditionally. That means treating them all as fairly and kindly as possible every day, respecting their inherent worth, doing everything in our power to help them succeed. It means being willing to keep them safe, even to put ourselves—in an instant, without thought—between them and a shooter. It's sad that some teachers have actually had to do that.

  "If you guessed that it's emotionally exhausting to love that many people that way, you're right. But it also works in reverse; it's life-giving. And it's good practice at living well. It gives me a chance to get out of my own head and focus on serving others. A teacher might come into contact with several thousand kids over the course of her career. Maybe they'll remember something you said, even pass that on to their children. Maybe something you did will influence their decisions in a way you never imagined. Teaching isn't a career, but a way of living. You don't go to work and then come home and stop being a teacher. It's who you are. Teaching is that vital to my sense of self."—Maryland middle school English teacher

ACKNOWLEDGMENTS

Reuniting with editor extraordinaire Jill Schwartzman, brilliant and kind, and rock-star publicist Emily Canders is a dream come true. Jill's edits, as always, were thoughtful and wise, and I am immensely grateful for her architectural refinements and enthusiastic advocacy. And Emily, one of my all-time favorite publicists, works wonders with her creativity and savvy. I could not have asked for smarter, more talented partners for a book representing a cause so close to my heart. Also at Dutton, I thank Christine Ball, John Parsley, Carrie Swetonic, Amanda Walker, Jamie Knapp, Nicole Jarvis, Yuki Hirose, Susan Schwartz, Alice Dalrymple, Melanie Koch, Bonnie Soodek, Patricia Clark, Steven Meditz, Amy Ryan, Marya Pasciuto, and Charlotte Peters.

Miguel, Rebecca, and Penny—wonderful people, remarkable teachers—were incredibly generous with their time and candor despite their intensely busy schedules. I thank them wholeheartedly for sharing their lives with readers and their expertise with me. I hope you grew to care for them as I do.

You never forget your most influential K–12 teachers. Here are mine: Robin Caropreso (1st grade), Marion Richter (K and 1st grade reading), Carl Baskerville (3rd grade), Deborah Grandy (6th grade English), Dean Westcoat (7th grade science), Bobbi Bounford (middle school PE and soccer coach), Bonnie Butler and Susan Wildstrom (high school algebra and calculus), and the late Martin Galvin (10th and 12th grade English) and Robert Atwood (10th through 12th grade journalism). Thank you for the fond memories and for helping me learn and grow.

Acknowledgments

I cannot emphasize enough how game-changing it was to have talented, caring colleagues who made it fun to teach full-time. My endless appreciation and admiration go to my phenomenal team leader Marni O., dynamite teammates Rev C. and Sam K., and the terrific educators who directly worked with some of my 3rd grade students: Karen J., Felice G., Lisa S., as well as to the teachers who provided invaluable advice, help, copier/laminator/spiral binder machine tutorials, and classroom decor: Maura B., Arielle B., Cheryl J., Amanda L., Deirdre S., Alana K., Enit C., Heather W., Hilary J., Nancy B., Joan I., Lori M., Colleen C., with thanks to Kim T., Charlene P., Nancy H., Mariam J., Maria B., Jenny F., Dana M., Noah D., and James L.

All of the following educators have also personally inspired me: Maura B., Marni O., Zach T., Michelle K., Allison J., Ricky S., Randi V., Sandra G., Marie T., Amanda L., Lindsey S., Alana K., Stephanie H., Mary K., Heather W., Pat B., Judy S., Hei-Jung K., Nancy B., Susan L., Jen P., Kerry C., Lorraine M., Kathy M., Michael D., Robert N., Katie F., Rebecca G., Liz G., Catherine H.-R. (the greatest substitute teacher of all time), Spencer E., Jim M., Robert T., Alison S., Michelle H., Corinne G., Margaret F., Deb B., Sam W., and Erin S.

Knowledgeable and supportive, Gail Ross is a top-notch agent with a top-notch team; I'm grateful to Howard Yoon, Dara Kaye, and especially Shannon O'Neill for her helpful insights. I'm also indebted to the great Michael Prevett, who has been a steady, fantastically innovative presence in my literary career for almost 20 years. Cheers to Maura Backenstoe, Isabel Hernandez-Cata, and Gina Tomaine for their valuable editorial input. Thank you also to the amazing booksellers and librarians who work so hard to pair books with people, opening their worlds and changing their lives.

Nobody makes me laugh like my brother does, a trend that continued with his side comments when he read my manuscript in progress. He insisted on spending time he didn't have in order to offer the kind of constructive, persnickety word-choice suggestions I favor.

Acknowledgments

I'm also eternally grateful to my parents and sister for their continuous support, love, and humor.

Every day I'm thankful for the friends who regularly brighten my week with catch-ups, lunchings, deck drinks, ridiculous outings, and meandering walks: Laura R., Ruth K., Chris S., Lyndsy P., Paula M., John M., Erin K., Alice A., Laurel R., Kim R., Erica O., Dana E., Tom M., Anna H., Haley F., Anna M., Abbey P., Tom B., Michel G., Marcela C., and Lakshmi K. For Nick B., Andi B., Vicki A., Amy L., and Andey D. from afar. And for MEO, who knows why.

Year after year, my family puts up with the challenges, twists, and idiosyncrasies of my weird career. With this book, they got hit by a double whammy as I attempted to report and write while separately teaching at the same time. I could not have done either of these jobs without their steadfast patience and support. I thank them for all their efforts to bolster me throughout this project, and for bringing so much joy and love into my life. They know how I feel.

Readers, you're the most thoughtful, engaging community an author could ask for and I appreciate our social media interactions more than you know. Some of you have been with me since my first book was published more than 20 years ago and some of you are new to my work. Either way, I'm grateful for your support.

And to Teachers:

There are not enough words to properly thank you for all that you do, but I hope this book is a start. You are so very much appreciated.

To "My" Students

I would like to add a special thank-you to the 3rd grade students who taught me about teaching. I am always here for you, Aydin Bocchicchia, Arushan Muthukumar, Dhilan Parasuraman,

Acknowledgments

Elliot Lange, Erin Hasse, Hailey Nyaboke Mwangi, Irene Saberi, Kate Zhou, Maura Sheeran Paton, Micah Letscher, Nicoletta Adamantiades, Patrick Bootz, Rafael Aguilar González, Scarlett Velez, Una Dulany—and bienvenida a la familia to Inés Bárcena.

I have one last surprise for you: You asked me to write a fable about our class mascot (and asked me and asked me and asked me . . .). Here it is! I hope each of you wonderful storytellers continue to share your unique, important voices in your own stories. I can't wait to read them.

How Apple Got His Skis

Once there was an apple who did not want to fall from his tree. As the fading summer sun lost its grip on the small, peaceful orchard, neighboring apples began to tumble from their perches.

One September morning, Squirrel raced atop Apple's branch, then did a double take when she spotted Apple. "Zip-zip-zing . . . Whoa! Why are you still here?" she asked through a mouthful of acorns.

"I do not want to let go," Apple explained.

Squirrel considered Apple's predicament. "I could quickly roll you down the branch—lickety-split!—to my hole in the trunk, where you may spend the winter," she offered.

"No, thank you. I would love to have some company, but if I tumble and bruise on the way down, I would become an apple turnover. Besides, apples can't live in a hole."

"Can't or haven't yet?" Squirrel asked. When Apple shrugged, she scurried on. Apple wished he could race like Squirrel.

Weeks passed. As the orchard blazed sienna and cinnamon, vermilion and gold, its creatures prepared for the change of the season. Apple doggedly held tight to the branch with all the might of his tiny stem.

Acknowledgments

Porcupine waddled among the branches, contentedly fattened in advance of the freeze. When he encountered Apple, his eyes widened. "Why are you still here?" he asked.

"I do not want to let go," Apple explained.

Porcupine thought for a moment. "I could carry you on my back so that you may wander the orchard with me," he suggested.

"No, thank you. I would love to venture beyond this tree, but if your quills pierced my flesh, I would become apple slices. Besides, apples can't wander."

"Can't or haven't yet?" Porcupine asked.

When Apple gave him an apologetic smile, Porcupine politely bowed and continued on his way. Apple wished he could be helpful like Porcupine.

The orchard leaves crisped and curled at the approach of winter's chill, yet still Apple clung to his tree. As the last leaves dropped, Bird paused her flight south to rest on Apple's branch. When she saw Apple, her beak opened in surprise. "Why are you still here?" she inquired.

"I do not want to let go," Apple explained.

Bird cocked her head. "Why don't you fly like me?"

"No, thank you. I would love to soar, but if I fell to the hardened ground, I would become applesauce. Besides, apples can't fly."

"Can't or haven't yet?" Bird asked.

When Apple looked at her skeptically, she resumed her journey. Apple wished he could travel like Bird.

At year's end, snow blanketed the orchard like fresh dough across an unbaked pie. Apple watched the white world glisten. He was grateful for the view yet disappointed he could see it from only one perspective. The orchard hushed, muffled beneath winter's weight.

Then Smushy Potato flew by with a propeller sticking out of his head.

Now Apple did a double take. "Come back!" he called. "You are spectacular! How are you flying?"

Smushy Potato *tut-tut-tutted* back to Apple, his propeller whirling cheerfully. "Well, I wanted to be a potato copter," Smushy Potato said. "So I am."

"Forgive me for saying so, but you are a little bit smushy," Apple said, though he secretly admired the potato's confidence.

"That is true. The first time I tried to use the propeller, I failed. After all, I am a potato."

"What happened?" Apple asked.

"I learned," Smushy Potato answered. "I got up and tried again."

Apple nodded. "I would like to race and be helpful. I would like to travel and learn."

"Join me, then," Smushy Potato proposed.

Apple scrunched his face in concentration. He pushed until his skin puckered with effort. After a bit of time and focus, from the bottom of his core came a *squirt* and a *ploop!*—and out from Apple popped two teeny skis.

Apple beamed at Smushy Potato. He spun off his stem, leapt from the tree, and glided smoothly to a stop at a slightly sloped bank of snow, the potato hovering by his side. The two new friends eagerly set off to explore the glorious wild beyond the orchard, to meet endless new creatures, to experience diverse points of view.

And that was how Apple became Apple on Skis.

Moral: Just because you haven't yet does not mean that you can't.

NOTES

Prologue

2 *blood donation center*: *Time* magazine also publicized this phenomenon in Katie Reilly, " 'I Work 3 Jobs and Donate Blood Plasma to Pay the Bills': This Is What It's Like to Be a Teacher in America," *Time*, September 13, 2018.

4 *"Other countries treat teachers"*: Interview with the author.

Chapter 1: August

5 *A Maryland administrator*: The quotes that begin each chapter were shared with the author during interviews.

5 *"summers off"*: Examples abound across social media and other outlets. For brevity, I have left social media sources out of this section. See, for example, "Do School Principals Get Summers Off?" ZipRecruiter.com; "15 Jobs to Consider if You Want Summers Off Work," Indeed editorial team, February 22, 2021; Savannah Byer, "Ten Benefits of Being a Teacher," *T Bird Nation Blog*, Southern Utah University, February 25, 2020.

5 *"they're off four months a year"*: Chris Christie, "On K–12 Education," Goffstown, NH, June 8, 2015, https://www.youtube.com/watch?v= LT2xwFlpixA.

5 *"paid vacation"*: Randy Rossi, "The Damage Caused by Teachers Unions," *Chicago Tribune*, July 24, 2017.

5 *"part-time job"*: Chris Christie also erroneously claimed that teachers get "a full-time salary for a part-time job." See also, for example, Jeff Rohwer, "Vote No on September 9 Bettendorf Schools Levy," *Quad City Times* (Davenport, IA), September 6, 2014.

5 *for "only 180 days"*: John P. Cardie, "Teachers Should Work More if They Want More Money," *Daily Camera*, August 17, 2018; Segann March, "DeSoto Ranks First in Starting Teacher Pay Locally," *Shreveport Times*, November 13, 2015.

Notes

5 *"to do is show up the next year"*: Andover, MA, Finance Committee chairman Jon Stumpf, in Gabriella Cruz, "Hidden Costs of Teachers' Contract," *Andover Townsman*, November 17, 2016.

9 *teachers did not work*: See, for example, "Voice of the People," *Chicago Tribune*, August 14, 2016.

26 *Western was an urban Title I school*: "Improving Basic Programs Operated by Local Educational Agencies (Title I, Part A)," U.S. Department of Education, last modified October 24, 2018, https://www2.ed.gov/programs/titleiparta/index.html.

36 *LeVar's workday didn't end*: Interviews with the author. Note: Some of the material in the introduction, including information from my first interviews with LeVar (I interviewed him again in 2022), was initially published in Alexandra Robbins, "Teachers Deserve More Respect," *The New York Times*, March 20, 2020.

37 *approximately four million K–12 teachers*: "Characteristics of Public School Teachers," *Condition of Education*, National Center for Education Statistics at IES, updated May 2021, cites 3.5 million public school teachers; "Fast Facts: Teacher Characteristics and Trends," National Center for Education Statistics, has 509,200 private school teachers.

37 *"Teachers feel more voiceless than ever"*: Interview with the author.

37 *As school staff fled the profession*: The U.S. Bureau of Labor Statistics reported that between January 2020 and February 2022, the number of educators working in public education dropped from about 10.6 million to 10.0 million. See, for example, Tim Walker, "Survey: Alarming Number of Educators May Soon Leave the Profession," *NEA Today*, February 1, 2022. See also Mark Lieberman, "How Staff Shortages Are Crushing Schools," *Education Week*, October 15, 2021.

37 *teachers to take on additional roles*: See, for example, Donna St. George, "Teachers Protest Staffing Shortages in Maryland School System," *The Washington Post*, October 27, 2021; Lieberman, "How Staff Shortages Are Crushing Schools"; Donna St. George and Valerie Strauss, "The Principal Is Cleaning the Bathroom: Schools Reel with Staff Shortages," *Washington Post*, December 5, 2021; interviews with the author.

37 *567,000 fewer public school educators*: Eric Jotkoff, "NEA Survey: Massive Staff Shortages in Schools Leading to Educator Burnout; Alarming Number of Educators Indicating They Plan to Leave Profession," NEA press release, February 1, 2022.

37 *three-quarters of its members*: Walker, "Survey: Alarming Number of Educators May Soon Leave the Profession." See also Lieberman, "How Staff Shortages Are Crushing Schools."

37 *"my job is not important"*: Interviews with the author.

38 *"a very different profession"*: Interviews with the author.

38 *U.S. teachers' salaries*: Organisation for Economic Cooperation and Development, *Education at a Glance 2021: OECD Indicators* (Paris: OECD Publishing, 2021).

38 *average teacher salary dropped 4.5%*: Cindy Long, "Average Teacher Salary Down 4.5% Over Past Decade," *NEA Today*, April 29, 2019.

38 *college costs and student loans ballooned*: "The Hidden Impact of COVID-19 on Educators: Rising Health Concerns, Lower Risk Tolerance and Benefit Gaps: Insights from the Horace Mann Educator Health and Well-Being Study," Horace Mann Educators Corporation, November 2020.

38 *"teacher pay gap"*: Sylvia Allegretto, "The Teacher Pay Penalty Hits a New High," Economic Policy Institute, August 16, 2022; Allegretto and Lawrence Mishel, "The Teacher Weekly Wage Penalty Hit 21.4 Percent in 2018, a Record High," Economic Policy Institute, April 24, 2019.

38 *"real, large and growing"*: Emma García and Elaine Weiss, "The Teacher Shortage Is Real, Large and Growing, and Worse than We Thought," Economic Policy Institute, March 26, 2019.

38 *teacher pay gap was 6% in 1996*: Sylvia A. Allegretto and Lawrence Mishel, "Teacher Pay Penalty Dips but Persists in 2019," Economic Policy Institute, September 17, 2020.

38 *it hovers at about 20%*: Allegretto and Mishel, "Teacher Pay Penalty Dips but Persists in 2019."

38 *average teacher's starting salary*: Reggie Wade, "State by State Data Show Gaps in Teacher Salaries, Student Spending: NEA," *Yahoo News*, April 27, 2021.

38 *even the highest-paid*: Emma Goldberg, "What It's Like to Be a Teacher in 2020 America," *The New York Times*, October 5, 2020.

38 *"I'm a single mom"*: Interviews with the author.

38 *more than $7,000 per year*: Alvin Chang, "Teacher Pay Is Falling. Their Health Insurance Costs Are Rising," *Vox*, March 16, 2018.

39 *in California, Oklahoma*: Madeline Will, "Sick Teachers Paying for Substitutes: Where and Why It's Happening," *EdWeek*, May 17, 2019; interviews with the author.

39 *"stay home with my kids"*: Interviews with the author.

39 *"a shortage of teachers"*: Jocelyn Gecker, "COVID-19 Creates Dire US Shortage of Teachers, School Staff," Associated Press, September 22, 2021.

39 *outgrew supply by more than 100,000*: Adam Edelman, "Biden Wants to

Fix the Nation's Teacher Shortage. Educators Say the Problem Is Worsening," NBC News, June 6, 2021.

39 *completion of teacher preparation programs*: Edelman, "Biden Wants to Fix the Nation's Teacher Shortage."

39 *13% of educator preparation programs*: "Survey Shows Positive Trends and Lingering Effects of COVID in Educator Preparation," AACTE Research Reports and Briefs, February 2, 2022.

39 *The pandemic also hastened the exodus*: See Gecker, "COVID-19 Creates Dire US Shortage of Teachers, School Staff," though examples abound.

39 *A 2022 NEA survey*: Walker, "Survey: Alarming Number of Educators May Soon Leave the Profession."

39 *55% of educators*: Tim Walker, "Teacher Spending on School Supplies: A State-by-State Breakdown," *NEA Today*, August 26, 2019. Similarly, an *Education Week* national survey of K–12 teachers and administrators found that 54% were considering leaving the field in the next two years—a 20% rise over pre-pandemic rates: Liana Loewus, "Why Teachers Leave—or Don't: A Look at the Numbers," *Education Week*, May 4, 2021.

40 *"Teachers, as well as building and district leaders"*: Cresencio Rodriguez-Delgado et al., "Schools Across the Country Are Struggling to Find Staff. Here's Why," *PBS NewsHour*, Nov 23, 2021.

40 *Oregon issued a statewide emergency*: Giulia Heyward, "Substitute Teachers Never Got Much Respect, but Now They Are in Demand," *The New York Times*, November 11, 2021.

40 *"Teachers are drowning"*: Interviews with the author. This quote originally was included in Robbins, "Teachers Deserve More Respect."

40 *five times more likely*: Rick Hampson et al., "We Followed 15 of America's Teachers on a Day of Frustrations, Pressures and Hard-Earned Victories," *USA Today*, October 17, 2018/December 14, 2019.

40 *nearly 70% of teachers*: "Voices from the Classroom 2020: A Survey of America's Educators," Educators for Excellence.

40 *had to work a side hustle*: Interviews with the author.

41 *whose only meal of the day*: Interviews with the author.

41 *scarcity of special education*: Interviews with the author.

41 *Approximately 14% of students*: See, for example, Holly Rosenkrantz, "What Is Special Education?" *U.S. News & World Report*, December 9, 2021.

41 *"free appropriate public education"*: "About IDEA," IDEA, Individuals with Disabilities Act, U.S. Department of Education, https://sites.ed.gov/idea/about-idea/.

41 *"least restrictive environment"*: Section 1412 (a) (5), IDEA, U.S. De-

partment of Education, https://sites.ed.gov/idea/statute-chapter-33
/subchapter-ii/1412/a/5.

41 *Individualized Education Program*: "A Guide to the Individualized Education Program," U.S. Department of Education, https://www2.ed.gov
/parents/needs/speced/iepguide/index.html.

41 *About 65% of six- to 21-year-old students*: National Center for Education Statistics, https://nces.ed.gov/programs/digest/d20/tables/dt20
_204.60.asp.

42 *"I'm really over"*: Interviews with the author.

42 *"told they can't leave classroom doors open"*: Confirmed with Gabriel
Debenedetti.

42 *bring their own toilet paper*: Interviews with the author.

42 *two days of paid maternity leave*: Agreement Between Montgomery
County Education Association and Board of Education of Montgomery County, Rockville, Maryland, School Years 2021–2022.

43 *"spent thirty-two thousand dollars"*: Interviews with the author.

43 *"I see the difference"*: Interviews with the author.

43 *LeVar is trying*: Interviews with the author.

Chapter 2: September

53 *Kahoot*: https://kahoot.com/.

65 *a Pennsylvania high school English teacher*: Interview with the author.

66 *"Parents see teachers"*: Interviews with the author.

66 *"The belittling and blaming"*: Interview with the author.

67 *berate him after his daughter scored a 93*: Interview with the author.

67 *In just the first six weeks*: Jeffrey Sachs and Jonathan Friedman, "Educational Gag Orders Target Speech About LGBTQ+ Identities with New
Prohibitions and Punishments," PEN.org, February 15, 2022.

67 *"Parental Rights in Education"*: Dana Goldstein, "Opponents Call It the
'Don't Say Gay' Bill. Here's What It Says," *The New York Times*, March
18, 2022; Mary Ellen Klas, "A Breakdown of the Language in Florida's
So-Called 'Don't Say Gay' Bill," Tampabay.com, March 29, 2022.

68 *Several other states*: Kalyn Belsha, "'Am I Not Allowed to Mention Myself?' Schools Grapple with New Restrictions on Teaching About Gender
and Sexuality," *Chalkbeat*, April 12, 2022; Marta W. Aldrich, "Tennessee Governor Signs Bill Restricting How Race and Bias Can Be Taught
in Schools," *Chalkbeat*, May 25, 2021.

67 *"put LGBTQ teachers"*: Terry Gross, "From Slavery to Socialism, New
Legislation Restricts What Teachers Can Discuss," *Fresh Air*, February
3, 2022.

67 *"a climate in which some teachers"*: Belsha, "'Am I Not Allowed to Mention Myself?'"

68 *Moms for Liberty offered a $500 bounty*: Gross, "From Slavery to Socialism."

68 *state department of education's establishment*: Sarah Gibson, "Offer of Cash Prize for Allegations Against N.H. Teachers Draws Rebuke," New Hampshire Public Radio, November 18, 2021.

68 *Virginia governor Glenn Youngkin*: See, for example, Valerie Strauss, "Youngkin's 'Tip Line' to Snitch on Teachers Suffers from This, Too," *The Washington Post*, January 28, 2022.

68 *"parents to send us any instances"*: "Gov. Glenn Youngkin Unplugged on Masks, VA Election Board and Illegals," *The John Fredericks Show*, January 24, 2022.

68 *state representative Barbara Gleim suggested*: Naomi Creason, "Gleim Stands by Circulated Substitute Teacher Comment on Social Media," *The Progress*, April 7, 2022.

68 *hosted "volunteer training"*: This ad was posted on social media. In a July 8, 2022, press release, CCDF justified the training with the statement: "self-published public content on social media is like an open window revealing your beliefs, interests, and actionable expressions," http:// ccdfusa.com/offical-statement-ccdf-usa-nueces-county-education -division-listens-to-citizens-interests-and-concerns.

68 *2022 legislative proposals*: See, for example, Sarah Schwartz and Eesha Pendharkar, "Here's the Long List of Topics Republicans Want Banned from the Classroom," *Education Week*, February 2, 2022; Aallyah Wright, Stateline.org, "Educators Warn Bills to Give Parents More Power Could Push Teachers Out," *Yahoo News*, February 11, 2022, https://news .yahoo.com/educators-warn-bills-parents-more-045900679.html.

68 *An Indiana bill passed by the state house*: See, for example, Arika Herron, "Indiana Senate Guts CRT-Inspired Bill, but Finds Little Support for What's Left," *Indianapolis Star*, February 16, 2022.

69 *not by the senate*: See, for example, Aleksandra Appleton, "Indiana Bills Seek to Regulate Teaching Race in Upcoming Session," *Chalkbeat Indiana*, January 3, 2022.

69 *"textbooks, books, articles"*: Wright, "Educators Warn Bills to Give Parents More Power Could Push Teachers Out."

69 *in the name of "parents' rights"*: See, for example, Jack Schneider and Jennifer Berkshire, "Parents Claim They Have the Right to Shape Their Kids' School Curriculum. They Don't," *The Washington Post*, October 21, 2021.

69 *"They're packaging some"*: Schwartz and Pendharkar, "Here's the Long List of Topics Republicans Want Banned from the Classroom."

69 *The majority of public school students*: "Enrollment and Percentage Distribution of Enrollment in Public Elementary and Secondary Schools, by Race/Ethnicity and Level of Education," Table 203.60, National Center for Education Statistics.

69 *following mass protests*: See, for example, Schwartz and Pendharkar, "Here's the Long List of Topics Republicans Want Banned"; Jonathan Friedman and James Tager, *Educational Gag Orders: Legislative Restrictions on the Freedom to Lead, Learn, and Teach*, PEN America report, January 18, 2022, https://pen.org/wp-content/uploads/2022/02/PEN _EducationalGagOrders_01-18-22-compressed.pdf.

69 *"a framework that denotes"*: "Critical Race Theory: Frequently Asked Questions," NAACP Legal Defense and Education Fund, https://www .naacpldf.org/critical-race-theory-faq/.

69 *not taught in K–12 schools*: See, for example, Phil McCausland, "Teaching Critical Race Theory Isn't Happening in Classrooms, Teachers Say in Survey," NBC News, July 1, 2021.

69 *galvanizing parents co-opted the term*: See, for example, Schwartz and Pendharkar, "Here's the Long List of Topics Republicans Want Banned"; Friedman and Tager, *Educational Gag Orders* report.

70 *"unprecedented" efforts to ban*: Stephanie Hlywak, "The American Library Association Opposes Widespread Efforts to Censor Books in U.S. Schools and Libraries," ALA News, November 29, 2021.

70 *banned nearly 1,600 books*: Ariana Figueroa, "More than 1,500 Books Have Been Banned in Public Schools, and a US House Panel Asks Why," WTOP.com, April 8, 2022.

70 *sought to ban entire book categories*: Constance Grady, "How the New Banned Books Panic Fits into America's History of School Censorship," *Vox*, February 17, 2022.

70 *targeted books featured race, gender*: See, for example, David Montgomery, Stateline.org, "Librarians Fight Back Against Efforts to Ban Books in Schools," *Education Week*, January 18, 2022; Elizabeth A. Harris and Alexandra Alter, "Book Ban Efforts Spread Across the U.S.," *The New York Times*, January 30, 2022; Hlywak, "The American Library Association Opposes Widespread Efforts to Censor Books in U.S. Schools and Libraries"; Figueroa, "More than 1,500 Books Have Been Banned in Public Schools."

70 *Tennessee district also struck Maus*: See, for example, Marilisa Jiminéz

Garcia, "Book Bans Are Targeting the History of Oppression," February 2, 2022.

70 *"No one has the right"*: This quote was originally included on the #FReadom Fighters website. For more about the #FReadom Fighters, see freadom.us/home.

70 *verbal and physical abuse*: See, for example, Paul LeBlanc, "McConnell Challenges Garland on DOJ Effort to Address Threats Against Public School Board Members and Teachers," CNN.com, October 9, 2021; teacher interviews with the author.

70 *a third of teachers had been victimized*: Susan McMahon et al., "Addressing Violence Against Teachers: A Social-Ecological Analysis of Teachers' Perspectives," *Psychology in the Schools*, April 2020.

70 *"there are 'problem parents'"*: Interviews with the author.

70 *After a 2017 parent-teacher conference*: WPXI.com, "Enraged Parents Attack Teacher with a Brick After Cellphone Taken from Student," *The Atlanta Journal-Constitution*, October 20, 2017.

70 *a mother sprayed lighter fluid*: Ron Gallagher, "Parent Threatened to Set Teacher Afire After Squirting Lighter Fluid, Police Say," *Charlotte News & Observer*, April 27, 2017.

70 *there was a marked increase*: See, for example, Jaclyn Peiser, "After Texas Parent Rips Mask Off Teacher's Face, School Official Warns: 'Do Not Fight Mask Wars in Our Schools,'" *The Washington Post*, August 18, 2021; Wilson Wong, "Parent Attacks Teacher After Mask Dispute on First Day of School in California District, Official Says," NBC News, August 13, 2021; Perry Vandell, "3 Charged After Threatening Tucson Principal with Arrest, Zip Ties over COVID-19 Rules," *Arizona Republic*, September 7, 2021.

71 *threatening school staff*: During the 2020–2021 academic year, despite less face time because many districts conducted remote learning for months, 42% of school administrators surveyed by the APA reported being harassed or threatened with violence by parents. "Teachers, Other School Personnel, Experience Violence, Threats, Harassment During Pandemic," American Psychological Association, March 17, 2022.

71 *"as a public enemy"*: Anne Lutz Fernandez, "School Covid Mask Rules Have Sparked Parent-Teacher Violence. We Can't Ignore It," NBC News, August 23, 2021.

71 *"thrash the teacher"*: William Vaillancourt, "Tucker Suggests Dads Should 'Thrash' Kids' Teachers," *Daily Beast*, April 9, 2022.

71 *Attorney General Merrick Garland*: Attorney General Merrick Garland, "Memorandum for Director, Federal Bureau of Investigation, Direc-

tor, Executive Office for U.S. Attorneys Assistant Attorney General, Criminal Division, United States," October 4, 2021.

71 *McConnell minimized the violence*: Letter from McConnell to Garland dated October 7, 2021, https://www.republicanleader.senate.gov/imo/media/doc/Garland%20Letter%20CRT%2010.7.21.pdf.

71 *An Iowa parent*: Interview with the author.

72 *An assistant principal made three Texas teachers*: Interviews with the author.

72 *"online grades have created monsters"*: Interview with the author.

72 *"Punch him"*: Interview with the author.

73 *A prominent Louisiana parent*: Interviews with the author.

73 *because they were Black*: Joel Brown, "Chapel Hill Students, Parents Say Racism at Heart of Teacher Removal Controversy," ABC 11, December 2, 2021.

73 *97% of Black math teachers*: Toya Jones Frank, "Exploring Racialized Factors to Understand Why Black Mathematics Teachers Consider Leaving the Profession," *Educational Researcher*, February 2021. Seen in Youki Terada, "Why Black Teachers Walk Away," *Edutopia*, March 26, 2021.

73 *Kentucky Teacher of the Year*: Matt Lavietes, "Kentucky's 2022 Teacher of the Year Quits Profession, Citing Homophobia," NBC News, June 27, 2022.

73 *An Illinois Catholic school fired*: "'Never Felt So Demeaned': Gay Teacher Says Dismissal Was Over Marriage," WAND-TV, March 28, 2022.

73 *they medicate fevered children*: Confirmed via interviews with school staff, parents, and an educator association.

73 *knowingly sent sick children*: Nicole Lyn Pesce, "7 in 10 Parents Admit to Sending Sick Kids to School, but They Have 3 Good Reasons Why," *MarketWatch*, September 26, 2019; Gemma Francis, "Millions of Parents Putting Children at Risk by Sending Their Sick Kids to School," *Mirror*, September 17, 2019.

73 *pick up their kids*: Interviews with the author.

74 *sent COVID-positive students*: See, for example, Reese Oxner, "Child Positive for Coronavirus Was Sent to School Anyway. Others Quarantining Now," NPR (WAMU), September 17, 2020; Rob Jennings, "N.J. Superintendent Scolds Parents for Keeping Quiet About Kids with COVID-19, Holiday Travel," NJ.com, December 3, 2020; Caroline Reinwald, "Health Officer: Parents Sending Sick, Symptomatic Kids to School," ABC12 (Wisconsin), September 22, 2020; Dawson White, "Student with COVID-19 Knowingly Attends First Day of High School, Oklahoma Officials Say," *The Kansas City Star*, August 16, 2020;

Mary Adeline Dela Cruz, "Parents Who Knowingly Sent COVID-Infected Child to School, Spawned Class Outbreak Could Face Charges," *Latin Times*, December 13, 2021.

74 *"I think sometimes parents"*: Interview with the author.

74 *"There's this crazy dichotomy"*: Interview with the author.

74 *the most frequent perpetrators*: Interviews with the author.

77 *"charter school refugees"*: Note: "Charter schools are less likely to respond to application inquiries from parents of students with severe disabilities . . . Schools were also less likely to respond to parents with Hispanic-sounding names, especially if the schools had a mostly white student population." Arianna Prothero, "Schools More Likely to Ignore Special Education Applicants, Study Finds," *Education Week*, December 20, 2018.

Chapter 3: October

105 *"the bond really grew"*: Interview with the author. See also Michelle Matthews, "Teacher Adopts Favorite Student: 'She Was Born for Me,'" Alabama.com, December 16, 2020. Readers who would like to contribute to Jamie's college fund can send a check made payable to The American Fund, c/o Jeremy Young, Legacy Advisory Group, 36 Manning Place #200, Birmingham, AL 35242.

106 *donated kidneys*: See, for example, Bopha Phorn, "'Hero' Teacher Donates Kidney to His 6th-Grade Student," ABC News, August 22, 2018; Jillian Idle, "Duncan Middle School Teacher Donates His Kidney to Former Student," WPTV, August 15, 2018; Mitch Stacy, "Fourth-Grade Teacher Donates Kidney to Save Student's Life," Associated Press, May 21, 2018; Gabriel Kinder, "Teacher Donates a Kidney to Her Student's Mother. Now Both Women Are Hoping to Find a Kidney for a Neighbor," CNN, August 26, 2020; WTHR.com staff, "Teacher Donates Kidney to Save Life of Student's Father," WTHR, October 17, 2019.

106 *"kids crawl right inside"*: Interviews with the author.

106 *press release about Teacher of the Year*: "TONIGHT: MCPS to Name Teacher of the Year," MCPS Public Announcements, April 27, 2021.

107 *Counselor of the Year*: "Counselors of the Year Announced," *MCPS Bulletin*, June 9, 2021.

107 *"I don't love being called a hero"*: Steven Singer, "I Love Teaching, but . . . ," *Badass Teachers Association Blog*, December 26, 2021. Thank you to Steven Singer, author of the book *Gadfly on the Wall: A Public School Teacher Speaks Out on Racism and Reform* (New York: Garn Press, 2017).

Notes

108 *"none of which are reasons"*: Interviews with the author.

108 *"exoticizes youth and positions them"*: Kenya Downs, "What 'White Folks Who Teach in the Hood' Get Wrong About Education," *PBS NewsHour*, March 28, 2016.

108 *"wholly visible to each other"*: Christopher Emdin, *For White Folks Who Teach in the Hood . . . and the Rest of Y'all Too* (New York: Beacon Press, 2016).

108 *workforce may be white women*: See, for example, Madeline Will, "Still Mostly White and Female: New Federal Data on the Teaching Profession," *Education Week*, April 14, 2020.

109 *"rendered superhumanly responsible"*: Alan Block, "Hey, I'm No Superman: The Teacher as Hero," *Journal of Curriculum Theorizing*, May 2014.

109 *bought eyeglasses, furniture*: Interviews with the author.

110 *nearly $500 per year*: See, for example, Tim Walker, "Teacher Spending on School Supplies: A State-by-State Breakdown," *NEA Today*, August 26, 2019.

110 *at least 94% of public school teachers*: Niraj Chokshi, "94 Percent of U.S. Teachers Spend Their Own Money on School Supplies, Survey Finds," *The New York Times*, May 16, 2018.

110 *gives his personal cell phone number*: Interviews with the author.

112 *11% of new teachers*: Richard M. Ingersoll et al., "Seven Trends: The Transformation of the Teaching Force," CPRE Research Reports, Consortium for Policy Research in Education, updated January 2021. Note: The last pre-pandemic Phi Delta Kappa poll found that half the country's public school teachers and 61% of high school teachers seriously considered quitting the profession in recent years.

112 *A study of seven districts*: Paul Landsbergis et al., "Organizational Policies and Programs to Reduce Job Stress and Risk of Workplace Violence Among K–12 Education Staff," *New Solutions: A Journal of Environmental and Occupational Health Policy*, February 2018.

112 *"made an effort"*: Interviews with the author.

113 *Adverse Childhood Experiences*: For more information on ACE, see Laura Starecheski, "Take the ACE Quiz—and Learn What It Does and Doesn't Mean," NPR, March 2, 2015, https://www.npr.org/sections/health-shots/2015/03/02/387007941/take-the-ace-quiz-and-learn-what-it-does-and-doesnt-mean.

113 *The psychologist shared*: Interviews with the author.

114 *AP Language and Composition*: Interviews with the author.

114 *When a California middle school math teacher*: Interviews with the author.

Notes

Chapter 4: November

124 *mandated compliance trainings*: See, for example, Evie Blad, "Growing Requirements for Trainings on Non-Academic Issues—Everything from Food Allergies to Sexual Assault—Have Made It Hard for Schools and Teachers to Keep Up," *Education Week*, May 14, 2019.

126 *"pressure" governors*: See, for example, Brett Samuels and Jessie Hellmann, "Trump Says White House Will Pressure Governors to Open Schools," *The Hill*, July 7, 2020.

126 *threatened to withhold funding*: See, for example, Suzanne Smalley, "School Officials in Frantic Scramble to Plan—and Pay for—Reopening," *Yahoo News*, July 13, 2020.

126 *"fully operational"*: "DeVos Says Schools Must 'Fully Open' and Be 'Fully Operational.'" NBC News, July 8, 2020.

126 *"dead on arrival"*: Smalley, "School Officials in Frantic Scramble."

126 *"teachable moment"*: Interviews with the author; Calvert Education Association, "Calvert Board of Education Refuses Safety Negotiations with Teachers and Staff," TheBaynet.com, October 19, 2020.

126 *"new" PPE was several months expired*: Calvert Education Association, "Calvert Board of Education Refuses Safety Negotiations."

126 *"personal interest group"*: Pamela Wood et al., "Maryland Officials Say All Public School Systems Meet New Set of Benchmarks for Some In-Person Instruction," *Baltimore Sun*, August 27, 2020.

126 *state and local correctional departments*: John Eligon, "'It's a Slap in the Face': Victims Are Angered as Jails Free Inmates," *The New York Times*, April 24, 2020; Brennan Center, "Reducing Jail and Prison Populations During the Covid-19 Pandemic," March 27, 2020; Wilson Wong, "More Than 2,000 New Jersey Inmates Released to Slow Spread of Coronavirus in Prisons," NBC News, November 4, 2020.

127 *one in four teachers*: Gary Claxton et al., "How Many Teachers Are at Risk of Serious Illness if Infected with Coronavirus?" Kaiser Family Foundation, July 10, 2020.

127 *preparing their wills*: Hilary Shenfeld, "'Panicked' Teachers Prep Wills, Goodbye Letters Before Their Schools Reopen: 'I'm Scared as Hell,'" *People*, July 17, 2020; see also Adrienne Vogt, "'Right Now, I Am Actually Afraid for My Life,' Georgia Teacher Says," CNN.com, August 5, 2020.

127 *districts told medically high-risk teachers*: See, for example, Aliyya Swaby and Emma Platoff, "Texas Schools Tell Teachers with Medical Risks They Must Return to Classrooms During the Pandemic," *The Texas Tribune*, October 20, 2020; Liz Schlemmer, "Teachers with Health Risks Resign, Retire or Chance Their Lives and Loved Ones," North

Carolina Public Radio, October 27, 2020; Ari Odzer, "Broward Teachers Union Files Suit to Prevent High-Risk Educators from Returning to Classrooms," NBC6 (Miami), January 7, 2021.

127 *"The standard was bend the curve"*: Amy Cherry, "Brandywine School Board Member Tells Teachers to Find 'a New Career' if They 'Can't Handle the Risk' of Returning to Classroom," WDEL.com, July 30, 2020.

127 *"Teachers in Fairfax Revolt"*: Hannah Natanson, "Teachers in Fairfax Revolt Against Fall Plans, Refusing to Teach In-Person," *The Washington Post*, June 26, 2020.

128 *"For Athletes, Decision to Opt Out"*: Kareem Copeland, "For Athletes, Decision to Opt Out Is Fraught with Health Concerns and Pull of Social Activism," *The Washington Post*, July 1, 2020.

128 *got free virus testing*: Tom Haberstroh, "COVID Testing Priority a Potential Issue for NBA," NBCSports.com, July 9, 2020.

128 *Teachers would have strongly preferred*: Interviews with the author.

128 *hybrid or "concurrent"*: Interviews with the author.

128 *social-emotional development*: Michael Osterholm and Cory Anderson, "It's Time to Acknowledge Reality . . . ," *The Washington Post*, January 12, 2022.

129 *signs of child abuse*: Educators take annual compliance trainings on these topics.

129 *school ventilation systems*: Even by 2022, most educators reported that their schools had not improved their ventilation systems. Eric Jotkoff, "NEA Survey: Massive Staff Shortages in Schools Leading to Educator Burnout," National Education Association, February 1, 2022.

129 *Teachers were "absolutely right"*: Interview with the author.

129 *"sitting on top of each other"*: Eddie Burkhalter, "Worst Fear Come True: Two Alabama Public School Teachers Lose Parents to COVID-19," *Alabama Political Reporter*, October 14, 2020.

130 *"critical infrastructure workers"*: Jeff Amy, "New Trump Administration Guidance May Force Virus-Exposed Teachers Back to Classrooms," NBC4 Washington, August 20, 2020.

130 *nearly 22% of educators*: Horace Mann, Educator Health and Well-Being Study, November 2020 report, *The Hidden Impact of COVID-19 on Educators*.

130 *During a 10-day stretch*: Mary Papenfuss, "15 Miami-Dade Public School Staff Members Die of COVID in Just 10 Days," *Huffpost*, September 4, 2021.

130 *One in five educators*: Mark Lieberman, "1 in 5 Educators Say They've Experienced Long COVID," *Education Week*, April 27, 2022.

Notes

131 *30,000 public school teachers*: Kate Gibson, "Teacher Shortages—Made Worse by COVID-19—Shutter Schools Across U.S.," CBS News, November 12, 2021.

131 *Florida had 67% more teacher vacancies*: Elizabeth Stuart, "Florida Is Short More Than 5,000 Teachers, Education Group Says. The Pandemic and Low Pay Are to Blame," CNN.com, October 12, 2021.

131 *California's largest school district*: Jocelyn Gecker, "COVID-19 Creates Dire US Shortage of Teachers, School Staff," Associated Press, September 22, 2021.

131 *Fort Worth, Texas, was close*: Michael Sainato, "'Exhausted and Underpaid': Teachers Across the US Are Leaving Their Jobs in Numbers," *The Guardian*, October 4, 2021.

131 *A small Michigan district*: Gecker, "COVID-19 Creates Dire US Shortage of Teachers, School Staff."

131 *44% increase in midyear*: Sainato, "'Exhausted and Underpaid.'"

131 *some schools across the country temporarily closed*: Cresencio Rodriguez-Delgado et al., "Schools Across the Country Are Struggling to Find Staff. Here's Why," *PBS NewsHour*, Nov 23, 2021; Mark Lieberman, "How Staff Shortages Are Crushing Schools," *Education Week*, October 15, 2021; Gibson, "Teacher Shortages—Made Worse by COVID-19— Shutter Schools Across U.S."; interview with Michael Osterholm.

131 *asked the National Guard to fill in*: Deepa Shivaram, "New Mexico Is Calling on the National Guard to Fill In as Substitute Teachers," NPR, January 21, 2022; "School Bus Driver Shortages Affecting Families Across the Country," CBS News, January 22, 2022.

132 *"We cannot be everything"*: Interview with the author.

132 *"The disregard of teachers' shared"*: Diana D'Amico Pawlewicz, "The School Reopening Debate Reveals That We Don't Listen to Teachers About Schools," *The Washington Post*, July 10, 2020.

132 *"the teacher is considered"*: Pawlewicz, "The School Reopening Debate Reveals That We Don't Listen to Teachers About Schools."

133 *"true martyr fashion"*: Emma Reinhardt, "A Martyr Complex," *The Clearing House: A Journal of Educational Strategies, Issues and Ideas*, May 1957.

133 *society valued their work*: Seen in Susan McMahon et al., "Addressing Violence Against Teachers: A Social-Ecological Analysis of Teachers' Perspectives," *Psychology in the Schools*, April 2020.

133 *their opinions at work*: Anthony Cody, "John Thompson: Gallup Poll Finds Majority of Teachers 'Not Engaged,'" *Education Week*, April 16, 2014.

133 *major source of stress*: Quality of Worklife Survey, American Federation of Teachers and Badass Teachers Association, 2015.

133 *teacher protests and walkouts*: Madeline Will, "From 'Rotten Apples' to Martyrs: America Has Changed Its Tune on Teachers," *Education Week*, September 28, 2018.

133 *hostile White House administration*: See, for example, Valerie Strauss, "Why Donald Trump Jr.'s 'Loser Teachers' Comment Was 'a Chilling Moment' for Educators Around the World," *The Washington Post*, February 16, 2019; Kami Spicklemire and Stephenie Johnson, "Are Trump and DeVos Waging a War on Teachers?" *American Progressive*, June 5, 2017; Danielle Sklarew, "Tone Deaf DeVos Disrespects Educators in South Carolina," NEA, July 19, 2019; Brooke Seipel, "Trump: 'Children Are Taught in School to 'Hate Their Own Country,'" *The Hill*, July 30, 2020.

133 *"have my profession mocked"*: Interviews with the author.

134 *California 3rd grade teacher*: Interviews with the author. Originally reported in Alexandra Robbins, "Teachers Deserve More Respect," *The New York Times*, March 20, 2020.

135 *"I chose your child"*: Thank you to teacher, author, and poet Jason Fisk for permission to abridge and include his October 30, 2020, post. His latest book is *The Craiglist Incident* (Portland, OR: Unsolicited Press, 2022).

Chapter 5: December

148 *"People think librarians"*: Interview with the author.

148 *Many schools celebrate*: Interviews with the author.

149 *15 states require*: EveryLibrary Institute, "Requirements to Become a School Librarian by State."

149 *"like Beyoncé must feel after a concert"*: Interview with the author.

149 *impact studies have linked*: See, for example, Keith Curry Lance and Debra E. Kachel, "Why School Librarians Matter: What Years of Research Tell Us," *Phi Delta Kappan*, March 26, 2018; "School Libraries and Student Achievement," Library Research Service, 2013.

150 *qualified school librarian*: See, for example, Lance and Kachel, "Why School Librarians Matter"; Tricia Kuon, Juanita Flores, and Janie Pickett, "The Biggest Classroom in the Building," *Phi Delta Kappan*, April 1, 2014; Keith Curry Lance and Bill Schwarz, "How Pennsylvania School Libraries Pay Off: Investments in Student Achievement and Academic Standards," Pennsylvania School Library Project, October 2012; Stephanie Cohen et al., "Roles of the School Librarian: Empowering

Student Learning and Success," NY State Library Informational Brief, September 2019.

150 *student scores were higher*: Lance and Kachel, "Why School Librarians Matter."

150 *More than 90% of principals*: Debra E. Kachel, "A Perfect Storm Impacts School Librarian Numbers," *School Library Journal*, March 16, 2018; Melanie Lewis, "Professional Learning Facilitators in 1:1 Program Implementation: Technology Coaches or School Librarians?" *School Libraries Worldwide*, July 2016.

150 *A Nebraska district curriculum specialist*: Interviews with the author.

151 *"'keeper of books'"*: Lance and Kachel, "Why School Librarians Matter."

151 *In the 1980s*: "AASL Reclaims Basic Terminology: School Librarian," *American Libraries*, January 26, 2010.

151 *Today a school librarian*: Debra E. Kachel and Keith Curry Lance, "Changing Times: School Librarian Staffing Status," *Teacher Librarian*, April 2018.

151 *"I hold a BA"*: Interviews with the author.

152 *"All of that is a big joy"*: Interview with the author.

152 *Yet "classroom teachers"*: Interviews with the author.

153 *"the teachers have planning meetings"*: Interview with the author.

153 *"mystery to most teachers"*: Kelly Ahlfeld, "They Paved Paradise: School Librarians and School Libraries Are Disappearing and We Won't Know What We've Lost Until It's Gone," *Journal of Library Administration*, October 2019.

153 *9,000 full-time school librarian positions*: Kachel and Lance, "Changing Times"; Keith Curry Lance, "School Librarian, Where Art Thou?" *School Library Journal*, March 16, 2018.

153 *20% of full-time librarians*: Debra E. Kachel and Keith Curry Lance, "Investigating the Status of School Librarian Employment," *School Library Connection*, August 2021.

153 *45% of library support staff*: Lance, "School Librarian, Where Art Thou?"

153 *don't have full-time librarians*: Ahlfeld, "They Paved Paradise."

153 *31% of school districts*: Kachel and Lance, "Investigating the Status of School Librarian Employment."

153 *8,830 public schools*: "School Libraries & Education," American Library Association, https://www.ala.org/advocacy/school-libraries, updated January 2022.

153 *more than half of charter schools*: Kachel, "A Perfect Storm Impacts School Librarian Numbers."

154 *Spokane, Washington, eliminated*: Kelly Jensen, "Spokane Eliminates

School Librarians, Continuing Trend of Disappearing School Libraries," *Book Riot*, April 16, 2019; Associated Press, "Spokane Announces Elimination of School Librarian Positions," *Seattle Times*, April 14, 2019.

154 *Michigan, where 92% of schools*: Koby Levin, "Amid a Literacy Crisis, Michigan's School Librarians Have All but Disappeared," *Chalkbeat Detroit*, August 8, 2019; *State of America's Libraries 2020*, American Library Association; Kathy Lester, "To Boost Literacy, Michigan Must Invest in School Librarians," *Bridge Michigan*, May 3, 2021. Thank you to Michigan Association for Media in Education president Erica Trowbridge.

154 *reading scores in the Midwest*: Levin, "Amid a Literacy Crisis, Michigan's School Librarians Have All but Disappeared."

154 *require prisons to employ librarians*: Levin, "Amid a Literacy Crisis, Michigan's School Librarians Have All but Disappeared." States other than Michigan were researched separately.

154 *When instructional technology specialists*: Melissa Johnston, "Blurred Lines: The School Librarian and the Instructional Technology Specialist," *TechTrends*, May 2015.

154 *30% in five years*: Kachel, "A Perfect Storm Impacts School Librarian Numbers." See also Kachel and Lance, "Changing Times."

154 *students in high-poverty schools*: *State of America's Libraries 2019*, American Library Association.

154 *"The benefits associated with"*: Lance and Kachel, "Why School Librarians Matter."

154 *districts with high percentages*: See, for example, Sarah D. Sparks and Alex Harwin, "Schools See Steep Drop in Librarians, New Analysis Finds," *Education Week*, May 16, 2018.

155 *Washington State study*: Elizabeth Coker, "Certified Teacher Librarians, Library Quality and Student Achievement in Washington State Public Schools," Washington State School Library Impact Study, Washington Library Media Association, April 1, 2015.

155 *expose them to diverse perspectives*: See, for example, Ahlfeld, "They Paved Paradise."

155 *applies for grants to host presentations*: Interview with the author.

156 *"I get to have them"*: Interview with the author.

156 *"a war on books"*: David Montgomery, Stateline.org, "Librarians Fight Back Against Efforts to Ban Books in Schools," *Education Week*, January 18, 2022.

156 *"might make students feel discomfort"*: Brian Lopez, "Texas House Committee to Investigate School Districts' Books on Race and Sexuality," *The Texas Tribune*, October 26, 2021.

Notes

156 *champion diverse and inclusive books*: See, for example, Pamela Brill, "Texas Book Ban Prompts School Librarians to Launch #FReadom Fighters," *Publishers Weekly*, February 8, 2022.

156 *support readers*: Becky Calzada and Nancy Jo Lambert, "The #FReadom Movement," *Knowledge Quest: Journal of the American Association of School Librarians*, January 3, 2022; see also https://www.freadom.us.

157 *"The library is really the heart"*: Interview with the author.

157 *Washington, DC, school librarians*: John Chrastka, "School Librarians Must Treat the Fight for Their Future Like the Political Campaign It Is," *Publishers Weekly*, October 8, 2021.

157 *presents at PTA meetings*: Interview with the author.

157 *chief information officer*: Lance and Kachel, "Why School Librarians Matter." See also Cohen et al., "Roles of the School Librarian."

158 *librarians' impact was most significant*: See, for example, Mirah J. Dow et al., "School Librarian Staffing Levels and Student Achievement as Represented in 2006–2009 Kansas Annual Yearly Progress Data," *School Library Research*, August 1, 2012; Bill Wilson et al., *Delaware School Libraries Master Plan*, Delaware School Libraries Council, August 2016; Lance and Kachel, "Why School Librarians Matter."

172 *"treated me like garbage"*: Interview with the author.

172 *"PE teachers often struggle"*: K. Andrew R. Richards et al., "The Socialization of Teachers in Physical Education: Review and Recommendations for Future Works," *Kinesiology Review*, January 2014.

173 *"low status" subject*: Christa Spicer and Daniel B. Robinson, "Alone in the Gym: A Review of Literature Related to Physical Education Teachers and Isolation," *Kinesiology Review*, February 2021.

173 *"less important than others"*: Richards et al., "The Socialization of Teachers in Physical Education."

173 *dance teachers' bodies*: Interviews with the author.

174 *Some kindergarten teachers*: Interviews with the author.

175 *psychologically and physically isolated*: See, for example, Spicer and Robinson, "Alone in the Gym"; Alfredo Bautista et al., "Policy Strategies to Remedy Isolation of Specialist Arts and Music Teachers," *Arts Education Policy Review*, 2021.

175 *"Emotional isolation is experienced"*: Sian Chapman et al., "'I'm Really Worried for My Teaching Spirit': Professional Agency, Curriculum Change and the Primary Arts Specialist Teacher," *Journal of Curriculum Studies*, 2020.

176 *"egg-crate isolation"*: See, for example, Bautista et al., "Policy Strategies to Remedy Isolation of Specialist Arts and Music Teachers."

176 *"In other professions"*: Interviews with the author.

176 *at the end of the building*: This is common. See, for example, Richards et al., "The Socialization of Teachers in Physical Education."

176 *music, arts*: See, for example, Bautista et al., "Policy Strategies to Remedy Isolation of Specialist Arts and Music Teachers."

176 *online professional learning communities*: Bautista et al., "Policy Strategies to Remedy Isolation of Specialist Arts and Music Teachers."

176 *Catherine Bell-Robertson*: Catherine Bell-Robertson, "'Staying on Our Feet': Novice Music Teachers' Sharing of Emotions and Experiences Within an Online Community," *Journal of Research in Music Education*, January 2014.

176 *"I'd appreciate more time"*: Interviews with the author.

177 *Researchers additionally suggest*: K. Andrew R. Richards et al., "Addressing Physical Education Teacher Socialization Through Standards-Based Reform of Physical Education," *Teacher Education*, January 2018; Spicer and Robinson, "Alone in the Gym"; K. Andrew R. Richards et al., "Understanding the Realities of School Life: Recommendations for the Preparation of Physical Education Teachers," *Quest*, October 2013.

177 *"to work collaboratively"*: Spicer and Robinson, "Alone in the Gym."

177 *"the most profound things"*: Mary Ellen Flannery, "Lean on Me: How Mentors Help First Year Teachers," *NEA Today*, June 19, 2017.

177 *"teaching is a socio-emotional practice"*: Bautista et al., "Policy Strategies to Remedy Isolation of Specialist Arts and Music Teachers."

177 *Administrators can fold*: See, for example, K. Andrew R. Richards et al., "Personal Accomplishment, Resilience, and Perceived Mattering as Inhibitors of Physical Educators' Perceptions of Marginalization and Isolation," *Journal of Teaching in Physical Education*, January 2018.

178 *"You look familiar"*: Interviews with the author.

Chapter 6: January

185 *wiggle room*: See, for example, Alyson Klein, "The Every Student Succeeds Act: An ESSA Overview," *Education Week*, March 31, 2016.

193 *When the high school bell rings*: Interviews with the author.

193 *"terrible, dark, dirty little secret"*: Interviews with the author.

193–94 *observed workplace bullying*: See, for example, Cynthia Kleinheksel and Richard Geisel, "An Examination of Adult Bullying in the K–12 Workplace: Implications for School Leaders," *School Leadership Review*, 2019; Sandra Malahy, "Workplace Bullying: Teacher-to-Teacher" (PhD diss., Western Illinois University, 2015).

194 *percentage of surveyed K–12 staff*: Kleinheksel and Geisel, "An Examination of Adult Bullying in the K–12 Workplace."

194 *Workplace Bullying Institute*: Gary Namie, Workplace Bullying Institute.

194 *particularly verbal abuse*: Eurofound, "Gender Equality at Work," European Working Conditions Survey 2015 series, 2020. Thank you to Jorge Cabrita for assistance with accessing this research.

194 *"repeated, unreasonable actions"*: "Workplace Bullying," American Federation of Teachers, www.aft.org/position/workplace-bullying.

194 *wide range of behaviors*: See, for example, Srinivas Konda et al., "Nonphysical Workplace Violence," *Journal of School Health*, June 2020; Amy Orange, "Workplace Bullying in Schools: Teachers' Perceptions of Why They Were Mistreated," *Educational Forum*, September 2018; Corene De Wet, "Educators' Understanding of Workplace Bullying," *South African Journal of Education*, February 2014; Jo Blase and Joseph Blase, "Workplace Bullying and Mobbing in K–12 Settings: School Principal Mistreatment and Abuse of Teachers," in *Workplace Bullying and Mobbing in the United States*, eds. Maureen Duffy and David Yamada (New York: Praeger, 2018); interviews with the author.

194 *65% of teachers*: Kleinheksel and Geisel, "An Examination of Adult Bullying in the K–12 Workplace."

195 *"It's toxic"*: Interview with the author.

195 *"extraordinarily destructive"*: Interview with the author.

195 *"stress it created for them"*: Mary E. Thornton and Pat Bricheno, *Crying in Cupboards: What Happens When Teachers Are Bullied* (Kibworth Beauchamp, UK: Troubador, 2016); Mary Thornton, "How a Culture of Bullying Is Driving Teachers from Their Jobs," *The Conversation*, November 22, 2016.

195 *underperforming North Carolina elementary school*: Interview with the author.

196 *leave the education field*: Konda et al., "Nonphysical Workplace Violence."

196 *most frequent workplace bullies*: See, for example, De Wet, "Educators' Understanding of Workplace Bullying."

196 *"They lack peer support"*: Interviews with the author.

197 *"MO was to turn people"*: Interviews with the author.

197 *arsenal can expand*: Blase and Blase, "Workplace Bullying and Mobbing in K–12 Settings"; see also, for example, Orange, "Workplace Bullying in Schools"; De Wet, "Educators' Understanding of Workplace Bullying"; interviews with the author (Blase and teachers).

197 *"boys club"*: Interview with the author.

Notes

198 *"more direct in their bullying"*: Interview with the author.

198 *"the worst and most emotionally trying"*: Interview with the author.

199 *principal bullied her*: Interview with the author.

199 *"People become suicidal"*: Interview with the author.

199 *"The professional weakness"*: Raymond E. Callahan, *The Superintendent of Schools—A Historical Analysis* (St. Louis: Washington University, Graduate Institute of Education, 1966).

199 *"teacher-proof the schools"*: Diana D'Amico Pawlewicz, "The School Reopening Debate Reveals That We Don't Listen to Teachers About Schools," *The Washington Post*, July 10, 2020.

200 *Female educators*: See, for example, Brenda Iasevoli, "Even in Female-Dominated Education Workforce, Women Earn Less Than Men," *Education Week*, March 13, 2018.

200 *three quarters of K-12*: "Characteristics of Public School Teachers," *The Condition of Education 2020*, National Center for Education Statistics.

200 *73% of superintendents*: Andre Perry, "Education Needs More Ambitious Women," *Hechinger Report*, August 18, 2020.

200 *didn't teach a single class*: Interview with the author.

200 *Paulo Freire theorized*: Paulo Freire, *Pedagogy of the Oppressed* (New York: Herder and Herder, 1970). See also Linda Kay Matheson and Kathleen Bobay, "Validation of Oppressed Group Behaviors in Nursing," *Journal of Professional Nursing*, July–August 2007.

200 *disdain their own culture*: See Shellie Simons, "Workplace Bullying Experienced by Massachusetts Registered Nurses and the Relationship to Intention to Leave the Organization," *Advances in Nursing Science*, April–June 2008.

200 *oppressed group won't engage*: See, for example, Matheson and Bobay, "Validation of Oppressed Group Behaviors in Nursing."

200 *nurses are an oppressed population*: See, for example, Matheson and Bobay, "Validation of Oppressed Group Behaviors in Nursing"; Cheryl Y. Woelfle and Ruth McCaffrey, "Nurse on Nurse," *Nursing Forum*, July 2007; Janice E. Hurley, "Nurse-to-Nurse Horizontal Violence: Recognizing It and Preventing It," *NSNA Imprint*, September–October 2006.

200 *Since the 1800s, supervisors*: See, for example, Diana Pawlewicz, *Blaming Teachers: Professionalization Policies and the Failure of Reform in American History* (New Brunswick, NJ: Rutgers University Press, 2020).

201 *93% of teachers*: Seen in Alix Mammina, "Most Teachers Report High Levels of Stress, Study Finds," *Education Week*, April 26, 2018.

201 *"workplaces with high levels"*: Orange, "Workplace Bullying in Schools."

201 *"a fundamental disrespect"*: Interview with the author.

202 *"destructive game changer"*: Interviews with the author.

202 *"increased emphasis on interpersonal"*: Konda et al., "Nonphysical Workplace Violence." See also Lina Bernotaite and Valija Malinauskiene, "Workplace Bullying and Mental Health Among Teachers in Relation to Psychosocial Job Characteristics and Burnout," *International Journal of Occupational Medicine and Environmental Health*, June 2017.

202 *"originally created to allow teachers"*: Linda Myers, "What Happened to the Teacher Workday?" *Education Week*, February 28, 2018.

203 *"the best and brightest"*: Interview with the author. See also Kleinheksel and Geisel, "An Examination of Adult Bullying in the K–12 Workplace"; Les Parsons, *Bullied Teacher, Bullied Student: How to Recognize the Bullying Culture in Your School and What to Do About It* (Markham, ON: Pembroke Publishers, 2005).

203 *"a strong prosocial, do-gooder"*: Interview with the author.

203 *acceptable response from administrators*: See, for example, Konda et al., "Nonphysical Workplace Violence." For more on this issue, see Suzy Fox and Lamont Stallworth, "The Battered Apple: An Application of Stressor-Emotion-Control/Support Theory to Teachers' Experience of Violence and Bullying," *Human Relations*, July 2010. (The National Association of Elementary School Principals and the National Association of Secondary School Principals did not respond to repeated requests for comment about whether principals receive training on workplace bullying.)

203 *"We are behind much"*: Interview with the author.

203 *"Consider requesting a transfer"*: Catherine P. Bradshaw et al., "Prevention and Intervention of Workplace Bullying in Schools," National Education Association, 2012.

203 *"to feel so vulnerable"*: Interview with the author.

204 *"Teachers in general are very kind"*: Correspondence with the author.

Chapter 7: February

217 *"having a heart attack"*: Interview with the author.

218 *teachers' rates of "job strain"*: National Institute for Occupational Safety and Health (NIOSH), mentioned in Paul Landsbergis et al., "Organizational Policies and Programs to Reduce Job Stress and Risk of Workplace Violence Among K–12 Education Staff," *New Solutions: A Journal of Environmental and Occupational Health Policy*, 2018.

218 *nearly 80% of teachers*: Elizabeth D. Steiner and Ashley Woo, *Job-Related Stress Threatens the Teacher Supply: Key Findings from the 2021 State of the U.S. Teacher Survey*, Rand Corporation, 2021. Also, a survey released by

the AFT and the Badass Teachers Association revealed that almost two-thirds of educators find work "always" or "often" stressful, more than double the rate of the general public. "2017 Educator Quality of Work Life Survey," AFT, Badass Teachers Association.

218 *highest levels of job stress*: Joachim Stoeber and Dirk Rennert, "Perfectionism in School Teachers: Relations with Stress Appraisals, Coping Styles, and Burnout," *Anxiety, Stress, and Coping*, 2008.

218 *Merriam-Webster Dictionary's featured*: https://www.merriam-webster.com/dictionary/burnout.

218 *Social psychologists define burnout*: See, for example, Ariel Aloe et al., "Classroom Management Self-Efficacy and Burnout: A Multivariate Meta-Analysis," *Educational Psychology Review*, 2014; M. A. Steinhardt et al., "Chronic Work Stress and Depressive Symptoms: Assessing the Mediating Role of Teacher Burnout," *Stress Health*, December 2011. See also Tiina Soini, "Special Education Teachers' Experienced Burnout and Perceived Fit with the Professional Community: A 5-Year Follow-Up Study," *British Educational Research Journal*, June 2019.

218 *"It is confirmed that teachers"*: Lina Bernotaite and Valija Malinauskiene, "Workplace Bullying and Mental Health Among Teachers in Relation to Psychosocial Job Characteristics and Burnout," *International Journal of Occupational Medicine and Environmental Health*, June 2017.

218 *"Teacher burnout is a huge problem"*: Interviews with the author.

218 *causes of teacher burnout*: See, for example, Aloe et al., "Classroom Management Self-Efficacy and Burnout"; Eun-Young Park and Mikyung Shin, "A Meta-Analysis of Special Education Teachers' Burnout," *Sage Open*, April–June 2020; Claude Fernet et al., "Predicting Intraindividual Changes in Teacher Burnout: The Role of Perceived School Environment and Motivational Factors," *Teaching and Teacher Education*, May 2012; M. H. Fisher, "Factors Influencing Stress, Burnout, and Retention of Secondary Teachers," *Current Issues in Education*, May 2011; Donna Ault Jacobson, "Causes and Effects of Teacher Burnout" (PhD diss., Walden University, 2016); Rebecca Collie et al., "School Climate and Social-Emotional Learning: Predicting Teacher Stress, Job Satisfaction, and Teaching Efficacy," *Journal of Educational Psychology*, November 2012.

219 *"Teacher burnout results from"*: Alina Eugenia Iancu et al., "The Effectiveness of Interventions Aimed at Reducing Teacher Burnout: A Meta-Analysis," *Educational Psychology Review*, June 2018.

219 *"My time card says"*: Interviews with the author.

219 *Teachers who personally strive*: Stoeber and Rennert, "Perfectionism in School Teachers."

Notes

220 *"I felt overwhelmed"*: Interviews with the author.

220 *"burnout cascade"*: Patricia Jennings and Mark Greenberg, "The Prosocial Classroom: Teacher Social and Emotional Competence in Relation to Student and Classroom Outcomes," *Review of Educational Research*, Spring 2009.

220 *"significantly less socially and emotionally competent"*: Eva Oberle et al., "Do Students Notice Stress in Teachers? Associations Between Classroom Teacher Burnout and Students' Perceptions of Teacher Social-Emotional Competence," *Psychology in the Schools*, July 2020.

221 *"burnout contagion"*: Chloe Meredith et al., "'Burnout Contagion' Among Teachers: A Social Network Approach," *Journal of Occupational and Organizational Psychology*, June 2020.

221 *higher morning cortisol levels*: Eva Oberle and Kimberly Schonert-Reichl, "Stress Contagion in the Classroom? The Link Between Classroom Teacher Burnout and Morning Cortisol in Elementary School Students," *Social Science & Medicine*, June 2016.

221 *A* Quartz *article*: Adrienne Matei, "Stress in the Classroom Can Be as Contagious as the Flu," *Quartz*, September 6, 2016.

221 Time *magazine's coverage*: Alexandra Sifferlin, "Stress Is Contagious in the Classroom," *Time*, June 27, 2016.

221 *"teachers of those classrooms"*: Oberle and Schonert-Reichl, "Stress Contagion in the Classroom?"

222 *"some interaction partners"*: Meredith et al., "'Burnout Contagion' Among Teachers."

223 *compatible with family life*: See, for example, Lora Bartlett, "Expanding Teacher Work Roles: A Resource for Retention or a Recipe for Overwork?," *Journal of Education Policy*, September 2004.

223 *1983 Department of Education report*: *A Nation at Risk: The Imperative for Educational Reform*, A Report to the Nation and the Secretary of Education, United States Department of Education, by the National Commission on Excellence in Education, April 1983. See also Valerie Strauss, "'A Nation at Risk' Demanded Education Reform 35 Years Ago. Here's How It's Been Bungled Ever Since," *The Washington Post*, April 26, 2018; Tamim Ansary, "Education at Risk: Fallout from a Flawed Report," *Edutopia*, March 9, 2007.

224 *"equation of the expanded role"*: Bartlett, "Expanding Teacher Work Roles."

224 *"the worst federal education legislation"*: Diane Ravitch, "Today Is the Anniversary of the Worst Federal Education Law Ever Passed," *Huffpost*, January 8, 2018.

224 *Race to the Top*: Ravitch, "Today Is the Anniversary of the Worst Federal Education Law Ever Passed"; Nirvi Shah, "Report: 'Race to the Top' a Flop," *Politico*, September 12, 2013.

224 *The test scores did not rise*: Diane Ravitch, *Slaying Goliath: The Passionate Resistance to Privatization and the Fight to Save America's Public Schools* (New York: Alfred A. Knopf, 2020).

224 *112 standardized tests*: See, for example, Valerie Strauss, "Confirmed: Standardized Testing Has Taken Over Our Schools. But Who's to Blame?," *The Washington Post*, October 24, 2015.

225 *"not found in any high-performing nation"*: Ravitch, *Slaying Goliath*.

225 *Most states have eliminated*: Author interview with Bob Schaeffer, executive director of FairTest, the National Center for Fair and Open Testing.

225 *"unrelenting focus on standardized testing"*: Interview with the author.

225 *"tests whose individual sections"*: Interview with the author.

225 *most states resumed*: Interview with the author.

226 *superintendent humiliated teachers*: Interview with the author.

227 *"the term most commonly used"*: Doris Santoro, "The Problem with Stories About Teacher 'Burnout,'" *Phi Delta Kappan*, December 2019–January 2020.

228 *"enough to recharge me"*: Interviews with the author.

228 *"intervention effectiveness is generally small"*: Iancu et al., "The Effectiveness of Interventions Aimed at Reducing Teacher Burnout."

228 *when she needed extra time*: Interviews with the author.

228 *the importance of social support*: See, for example, Park and Shin, "A Meta-Analysis of Special Education Teachers' Burnout"; Soini, "Special Education Teachers' Experienced Burnout and Perceived Fit with the Professional Community"; Landsbergis et al., "Job Stress and Health of Elementary and Secondary School Educators in the United States"; Iancu et al., "The Effectiveness of Interventions Aimed at Reducing Teacher Burnout"; Sammy K. Ho, "Relationships Among Humor, Self-Esteem, and Social Support to Burnout in School Teachers," *Social Psychology of Education*, March 2016.

228 *"best support is a friend"*: Interviews with the author.

Chapter 8: March

243 *Prodigy Math*: https://www.prodigygame.com/main-en/.

250 *Teacher Confessions*: All of the information in this section was compiled from interviews with the author.

Notes

Chapter 9: April

266 *"world history with pictures"*: Interviews with the author.

276 *80% of K–12 teachers*: Susan D. McMahon et al., "Violence Directed Against Teachers: Results from a National Survey," *School Psychology*, June 2014. Note: The most recent European Working Conditions Study at the time of this writing also concluded that occurrences of verbal abuse and physical violence are particularly prevalent toward education staff, https://www.eurofound.europa.eu/surveys/european -working-conditions-surveys-ewcs.

276 *"It's a tough thing to study"*: Madeline Will, "When Students Assault Teachers, Effects Can Be Lasting," *Education Week*, February 7, 2018.

276 *"I love him dearly"*: Interviews with the author.

276 *high school teachers were more likely*: Eric M. Anderman et al., "Violence and Other Forms of Abuse Against Teachers: 5 Questions Answered," *The Conversation*, February 6, 2020.

277 *38% to 62% of teachers*: Susan McMahon et al., "Addressing Violence Against Teachers: A Social-Ecological Analysis of Teachers' Perspectives," *Psychology in the Schools*, April 2020.

277 Report on Indicators of School Crime and Safety: Véronique Irwin et al., *Report on Indicators of School Crime and Safety: 2020*, National Center for Education Statistics at IES, July 8, 2021.

277 *"because teachers may fear"*: Anderman et al., "Violence and Other Forms of Abuse Against Teachers."

277 *"filing incident reports"*: OSEA (Oregon State Education Association), "Work Shouldn't Hurt," http://www.osea.org/work-shouldnt-hurt/; Paul Landsbergis et al., "Organizational Policies and Programs to Reduce Job Stress and Risk of Workplace Violence Among K–12 Education Staff," *New Solutions: A Journal of Environmental and Occupational Health Policy*, 2018.

277 *discouragement of reporting injuries*: OSEA, "Work Shouldn't Hurt."

277 *"The discontinuation of counselors"*: John Rosales, "Threatened and Attacked by Students: When Work Hurts," *NEA Today*, June 20, 2019.

278 *240 gun incidents in schools in 2021*: K–12 School Shooting Database, Naval Postgraduate School's Center for Homeland Defense and Security, https://www.chds.us/ssdb/charts-graphs/.

278 *only nationwide substantive change*: This point was inspired by a May 24, 2022, tweet by communications consultant Zara Rahim. @ZaraRahim, "Insane how the only noticeable changes since Sandy Hook," Twitter, May 24, 2022, 6:16 p.m., https://twitter.com/ZaraRa him/status/1529224827646648320.

278 *"a sweeping push"*: Brittany Wallman and Megan O'Matz, "Violent Kids Take Over Florida's Classrooms, and They Have the Law on Their Side," *Sun Sentinel*, December 10, 2019.

279 *"Inclusion positively impacts"*: McMahon et al., "Addressing Violence Against Teachers."

279 *Florida law leaves dangerous students*: Wallman and O'Matz, "Violent Kids Take Over Florida's Classrooms."

279 *teacher victimization costs*: *A Silent National Crisis: Violence Against Teachers*, American Psychological Association brochure, 2016.

280 *"big girl panties"*: Will, "When Students Assault Teachers." (The quote in this book assumes the principal said "your." *Education Week* reported, "She says the principal told her to 'put on her big girl panties and deal with it.'")

280 *filed a restraining order*: Wallman and O'Matz, "Violent Kids Take Over Florida's Classrooms."

280 *for not controlling the student*: Wallman and O'Matz, "Violent Kids Take Over Florida's Classrooms."

280 *Washington, DC, charter school teacher*: Interview with the author.

280 *"If a student decides"*: Interviews with the author.

281 *"If we can't contact parents"*: Interview with the author.

281 *"ambush meetings"*: Interview with the author.

281 *administrators have told teachers*: Interviews with the author.

282 *"pack 'em deep"*: Interview with the author.

282 *At a mid-Atlantic school*: Interview with the author.

282 *"The buildings with the highest"*: Interview with the author.

283 *During a photo shoot*: Interview with the author.

Chapter 10: May

299 *"Do No Harm but Take No Crap"*: All of the tips in this section were mentioned in interviews with the author, except for the following.

299 *"Connect before you correct"*: Katherine Reynolds Lewis, *The Good News About Bad Behavior, Why Kids Are Less Disciplined Than Ever—And What to Do About It* (New York: Public Affairs, 2018).

307 *Teachers Pay Teachers*: https://www.teacherspayteachers.com/.

308 *whole-body movements can help*: Annie Murphy Paul, *The Extended Mind: The Power of Thinking Outside the Brain* (New York: Mariner Books, 2021).

Chapter 11: June

329 *"Oh my god, pay us"*: Interview with the author.

329 *significantly higher in districts*: Emma Garcia and Eunice S. Han,

"Teachers' Base Salary and Districts' Academic Performance: Evidence from National Data," *SAGE Open*, March 2022.

330 *"physical and social-emotional security"*: Paul Landsbergis et al., "Organizational Policies and Programs to Reduce Job Stress and Risk of Workplace Violence Among K–12 Education Staff," *New Solutions: A Journal of Environmental and Occupational Health Policy*, 2018.

330 *"The social, emotional, and academic pressures"*: Interview with the author.

330 *"So often, the government"*: Interview with the author.

331 *"Society gives respect to doctors"*: Interview with the author.

332 *recruit a more diverse workforce*: See, for example, Katherine Schaeffer, "America's Public School Teachers Are Far Less Racially and Ethnically Diverse Than Their Students," Pew Research Center, December 10, 2021.

332 *the only Asian man*: Interviews with the author.

332 *7% of public school teachers are Black*: "Characteristics of Public School Teachers," *Condition of Education*, National Center for Education Statistics, accessed in 2022; see also Youki Terada, "Why Black Teachers Walk Away," *Edutopia*, March 26, 2021.

332 *9% of public school teachers are Hispanic*: Madeline Will, "Latino Male Teachers: Building the Pipeline," *Education Week*, January 23, 2018.

332 *one Black teacher by 3rd grade*: Seth Gershenson et al., "The Long-Run Impacts of Same-Race Teachers," National Bureau of Economic Research Working Paper, revised February 2021.

332 *up to 39% less likely*: Center for Black Educator Development, https://www.thecenterblacked.org/.

332 *Mary Lou Fulton Teachers College*: Arizona Teachers Academy Scholarship, https://education.asu.edu/arizona-teachers-academy-at-asu; see also Christina Maxouris and Christina Zdanowicz, "Teachers Are Leaving and Few People Want to Join the Field. Experts Are Sounding the Alarm," CNN.com, February 5, 2022.

333 *"formidable task"*: Interview with the author.

333 *"beauty of their subject matter"*: Doris A. Santoro, "Teacher Demoralization Isn't the Same as Teacher Burnout," *Education Week*, November 12, 2020.

335 *"Why I Love Teaching"*: All of these testimonials were mentioned during interviews with the author.

ABOUT THE AUTHOR

Alexandra Robbins, the author of five *New York Times* bestselling books and a Goodreads Best Nonfiction Book of the Year, is an award-winning investigative reporter who has also been honored with the Distinguished Service to Public Education award. She has written for several publications, including *The New York Times, The New Yorker, The Wall Street Journal, The Washington Post,* and *The Atlantic,* and has appeared on hundreds of television shows, including *60 Minutes, Today, CBS Mornings, The Oprah Winfrey Show, The View,* and *The Colbert Report.*